Slow and Steady

Get Me Ready

Slow and Steady

Get Me Ready

A Parents' Handbook

For Children from Birth to Age 5

Author: June R. Oberlander

Illustrations by: Dr. Barbara Oberlander Jansen
                   and Teresa L. Selove

Publisher: Bio-Alpha, Incorporated
                   P.O. Box 7190
                   Fairfax Station, Virginia 22039

Second Edition

Printed in the United States of America

Revised Edition

Editor: Clyde G. Oberlander

Publisher: Bio-Alpha, Incorporated
                  P.O. Box 7190
                  Fairfax Station, VA 22039
                  Telephone: (703) 323-6142

<u>Acknowledgments</u>

At this time I want to express my gratitude to my friends, former teaching colleagues, my children and my husband who gave me encouragement to complete this challenging endeavor.

Without my husband's constant belief in me, I would not have had the motivation to develop this book for my children to use with their children.

Preface

A Special Note to the Readers of this Book

This handbook was written primarily to bridge the gap between home and school. It contains weekly activities to correspond to the developmental patterns of each age group from birth to age five. There are 260 sequential activities that use primarily household items for materials. Explicit directions are written in layman's language to ensure that people who use this book will understand HOW to implement each activity. A brief evaluation follows each experience so that the person will know what the desired outcome should be from each activity. Some activities may appear to be similar, but the intended concept for each activity is different. The title of the weekly activity and the evaluation of each should clarify any confusion.

The gender is addressed alternately on a yearly basis throughout the five years so that each entire year will flow consistently in a pattern. Thus, Parts I, III and V are addressed to males, and Parts II and IV are directed to females.

This book contains common sense activities. Many of these concepts and skills were originally taught by grandparents who lived within the home. However, society has changed. Many mothers work outside the home, and few grandparents live with their adult children. Therefore, many grandparents do not have the privilege of exposing their grandchildren to the many basic concepts of learning that are so necessary for a child to become well-rounded before entering school.

There are parents that try to teach concepts or skills too early and consequently frustrate the child. They may present other concepts too late or not at all; therefore, these parents have missed the optimum time to teach these concepts. Recent studies have confirmed that very early stimulation in young children gives them an enriched approach to learning which produces better scholars in school, but it must be done at the proper time.

As a retired kindergarten teacher with over twenty-five years of experience, I know that many gaps in learning can be prevented if children are subjected to brief, stimulating and challenging experiences at the appropriate age and developmental level. Basic concepts are more difficult for children to learn in school, because they may have experienced lags in developmental learning at home.

My daughter and daughter-in-law urged me to provide activities for them to use with their young children, ages five months and eighteen months. They wanted a sequential guide that explained HOW to implement activities since no one book seemed to contain what they desired.

I was inspired to write this book to ensure that my grandchildren would be exposed to a variety of enriching experiences that would stimulate and challenge them through meaningful play activities. Play is a child's work. It should be nurtured and guided skillfully with love and patience.

I sincerely hope that my book will help young parents, day care personnel, baby sitters and anyone who cares for young children to meet the needs of today's young children who will be our leaders of tomorrow.

Here are some suggestions to help to implement this handbook:

- Read through an entire weekly activity that is appropriate for the age of the child.

- Make certain that you understand the intended purpose of the activity.

- Collect and assemble the necessary materials.

- Decide how you plan to implement the activity.

- Have a pencil and paper ready to make notes of any observations, additions or comments regarding the activity and the child's responses.

- Review the brief evaluation of each activity and evaluate the child's progress.

- Administer an activity when the child appears to be ready. It may not be at the same time each day.

- Avoid too much structure but be consistent. Just doing an activity every now and then may prove to be ineffective.

- Remember, a child begins at birth with almost a non-existent attention span which gradually expands to approximately 15 seconds during the first few months. Subsequently, the period of attention slowly increases. By age four, the child may still only be able to engage in an activity for a brief time. It depends on the child. With guidance and patience a child's attention span can be increased.

- Repeat the same weekly activity or repeat previously suggested activities throughout a given week. Repetition is very important.

- Stop an activity when the child appears disinterested, frustrated or inattentive. Record this activity and try it again later. Feel free to alter the suggestions to meet the needs of the child.

- Avoid introducing activities too soon. Pace the activities slowly and steadily as you consistently administer the suggested activities with the child.

Slow and steady, the child will be ready.

Note: The author and publisher are not liable for any injury or death incurred due to the misuse of the suggested materials and directions. As with all child-related activities, materials should be selected with careful attention to child safety; adult supervision is essential.

Contents

Part I	Page Number

Introduction:	Birth to Age 1	1
Week 1	Move the Body Parts	2
Week 2	Response to Light	3
Week 3	Moving an Object	4
Week 4	Make a Cradle Gym	5
Week 5	Mirror and Pendulum	7
Week 6	The Sock Ball	8
Week 7	Response to a Noise Maker	9
Week 8	Awareness	10
Week 9	Interaction With Your Baby With Understanding	11
Week 10	Large Muscle Activities	13
Week 11	Eye-Hand Coordination	14
Week 12	Observing Different Faces	15
Week 13	The Face Observation	16
Week 14	Stomach Position and Free Movement	17
Week 15	Listening to Sounds	18
Week 16	Developing Grasp and Eye-Hand Coordination	19
Week 17	Listen and Do	20
Week 18	Nursery Rhymes	21
Week 19	Reach to Grasp	22
Week 20	More Awareness of Hands	23
Week 21	Awareness of Fingers	24
Week 22	Awareness of Toes	25
Week 23	Move to Grasp	26
Week 24	Drop and Fall	27
Week 25	Listen to the Sounds	28
Week 26	The Sock Ball Throw	29
Week 27	Toss the Ball Up and Watch	30
Week 28	Awareness of Feet	31
Week 29	Stacking and Falling	32
Week 30	Paper Noise	33
Week 31	Shake, Listen and Find	34
Week 32	Watch the Ball	35
Week 33	Bowl and Ball Roll	36
Week 34	Sizes	37
Week 35	Blowing Bubbles and Water Splash	38
Week 36	The Shoe Box House	39
Week 37	Feely Squares	40
Week 38	The Magic Mirror	41
Week 39	Faces	42
Week 40	Move and Roll	43
Week 41	Poking	44
Week 42	Drop It In a Container	45
Week 43	Pull and Let Go	46
Week 44	Name and Find	47
Week 45	Which Hand?	48
Week 46	Listen and Do More	49
Week 47	Command and Do	50
Week 48	Where Does It Belong?	51
Week 49	Point to It	52
Week 50	Home Sounds	53
Week 51	Over	54
Week 52	In and Out	55

Contents

Part II		Page Number
Introduction:	Age 1 to Age 2	56
Week 1	The Face and Head Game	57
Week 2	Spools	59
Week 3	Pick Up	60
Week 4	Containers and Lids	61
Week 5	Let's Play Ball	62
Week 6	Let's Go Walking	63
Week 7	Look at Me	64
Week 8	What Made That Sound?	66
Week 9	What's Outside?	67
Week 10	What is Moving?	69
Week 11	What Can I Smell?	70
Week 12	Let's Go Fishing	71
Week 13	Can I Dress Myself?	72
Week 14	Exploring With Dirt, Sand or Rice	73
Week 15	My New House	74
Week 16	Rhythm Band Music	75
Week 17	Exploring With Water	76
Week 18	Put It Through the Slit or Hole	77
Week 19	Finger Painting Can Be Fun	78
Week 20	Painting With a Brush	79
Week 21	Inside-Outside	80
Week 22	Upstairs and Downstairs	81
Week 23	Home Clay Exploration	82
Week 24	Cardboard Puzzles	83
Week 25	Drop Small Objects in a Bottle	84
Week 26	I Can Carry a Tray	85
Week 27	Put the Fish in the Boat	86
Week 28	Where Is the Room?	87
Week 29	Big and Little	88
Week 30	Stepping Stones	89
Week 31	Stencil Up and Down	90
Week 32	Vegetable Printing	91
Week 33	This Side, That Side	92
Week 34	On and Off	93
Week 35	Straw and Spool Stack	94
Week 36	Stuff It in the Box	96
Week 37	Clothespin Snap	97
Week 38	Shake and Find	98
Week 39	Flowers in the Basket	99
Week 40	Poke and Print	100
Week 41	Collect and Return	101
Week 42	Rip It	102
Week 43	Pans and Lids	103
Week 44	Funnel Fun	104
Week 45	The Big Button	105
Week 46	Fold It	106
Week 47	Find and Touch	107
Week 48	The Medicine Dropper	108
Week 49	Button, Zip, Snap, Velcro	109
Week 50	Listen and Draw	110
Week 51	Open and Close	111
Week 52	Find Me	112

Contents

Part III	Page Number

Introduction: Age 2 to Age 3 113

Week 1	Humpty Dumpty	114
Week 2	Jack in the Box	116
Week 3	Top and Bottom	118
Week 4	Big and Little	119
Week 5	Toss in the Can	120
Week 6	Let's Make a Necklace	121
Week 7	The Box Walk	122
Week 8	My Name	123
Week 9	What Color Am I Wearing?	124
Week 10	Moving Hands and Fingers	125
Week 11	Jump and Hop	126
Week 12	My Family	127
Week 13	I Can Paint	128
Week 14	Farm Animals	129
Week 15	Put It in a Line	130
Week 16	Jack Be Nimble	131
Week 17	Feely Bag Fun	132
Week 18	The Three Bears	133
Week 19	Sock Match	134
Week 20	Outline the Shape	136
Week 21	Up and Down	137
Week 22	What Belongs in the Drawer?	139
Week 23	Rub-A-Dub-Dub	140
Week 24	I Spy Red, I Spy Blue	142
Week 25	The Washing Machine	143
Week 26	Slide and Roll	145
Week 27	I Can Dress Myself	146
Week 28	Clapping Hands	147
Week 29	Spool Roll	148
Week 30	The Coat Hanger Hoop	149
Week 31	Ladder Walk	150
Week 32	Eggs in the Carton 1-2-3	151
Week 33	Fruits to See, Feel, Smell and Taste	152
Week 34	The One-Two Walk	154
Week 35	Tall and Short	156
Week 36	Is It Hot or Cold?	157
Week 37	Through the Tunnel	158
Week 38	Little and Big	159
Week 39	Bowling	160
Week 40	Paper Plate Pull	161
Week 41	Little Boy Blue	162
Week 42	Leaf Matching	163
Week 43	Place It On or Under	164
Week 44	How Far Can You Throw?	165
Week 45	My Color Booklet	166
Week 46	Belongings	168
Week 47	What is its Use?	169
Week 48	Food, Ordinals and Eating	170
Week 49	Foot Pushing	171
Week 50	Sequence Fun	172
Week 51	Tiptoe	173
Week 52	Color Pieces	174

Contents

Part IV		Page Number
Introduction:	Age 3 to Age 4	175
Week 1	Ball Bounce	176
Week 2	Early Skipping Fun	177
Week 3	Pound, Pound, Pound	178
Week 4	Animal Moves	179
Week 5	Match Pictures	181
Week 6	Colorful Fish	182
Week 7	Climb Up and Down	184
Week 8	Obstacle Line	185
Week 9	Day and Night	186
Week 10	Scissors	187
Week 11	Me	189
Week 12	Circle and Square	190
Week 13	Hit or Miss	191
Week 14	The Hole Punch Row	192
Week 15	Name the Sound	193
Week 16	Listen and Draw Book	194
Week 17	Guess What?	196
Week 18	Create With Tape	197
Week 19	Jumping Fun	198
Week 20	Where Does It Belong?	199
Week 21	Print Painting	200
Week 22	Nuts and Bolts	201
Week 23	Pouring	202
Week 24	Money Talk	203
Week 25	Which Egg is It?	205
Week 26	Two Parts Make a Whole	206
Week 27	In and Out of the Box	207
Week 28	On and Off	208
Week 29	Tearing Strips	209
Week 30	Three Triangles	211
Week 31	Hoops	213
Week 32	Foot Shapes	214
Week 33	How Does It Taste?	216
Week 34	Sort the Tableware	217
Week 35	Sink or Float	218
Week 36	The Alphabet Song	219
Week 37	Fabric Match	221
Week 38	Shadow Fun	222
Week 39	Gallop Fun	224
Week 40	Trace the Shapes	225
Week 41	I Can Do It	226
Week 42	Fold It and Discover	228
Week 43	Magnet Fun	230
Week 44	Yes or No	231
Week 45	Clothespin Toss	232
Week 46	Listen and Move	233
Week 47	What is Missing?	234
Week 48	Tell Me How	235
Week 49	Families	236
Week 50	Hopscotch Fun	238
Week 51	Finish It	240
Week 52	Actions	241

Contents

Part V	Page Number

Introduction: Age 4 to Age 5 242

Week 1	Playing With Shapes	243
Week 2	Junk Box	245
Week 3	A Dozen	246
Week 4	Mail	247
Week 5	Letters and Lines	248
Week 6	Sewing is Fun	250
Week 7	The Telephone	251
Week 8	More About Me	253
Week 9	Fun With Letter Aa	254
Week 10	Bouncing Bb	256
Week 11	Cc, Cc, Cc	258
Week 12	Dig Deep	260
Week 13	Eggs in the Basket	262
Week 14	Let's Go Fishing	264
Week 15	Goo Goo Goggles	266
Week 16	The Hat Game	268
Week 17	Indian Boy	270
Week 18	Jack-in-the-Box	272
Week 19	The Kite	273
Week 20	Lollipop Fun	275
Week 21	My Mittens	277
Week 22	Night Time	279
Week 23	Octopus	281
Week 24	The Pickle Jar	283
Week 25	My Quilt	285
Week 26	The Rocket	286
Week 27	Make a Snake	288
Week 28	Tree Tops	290
Week 29	The Umbrella	292
Week 30	The Pretty Vase	293
Week 31	My Wagon	294
Week 32	The Musical Xylophone	296
Week 33	Wind the Yarn	298
Week 34	Zero	300
Week 35	Finger Writing	302
Week 36	Labeling	304
Week 37	More Ball	305
Week 38	More Actions	306
Week 39	Listen and Name	307
Week 40	Rope Jumping	308
Week 41	Feel and Tell	309
Week 42	Foods	310
Week 43	Jumping a Distance	311
Week 44	Number Stairs and Counting	312
Week 45	The Clock	314
Week 46	Patterns	316
Week 47	Picture Puzzles	318
Week 48	My Name	319
Week 49	Listen	320
Week 50	Clothing	321
Week 51	ABC Actions	323
Week 52	The Traveling Bag	324

Tips for Solving Behavioral Dilemmas

These tips are designed for parents of young children who are old enough to understand rules. Parents learn as they parent their children. Therefore, it is beneficial to be aware of the characteristics, behaviors and development of young children. Parenthood is a challenging but rewarding task. In dealing with a young child, learn to control your emotions and refrain from punishment, if possible, until you have tried the following suggestions to calm down.

If you are frustrated:

Think of something you like and picture it in your mind.
Take a deep breath and exhale slowly.
Take more deep breaths as you count slowly to ten.
Try to seek a quiet place and rest until you have calmed down.
It may help to share your child's behavioral concern with another person.

Problem Solving:

What is the problem?
What are some ideas to solve the problem?
Which idea seems the best to do?
Try the selected idea and see if it works.
If it doesn't work, pick another idea and try it.

To guide a young child, make eye contact as you introduce a rule calmly but emphatically. Instruct the child to repeat the new rule to make certain that he heard it. Rules should be reasonable and altered if necessary, but children will test their parents at every stage of development. Keep calm and make your values clear to the child. Show interest, love, praise and above all, be consistent in following the rules you have established.

If the situation with a young child requires immediate behavior modification, the following behavioral dilemmas, using ideas from the book Slow and Steady, Get Me Ready, may help in changing the child's behavior. Perhaps it will motivate you to think of other ways to divert and alter the child's behavior. These suggested solutions for dilemmas can be adapted for any preschool age child.

The dilemmas are listed alphabetically with the name of the activity and the page number.

Bed and Nap Time Dilemma

Your child balks or cries at nap or bedtime, even though it is apparent that he is tired and rest is needed. What can you do? Refer to page 173 to the activity entitled Tiptoe. Calmly suggest to the child to pretend that he is a mouse and to be very quiet so that he will not wake the pretend sleeping cat. Begin singing or chanting, "Tippy, Tippy Tiptoe" and tell the child to tiptoe behind you as you tiptoe throughout the house and eventually go the child's room. Encourage the child to get in bed very quietly so that the cat will not hear him. Remind the child to be very quiet or he will disturb the cat.

Boisterous, Loud and Too Active Dilemma

You have tolerated the child's noise and rambunctious behavior. He needs to calm down and you need relief in order to keep your sanity. What can you do? Refer to page 75 to the activity entitled <u>Rhythm Band Music</u>. Encourage the child to divert his energy and use his hands to tap rhythmical patterns on his thighs or use a wooden spoon to tap the patterns out on a box or coffee can as suggested. This should ultimately control the overt behavior and uncontrolled noise. Pages 143, 173, 178 and 185 will give you other ideas as to how to control this type of behavior. Jumping in the house may be controlled by using activities on pages 116 and 131.

Biting Dilemma

Some children bite people in self-defense. What can you do? Refer to page 82 to the activity entitled <u>Home Clay Exploration</u>. To change negative behavior to positive behavior, give the child a piece of bread and encourage him to bite and view the impression his teeth have made and allow him to eat the bread. Use a pat of clay and ask the child to make deep impressions with a popsicle stick. The clay retains the impression, yet it cannot feel. Emphasize to the child that people can feel and that biting hurts and leaves an impression on the skin. Ask the child which of the three he can eat, the person he bit, the bread or the clay. Also, ask the child to suggest other ways he can defend himself instead of biting. Praise him with any positive response and discuss alternatives for self-defense other than biting.

Crayon Dilemma

Your child has found a crayon and begun coloring anything in sight--the walls, furniture, floor, etc. What can you do? Refer to page 166 to the activity entitled <u>My Color Booklet</u>. Calmly suggest that he make a color booklet as suggested, but allow the child to choose any one color crayon and draw whatever he wishes on each page. Praise the child for using the crayon correctly. Tell the child that crayons are to be used for drawing and coloring on paper and that the walls, furniture and floor, etc. are already colored and decorated.

Crying Dilemma

Your child has been crying for some time in order to get his way and you are at your wits end. What can you do? Try the <u>Magic Mirror</u> activity found on page 41. Look through the mirror and name objects that are visible in the room, including the child. Continue to do this and include the child's name using a calm voice with good voice inflection. The child may ultimately become interested in anticipating what you will name next and forget to cry. Invite the child to name objects by looking through the magic mirror. Pages 15 and 16 may give you additional ideas.

Destructive Dilemma

Your 1-1/2 year old has an early case of the "terrible twos." He is inclined to destroy his food, his toys and your house. What can you do? Refer to the activity entitled <u>Rip It</u> found on page 102 and turn the destructive child onto something he can really destroy. You have drawn your child's attention away from other things and you can use this activity to emphasize the very practical job of cleaning up.

Disobedience Dilemma

The child knows the rule that he should obey his parent or caregiver but he deliberately rebels. What can you do? Without scolding the child, instruct him to go to his room and think about the rule. If he refuses to go, calmly pick him up and carry him to his room. Tell him you would like to read or play a game with him when he is ready. Leave him in the closed room briefly until you think he has calmed down. Then read "Mary Had a Little Lamb" and talk about why the lamb was not allowed at school. Refer to the activity <u>Listen and Move</u> found on page 233 or develop some commands of you own and commend the child for following your "pretend rules."

Door Slamming Dilemma

Your child has discovered the disturbing habit of door slamming. He tries to close the door on you and his friends. What do you do? Before you lose an appendage, try the activity entitled <u>Open and Close</u> found on page 111. This activity directs your child to the workings of the door and away from the thrill of the loud slamming noise. It emphasizes, in a practical way, the many types of doors and allows the child some safe door closing and opening opportunities.

Flower Picking Dilemma

Your child has suddenly developed a passion for flowers. So he indiscriminately picks them all--the neighbor's tulip and the dandelions in your weed-strewn lawn. What can you do? Try the activity entitled <u>Flowers in the Basket</u> found on page 99 and teach him about the parts of the flower, as well as some discrimination about those he picks.

Food Playing Dilemma

Your child plays with food instead of eating and you feel that he should eat at least one bite of each food being served. Nothing else that you have tried has succeeded. What can you do? Try the activity <u>Food, Ordinals and Eating</u> found on page 170. Your child may respond because he, no doubt, will consider this a game. The activity entitled <u>Foods</u> found on page 310 may also be helpful.

Hitting Dilemma

Hitting seems to be a game that your child enjoys doing. You have said "stop" to him but he continues. What can you do? Refer to the activity entitled <u>Hit or Miss</u> found on page 191 and allow the child to hit the ball instead of people.

Lights On and Off Dilemma

Your child develops an interest in cutting lights on and off even though you may have told him not to do so. What can you do? Refer to the activity entitled <u>On and Off</u> found on page 208 and allow the child to switch lights on and off under your supervision in each room. This should serve to satisfy his curiosity about light switches. In addition, the <u>On and Off</u> activity on page 93 can be used to divert the child's attention from light switches.

Mouth and Objects Dilemma

Your child appears to put everything in his mouth. He doesn't seem to understand the word no. You want to correct this. What can you do? First of all, try to refrain from the excessive use of the word no. Refer to the activity entitled <u>Yes or No</u> found on page 231 or make up some yes and no statements of your own in which you ask the child questions about himself (e.g., "Are your eyes blue?" "Can you run?" "Can you read?" etc.) This will emphasize that the word no should be used appropriately. By answering yes to some statements implies that the word no is not always right.

Pinching Dilemma

Your child pinches people for no apparent reason and uses this objectionable behavior as a method of self-defense to get his own way. What can you do? Involve the child in the activity entitled Clothespin Snap found on page 97 and emphasize to the child that pinching a person hurts. Instead, he can exercise his fingers and hand and pinch with clothespins. Encourage the child to suggest other ways to defend himself and to achieve his objective instead of from pinching people.

Rock Throwing Dilemma

Your child is playing with some small rocks and picks up a handful or a single rock and suddenly throws the rock(s) at another child. Your child is attempting to develop his skill in throwing and has no idea of the damage that thrown rocks can cause. What can you do? Immediately inform your child about the damaging effects of thrown rocks and direct him to another activity that is safe. To improve his throwing skills, refer to the activity entitled Toss in the Can found on page 120.

Scissors Dilemma

Your child finds a pair of scissors and begins to attempt to cut everything in sight. What can you do? Refer to the activity entitled Scissors found on page 187 and instruct your child as to the proper use of scissors. If your child is not ready for paper cutting, refer to the activity entitled Home Clay Exploration found on page 82 and encourage your child to cut clay that has been rolled into thin "snakes." The child can also develop his cutting skills by cutting strips of cooked spaghetti. These activities will help to satisfy the urge to cut.

Spills and Slashes

Your child is fascinated by liquids such as juice or milk that he can spill, pour or splash on your kitchen floor. What can you do? To enrich your child's experience with filling and pouring, refer to the activity entitled Funnel Fun found on page 104 and the activity entitled Pouring on page 202. These activities will ultimately enrich your child's skill in holding a cup, thereby reducing the number of spills on the kitchen floor.

Visitors Dilemma

A child visits and picks up your treasured knickknacks. This child has not learned to leave these knickknacks alone. What can you do? Refer to the activity entitled Junk Box found on page 245 and direct the child to examine the "special" box of interesting things which he can examine to satisfy his curiosity, thereby leaving your knickknacks alone.

Wet Window Art Dilemma

You have just washed your windows. Condensation forms on a window and your child discovers this and begins to finger paint. What can you do other than say no? Refer to the activity entitled Finger Painting Can Be Fun found on page 78 and encourage the child to finger paint on paper instead of your window.

Part I

(Birth - One Year)

___

Introduction

Educators are beginning to believe that early and consistent stimulation is very important in a child's development. Your baby will mature eventually and be able to accomplish the suggested basic skill activities presented here in this book. However, if your baby appears to be unresponsive (not ready) to the activities suggested, try again each day. Be consistent and be aware that babies are not time clocks. They develop at different rates and not necessarily in the same areas at the same age.

On the other hand, your baby may show signs of being responsive (ready) to the skill activities at an earlier time than those suggested. Introducing skill activities that are a little more advanced is fine, but going too far ahead may not be the best thing for your baby. By going too far ahead, your baby may miss basic skills which would be a foundation for future developmental activities.

Repeating activities is far more advantageous. The more a baby repeats an activity, the more secure and responsive he will be. This is the baby's foundation for learning. It is called rote learning. An infant's thinking, reasoning and association processes are very immature. Rote learning will help develop these abilities to their fullest potential.

The developmental skill activities in this section are designed to help develop thinking, reasoning and association. The key to a baby's learning is introducing and developing skills at the right time. A gap in the learning and development of an infant is what educators believe causes many learning and behavior problems at home and at school. That optimum time is of the utmost importance. The child should be nurtured with love, gentleness and consistency. The recommended activities should be administered at appropriate times throughout the day. A set time is too regimented and may cause anxiety with mother, infant or both. The way a mother interacts with her child is very important. Good voice inflection with praise, consistency without pressure, gentleness and love will enable your child to grow with a positive attitude toward himself and his environment.

Note: The author and publisher are not liable for any injury or death incurred due to the misuse of the suggested materials and directions. As with all child-related activities, materials should be selected with careful attention to child safety; adult supervision is essential.

Age 0 – Week 1

Move the Body Parts

Observe the baby's movements of the head. Is it wobbly? Support it when the baby is not in a reclining position. Support the head with a collar, blanket, hand, lap or cradled arm. Does the baby turn his head from side to side? If not, gently turn the baby's head while he is in a reclining position. This helps the baby to become aware of both sides of his head.

Observe the baby's hand movements. Does the baby have a strong grasp? Let the baby grab and hold your finger. The baby is beginning to react to other people by feeling. The grasp is a prenatal reflex and will weaken as the baby's eye-hand coordination develops. When you are playing with or holding the baby put his left and right palms together. This helps to develop a feeling and awareness of both sides of his body.

Observe the baby's arm movements. Straighten the baby's left arm and note the baby's reaction. Straighten the baby's right arm and note the baby's reaction.

Observe the baby's legs. Straighten the left leg and note the baby's reaction. Straighten the right leg and note the baby's reaction.

Observe the baby's foot movements. Touch and hold the baby's left foot and note the baby's reaction. Touch and hold the baby's right foot and note the baby's reaction.

This week's activity is primarily for the observation of your baby's movements and reactions. By touching the baby's body parts you are enabling the baby to feebly be aware of his body through the sense of touch.

Wrap the baby securely in a blanket during the first weeks of life. For nine months the baby has been curled up. This makes a baby of this age feel secure. It is like a cocoon.

As you exercise your baby's body parts throughout the first few weeks, you will notice that the baby will stretch his arms and legs as he adjusts to his new environment. The secure blanket wrapping will not be as necessary.

Talk to your baby. Use brief phrases that reflect your personality. Sing or hum to your baby. If you prefer not to sing or hum, use a music box or a tape recorder and play soft lullabies. This stimulates your baby's sense of hearing.

Age 0 – Week 2

Response to Light

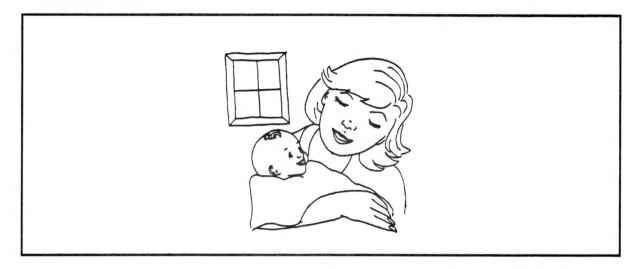

How does your baby respond to light? At birth a baby is sensitive to light, shiny and moving objects and will usually respond by turning his head to follow the stimulus. The baby's eyes may appear to be out of focus. However, there is no need for concern. Open the blinds, raise the shades or admit light from a window. Notice if your baby's head turns to the light. Close the blinds or shades and turn on a lamp on the other side of the room or use a flashlight. Avoid shining the light in the baby's eyes. Allow the light to shine on the wall. Notice if your baby's head turns toward the direction of the light. You are making your baby aware of left and right, and at the same time you are teaching your baby to react to a light stimulus. You are teaching him to move his head from side to side for a purpose. You will also note that your baby will learn to recognize and respond to his mother's voice at a very early age.

Repeat the above activities from time to time throughout the week. Being consistent with your interaction with your baby may help to prevent a learning lag.

Repeat all of the activities that were suggested in week 1. Babies learn best at this age by rote learning. That is, you repeat the same activities over and over. Gradually the baby will learn by other means.

Remember to talk, sing, hum or play music. Babies need this auditory stimulus.

4

Moving An Object

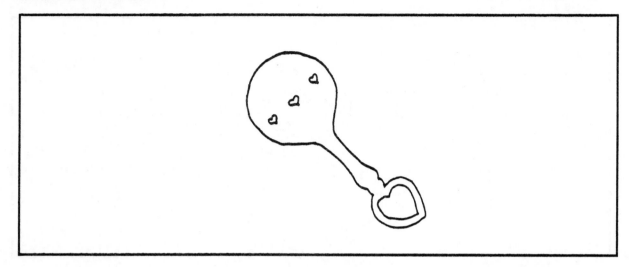

Observe your baby's eye responses. Does the baby fix his eyes on you? Hold a rattle or another object in front of the baby's line of vision. Does the baby look at it? Move the rattle from left to right. Do the baby's eyes follow from left to right?

If your baby's eyes do not react to the stationary or moving rattle, do not be concerned. Infants do not develop at the same rate in all areas. However, be sure and repeat this activity many times throughout the days and weeks to come, and observe the baby's reactions. This is the beginning of left to right eye movement training. This is a prerequisite for reading.

Repeat the exercises suggested in week 1. Touch and move the head from side to side gently. Touch and move the left and right arms. Place the hand palms together. Touch and move the left and right legs. Touch and move the left and right feet. Also repeat the eye/light exercises in week 2 and remember to talk, sing, hum or play soft music.

Age 0 – Week 4

Make a Cradle Gym

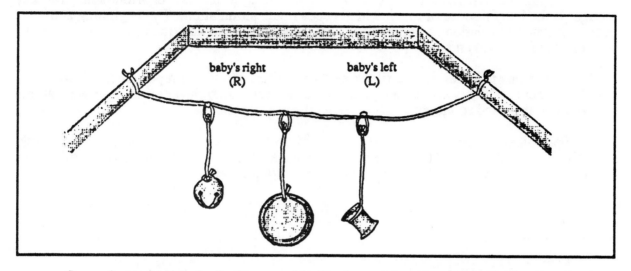

Cut a piece of 1/4 inch elastic several inches longer than the width of the crib. Tie three knots loosely in the elastic, approximately three or four inches apart, before tying each end to each side of the top rail of the crib. Cut and slip three shorter pieces of 1/4 inch elastic through the loose knots. Loosely tie two of the short pieces and retain these for later use. Tie a colored spool (or color one with a red felt marker) securely to the other loose knot. Pull the elastic and tighten the knot. The spool and the other two objects that will be attached should hang low enough so that the baby will be able to reach them when he is ready.

The first day try to interest the baby by moving the spool back and forth. Observe the baby's eyes. Does he watch the spool swing? Does the baby attempt to grasp the spool? Does your baby smile? Talk to your baby while you interact with him.

The second day attach a plastic lid that has been covered with shiny household aluminum foil securely to the knot beside the spool. Follow the same procedure for the lid as was done with the spool. Observe the baby's reaction. Then move both the spool and the lid back and forth. Observe to see if the baby responds in any way.

The next day attach a large jingle bell or rattle securely to the third loose knot. Move the bell to make a sound. Observe the baby's reaction. Does the baby attempt to touch the object that makes a sound?

For the remainder of the week and later, repeat the procedure with the spool, lid and bell. The baby will soon discover that the spool and lid make no sound when moved, whereas the bell makes a sound. This activity may serve to entertain the baby briefly at various times.

Observe your baby and become aware of any changes in his responses or movements. Have your baby's arms and legs straightened out? Does the baby turn his head more easily? Does the baby lift his head slightly? Does the baby follow a moving object? Does the baby tend to turn his head when you move throughout the room? Does the baby's whole body seem to lean in the direction that you move, the direction of light or sound?

Repeat all of the activities that have been suggested. Remember to begin on the left when moving the body parts so that body laterality continues to be established. Also continue to move the baby's entire body gently from left to right at various times to reinforce this. It is also important to repeat the light and eye exercises and to talk, sing, hum or play music to keep the baby's senses keen.

During the first month of life, a baby is adjusting to his new environment. The key thought is the baby's sense of touch which needs much stimulation. The beginning activities deal with touch in relation to body parts. The light and sound activities serve to initiate the stimulation of the eyes and ears.

At various times all of the first week's activities should be repeated to reinforce the baby's awareness of his whole body, body parts, left and right laterality, as well as his sensitivity to light and sound.

Periodically, you should move your baby from his stomach position onto his back. Also alternate positions by laying the baby at the head and foot of the bassinet or crib. This further stimulates the baby's sensations to his new environment.

Age 0 – Week 5

Mirror and Pendulum

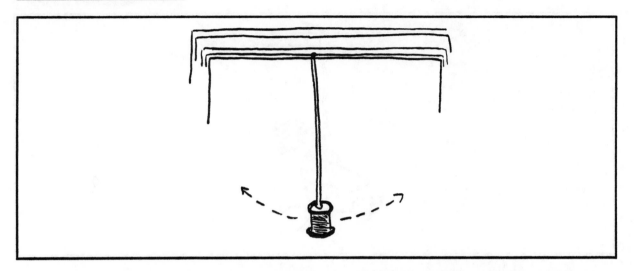

Use a mirror (preferably non-breakable) or hold the baby close enough to look at himself in a large mirror. Does the baby smile or coo? If he does, smile or coo back. Talk to the baby and call him by his name as you and the baby look in the mirror. Does the baby reach out for the image in the mirror? Use an expressive voice when you talk to your baby.

Prop the baby up in an infant seat or chair. Be sure to support the baby's head with an infant collar or rolled blanket. Hang a spool, funny face drawn on a paper plate or any safe object from a string or use a piece of 1/4 inch wide elastic that is attached to the top of a door, doorway, ceiling fan or something high. This must be in clear view of the baby's eyes.

Push the object on the string so that it swings back and forth like a pendulum. Try to encourage the baby to watch it move back and forth.

Repeat some of the first week's activities. You may be tired of them, but a baby needs much repetition for awareness and association.

The cradle gym used in the week 4 activity can be hung across a play pen. The pendulum can also be hung above the play pen or crib. These activities should serve to interest the baby for brief periods of time. However, do not offer both activities at one time. The baby needs only one activity at a time to avoid over stimulation and confusion.

These activities develop

- a baby's awareness of his own image
- beginning listening skills
- a baby's interest in making sounds by watching
- visual stimulation
- an awareness of movement initiating a response.

Age 0 – Week 6

The Sock Ball

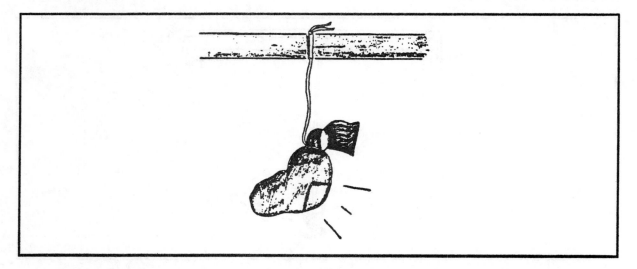

Take an old sock and fill it with fiberfill, newspaper, rags, or old stockings. Tie it securely to make a sock ball. Attach it very securely to the side top rail of the crib or play pen with string or sew a velcro strap to hold it. With the baby lying on his back move the attached sock ball back and forth from left to right and in clear view of the baby's eyes.

Does the baby look at the ball and watch it move? Does he attempt to touch or move it, or does he just ignore it? If the baby is not interested, try again later. Do not forget this activity. Keep trying each week until you meet success. If the baby is interested encourage the sock ball activity, but remember a baby's attention span is very brief. Be patient. Keep the sock ball, it can be used again later in another activity.

Throughout the week, reinforce the activities that you have done before. Observe your baby's responses. Can your baby raise his head slightly while he is resting on his stomach? You will notice that the baby's neck is stronger. Pat the baby's back and talk to him. Remember to use good voice inflection. This stimulates the baby's hearing. As you talk to the baby turn his body over several times and observe his head and neck. Throughout the ensuing weeks you will notice how much stronger your baby has become.

This activity develops

- beginning steps in eye-hand coordination
- an awareness of the sock ball and the movement of it
- an enhancement of the sense of touch
- a stimulus to encourage eye-hand movement

Age 0 – Week 7

Response to a Noise Maker

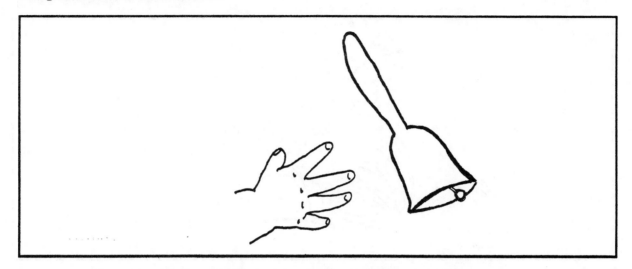

Make a sound with a noisy rattle or bell. Does the baby turn his head, eyes or body in the direction of the sound? Then make the sound on the left of the baby and observe. Then move to the right of the baby and make a sound. Do this several times. Move it first to the left of the baby, then in front of the baby, and then to the right of the baby. Let the baby touch the rattle or bell. Hold the rattle in front of the baby. Does the baby reach for it? If so, let the baby touch or attempt to grasp it. Hold the bell in front of the baby and observe as you did with the rattle. If the baby does not reach for it, move to the left and make a sound with the rattle or bell. Does the baby's head turn?

Be sure and repeat the previous weekly activities. These activities are necessary for sequential learning.

This activity develops

- the baby's listening awareness
- eye-hand coordination and association (This will be noted when the baby responds to the sound direction.)

Age 0 – Week 8

Awareness

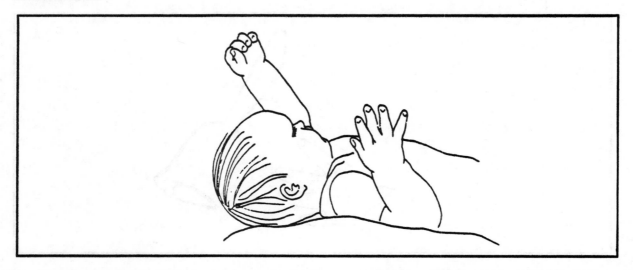

Lay the baby face down on a quilt or blanket that has been spread out on the floor. Talk to the baby or make a sound. Does the baby lift his head and try to face or see you? If not, try again. Good voice inflection varies the sound and serves to stimulate the baby's hearing. If the baby displays some response, try making the sound in different directions. Try first at the left, then in front of the baby and then to the right. It is not necessary to make the sound from the baby's back, because the baby cannot see you there. Be sure and observe any response the baby makes.

Turn the baby on his back and repeat the above activity. It is important to start on the left and move to the right. Early awareness of left and right laterality assists the baby in learning this concept early.

Stretch the baby's left arm out. Does it stay straight out or does it curl back? Next, do this with the right arm. Then do the same with the left and right legs. Be sure to alternate left then right to ensure that the baby is learning left and right laterality. This concept may be more difficult to teach at a later age.

Press the palms of the baby's hands together. Do they stay together? Or does the baby separate them and then put them back together? Separating and putting back together denotes the baby's awareness of his hands.

This activity develops

- an awareness of the source of the sound
- responses of body parts when moved
- an awareness of left and right laterality
- an awareness of hands

Age 0 – Week 9

Interaction With Your Baby With Understanding

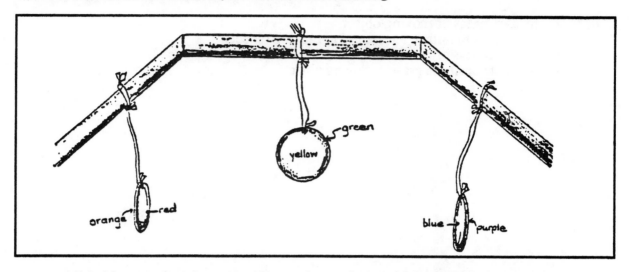

All babies cry, but do you understand your baby's crying? Crying is the only way a baby can communicate at first. Babies develop different kinds of cries and you should learn to distinguish between them. A baby may cry when he is hungry. He may cry when he has a stomachache. He may cry because he has a wet or dirty diaper. He may cry because he is angry or wants attention. Some babies cry when they are bored. These cues should be your signal to interact with your baby. This is a good time to be ready to do activities with your baby. It will not necessarily be the same time every day. You will learn from your baby when the optimum time is present.

Whatever cry the baby makes, respond to his needs with love, tenderness and a soft responsive voice. For example, you could call your baby by name, talk to him lovingly and comfort him.

Bright colors appeal to babies. Obtain red, orange, yellow, green, blue and purple construction or contact paper. Cover three plastic lids with the colored paper. Cut the pieces of paper the size of the three lids. Glue or staple the pieces to the front and back of each lid in the following manner. On the first lid use red on one side and orange on the other side. Use yellow and green on the second lid and blue and purple on the third lid. Punch a hole in the top of each lid. Loop a length of 1/4 inch wide elastic through each hole and tie a knot as you attach each lid. Cut another length of 1/4 inch elastic as described in week 4. Tie one of the three lids to each of the loose knots and secure the elastic to each side of the crib or play pen. Allow them to dangle so that the baby can focus on the objects, watch the movement of the lids and begin to distinguish color.

Touch the elastic to make the lids move slightly. Observe the baby's responses but allow him to play alone if possible. Observe if the baby attempts to reach for the moving lids. If he does appear to reach, does he miss or accidently touch one of the lids? If there is no response to the lids, try again later.

Try repeating the sock ball activity and some of the previous activities, and continue to initiate the colored lid activity. Does your baby show an interest in any of the activities? Make a note of which ones and reinforce these and try those that the baby is less responsive to later. Be sure and observe what happens when your baby responds. You may think of other activities to enrich his experiences.

This activity develops

- an awareness of moving objects
- a stimulus to initiate a response to moving objects
- an awareness of colors
- a remote desire to grasp a moving object

Age 0 – Week 10

Large Muscle Activities

Gross motor activities further develop the baby's sense of touch. Place the baby face down on a quilt or blanket that has been spread out on the floor. Gently straighten the baby's left arm and observe the baby's response. Gently straighten the baby's right arm and observe the baby's response. Do the same with the left and right legs. Does your baby lift his head and focus on his left and right arms when you move them? When you move the left and right legs, does the baby respond in any way? Repeat this activity throughout the week and note if there is any progress. If there is no response try again a little later.

When the baby shows some sign of response to the movement of the arms and legs, place a stuffed animal or any safe object in front of the baby. Does the baby attempt to reach for it or does he show no interest? Do not expect the baby to grab it. However, the baby may feebly attempt to do so. Continue to repeat these activities until the baby responds successfully.

This activity develops

- the baby's further awareness of his body and body parts
- more of an awareness of left and right laterality
- a vague awareness of hand grasping

Age 0 – Week 11

Eye-Hand Coordination

Retrieve the sock ball that was used in week 6 or make a new one. A bright colored sock ball will appeal more to the baby.

Lay the baby on his back. Put the sock ball on the baby's stomach. Roll it along the baby's body across the chest and up to the baby's neck. Watch the baby's eyes and hands. Does the baby attempt to reach for the sock ball, or do his eyes just watch the movement? Be patient, he will respond when he is ready.

This activity should be repeated at various times throughout the week even if the baby showed little or no response. Talk to your baby during the activity and observe and listen for any verbal response or a smile. Remember to repeat some of the previous activities. Although some activities may bore you, babies enjoy and need repetition. The baby will delight and gain confidence in doing simple activities.

This activity develops

- a tactile sensation that stimulates the baby to grasp a moving object
- skill in focusing on a moving object
- skill in listening to sounds when you talk to him
- rudiments of eye-hand coordination

Age 0 – Week 12

<u>Observing Different Faces</u>

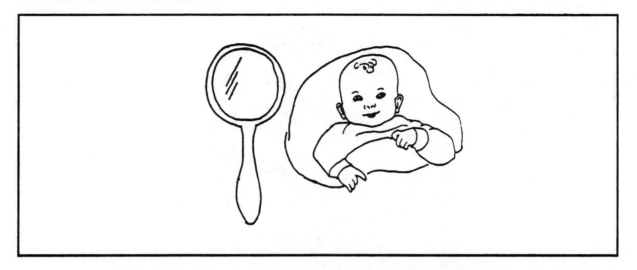

Use a large wall mirror or a non-breakable hand mirror and show the baby his face. Call the baby by name and say, "I see (baby's name)." With the baby still looking in the mirror, use a paper plate and block the baby's view. Gradually slide the plate from left to right so that the baby's face gradually comes into view. As you do this say, "Peek-a-boo, I see (baby's name)." Repeat this several times. Babies recognize and distinguish human faces, especially exaggerated facial expressions, at an early age and may attempt to respond to changes in facial expressions.

With the baby watching, try hiding your face with the plate and gradually expose your face by moving the plate. Once again say, "Peek-a-boo, I see (baby's name)." Be sure to observe the baby's reaction. Repeat this and the other activities at various times. The baby is learning to play a game. He looks. He listens. He responds. At the same time the baby is becoming more aware of his name.

This activity develops

- the baby's awareness of his face
- a purpose for looking and listening
- an interest in interacting with another person

Age 0 – Week 13

The Face Observation

Draw or glue a large colorful face on a paper plate. The face can be funny and should be only on one side. Show the baby the face on the lid. Turn it over and show the baby the blank side. Turn it back over (from left to right) and say, "Peek-a-boo" as the face gradually comes into view.

This simple game is making the baby aware of the front and the back of an object. Also the baby's eyes follow the movement of the face, thus visually training them from left to right.

You can extend this activity by using your hands to hide your face and play peek-a-boo with the baby. The baby may surprise you one day and hide his face to play the game with you.

Repeat this activity and the previous activities, especially those that the baby did not readily respond to. Repetition is very important for sequential learning, confidence and the mastery of basic concepts.

This activity develops

- more awareness of a face
- awareness of the concepts, front and back
- early motivation by initiating a purpose for observing

Age 0 – Week 14

Stomach Position and Free Movement

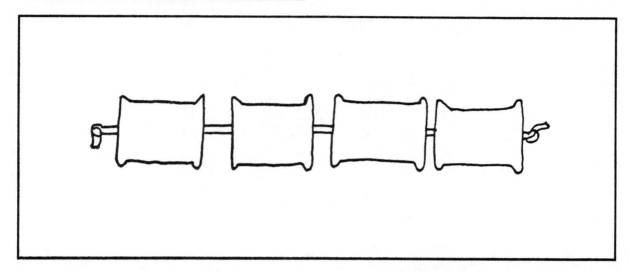

Place the baby face down on a soft mat or carpet and allow the baby to stretch his arms and legs to squirm. Place several large spools that have been strung with 1/4 inch elastic and tied securely at the ends, but leave enough slack so that the spools can be rolled. Roll the spools in front of the baby encouraging him to watch as you roll them. Does your baby watch you roll the spools? Does the baby wiggle slightly to grasp the spools? Make sure that the spools are in clear view and reach of the baby. If the baby attempts to reach for the rolling spools move them slightly away so as to encourage the baby to wiggle forward. You want to stimulate the baby enough so that he will attempt to stretch his arms, legs and torso and move toward the spools.

Pull the two end spools apart, stretching the elastic and slightly separating the spools. Tap the spools together to produce a tapping sound. Do this several times to interest the baby and encourage him to attempt to grasp the spools. Repeat this procedure and allow the baby to observe the spools and explore the spools independently.

Is the baby's head lifted in a wobbly fashion as the arms and hands extend and attempt to grasp the spools? Success with grasping is not likely at this age, but the idea is to motivate the baby to attempt to do so.

Repeat these activities often. These are the beginning steps of crawling.

This activity develops

• the baby's body muscles by using a stimulus to initiate stretching and squirming in an attempt to grasp
• an awareness of movement through the sense of touch
• A motivation to move forward.

Age 0 – Week 15

Listening to Sounds

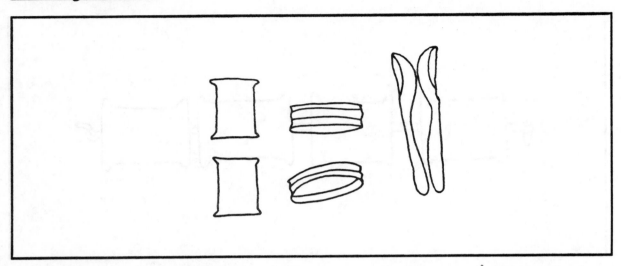

Clap your hands together to make a sound. Does the baby listen? Clap your hands again and observe the baby's response. Take the baby's hands and attempt to clap them together. Exaggerate the sound and say, "Clap" each time that you clap.

Take two spools and tap them together to make a sound. Does the baby listen? Hit the spools together again and observe the baby. Continue doing this until the baby appears to be watching.

Take two jar lids and tap them together to make a sound. Does the baby listen? Continue doing this until the baby shows some sign of a response.

Tap two spoons or something else that is safe to use and make a sound. Repeat the tapping with a rhythm of 1-2, 1-2. Talk to the baby and try to encourage him to listen.

At other times throughout the week, try tapping other objects together to the rhythm of 1-2, 1-2. Also clap your hands to this rhythm when you are holding or playing with your baby.

This activity develops

- an awareness of different sounds
- an awareness of the origin of the different sounds
- listening skills
- an awareness of the rhythm 1-2

Age 0 – Week 16

Developing Grasp and Eye-Hand Coordination

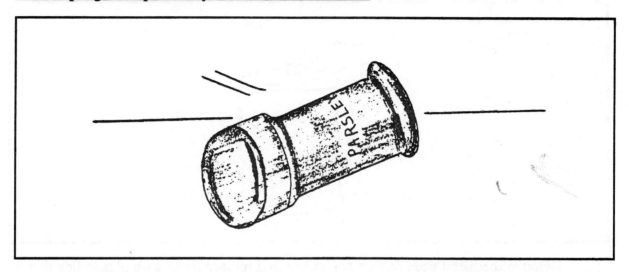

Use a round plastic spice container or one of similar size. Place the baby on his back. Roll the container over the baby's chest and down the abdomen and back up to the chest for tactile sensation. Repeat if the baby is responsive.

Place the baby on his stomach. Lay the plastic container on its side and roll it toward the baby. Make sure that the container is clearly visible to the baby. Try to encourage him to watch as you roll the container. Allow the baby to stretch his arms and legs to squirm. Does your baby watch you roll the container? Does he wiggle slightly in an attempt to grasp the container? For further awareness and stimulation, a jingle bell may be placed inside the container before rolling it to the baby. Allow the baby to touch and explore the container. Roll the container again to the baby and talk to the baby as you do this.

At this age the baby may prefer to be propped in a sitting position when the container is rolled. However, more free movement and the urge to move forward and grasp would be better if the baby were on his stomach.

Observe the baby's reaction as you continue to roll the container toward him. Does the baby make sounds, attempt to grasp the object or does he just watch? If the baby just watches, he is attending and eye coordination is taking place.

It is important to repeat some of the previous activities, especially those that produced very little response earlier.

This activity develops

- an awareness of a rolling object
- skill in watching a moving object
- rudimentary skill in attempting to grasp
- listening skill as you talk; this aids in vocabulary development

---

Age 0 — Week 17

Listen and Do

Remove the metal ends from a coffee can and replace them with plastic lids that fit snugly on each end. Set the can in an upright position in front of the baby. The baby should be in a propped sitting position.

With your hand, tap on the top of the plastic lid in a pattern or rhythm of 1-2, 1-2. Talk to the baby and encourage him to listen as you tap and say, "1-2, 1-2."

Does the baby pay attention? Repeat the tapping several times and try to encourage the baby to use his hand and tap to make a sound. Do not expect the baby to make a pattern. However, if you repeat this activity often enough the baby will be able to produce the pattern when he is a little older.

This activity develops

- an awareness of sound
- an awareness of a rhythmical pattern
- listening skills
- the sense of touch

Age 0 – Week 18

Nursery Rhymes

Buy or borrow a nursery rhyme book from the library. Choose some of your favorite rhymes and read, recite or sing these rhymes for your baby to hear. Repeat each one several times. The nonsensical words of these "catchy" rhymes will entertain the baby as he listens.

Show the baby the picture that corresponds to the rhyme. The brief glance at the pictures will serve to develop beginning associations of pictures and words. Rhymes and rhythms are useful in developing early listening skills.

Repeat the recitations of the nursery rhymes whenever it is possible. The baby will learn to listen. As he begins to talk, he will recite parts of his favorite rhymes spontaneously.

This activity develops

- language enrichment
- listening skills
- an interest in repetition
- an interest in rhythm

Age 0 – Week 19

Reach to Grasp

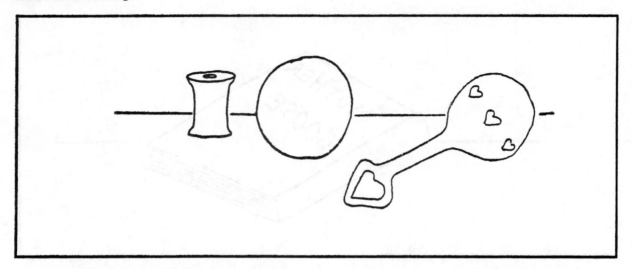

Prop the baby up in a sitting position on the floor. Place a spool, a ball and a rattle or three similar items in a row. It may be necessary to place these objects on a low table or stool so that they will be within easy reach of the baby.

Move the object on the left first to see if the baby will attempt to grasp or rake the object closer to him with his hand. Move the next object closer and observe the baby's response. Move the third object closer and again observe the baby's response. Does he reach for the third object or does he show a preference for one of the other two? Repeat this activity and encourage the baby to feel each object. It may be necessary for you to assist the baby as you encourage him to touch and grasp each object.

Substitute other objects and repeat this activity. Be sure to work from left to right as you move each object closer to the baby. This will give the baby a sense of left and right progression which is a prerequisite to reading and writing.

Continue to repeat some of the previous activities, particularly the ones associated with the movement of the body parts. Remember to move the left body part of each appendage first to ensure that the baby establishes a good sense of left and right laterality. As an extension of this concept, gently roll the baby's entire body from left to right several times.

This activity develops

- eye-hand coordination
- skill in making eye contact with a stationary and moving object
- an awareness of left and right
- enhancement of the sense of touch

Age 0 – Week 20

More Awareness of Hands

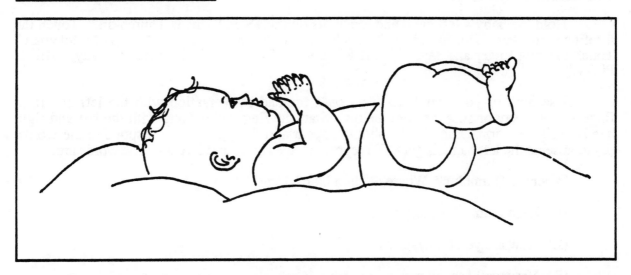

Hold the baby in your lap and encourage the baby to watch as you place your hands together. Move your hands apart and then together again. Repeat this several times so that the baby is aware of what you are doing. Continue to do this as you say, "Pat-a-cake, pat-a-cake, a baker's man. Bake me a cake as fast as you can. Roll it and pat it and mark it with a (B), and put it in the oven for Baby and me."

Repeat this several times and observe the baby. Does he appear to be interested? Does he attempt to clap his hands to play pat-a-cake? If not, encourage the baby to copy the pat-a-cake hand movement. If you substitute the initial letter of the baby's name and use the baby's name in the rhyme, he may listen more attentively.

You may need to gently hold the baby's wrists and assist him. With practice the baby will play pat-a-cake spontaneously.

Remember that babies enjoy and need much repetition.

This activity develops

- more of an awareness of hands
- listening skills
- an awareness of rhythm and rhyme
- observational skills

Age 0 – Week 21

Awareness of Fingers

Hold the baby's left hand and touch his thumb. Say, "This is Thumbkin." Touch the forefinger and say, "This is Pointer." Touch the middle finger and say, "This is Middleman." Touch the ring finger and say, "This is Ringman." Touch the little finger and say, "This is Pinky."

Use both of your hands to carry on a pretend conversation with the left and right fingers as you say or sing the song below. Start the finger play song with the left and right hands in fist position. Each finger should appear and disappear to correspond to the words. (L) represents the left hand fingers. (R) represents the right hand fingers. The words are:

Where is Thumbkin? Where is Thumbkin?

(L) Here I am. (R) Here I am.

(L) How are you today, sir?

(R) Very well I thank you.

(L) Run away

(R) Run away

Repeat the song for each finger and substitute the correct finger for the word, Thumbkin. For example, "Where is Pointer?," "Where is Middleman?," "Where is Ringman?," and "Where is Pinky?" Repeat this several times. Then place your hands behind you and sing the words as you move the correct fingers forward to correspond to the song. This activity will serve to interest the baby and at the same time enrich his learning.

This activity develops

- listening skills
- observational skills
- an awareness of associating finger movement
  with the words of the finger play song
- a further awareness of fingers
- more of an awareness of left and right

Age 0 – Week 22

Awareness of Toes

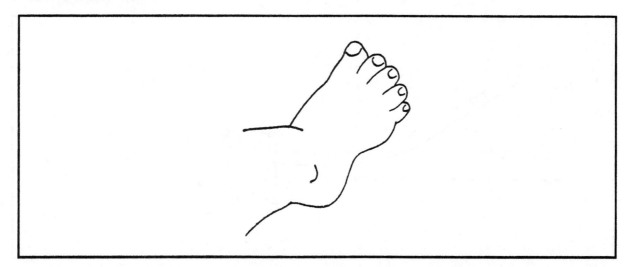

Touch the baby's bare right foot. Use good voice inflection to maintain the baby's attention. Even though you will be using the right foot, the progression will be from left to right. Begin with the big toe and move to the little toe and say the following rhyme.

This little piggy went to market. (touch the big toe)

This little piggy stayed home. (touch the second toe)

This little piggy had roast beef. (touch the third toe)

And this little piggy had none. (touch the fourth toe)

This little piggy cried, "Wee, wee, wee" all the way home. (touch the little toe)

Say the rhyme several times and repeat it many times in the future. The baby will soon begin to play with his hands, feet, fingers, and toes. The tactile sensation of touching each of the body parts will assist the baby in associating the body movement with the body parts. The baby will delight in watching the different body parts move, and will soon realize that he can initiate and control the movement of his body parts.

This activity develops

- more of an awareness of the toes and other body parts
- listening
- enhancement of the sense of touch

Move to Grasp

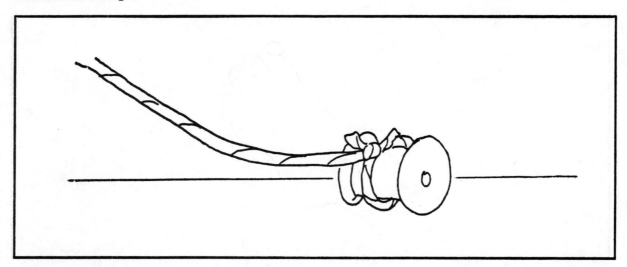

Prop the baby up in a sitting position on the floor. Use a strip of wide colored yarn or a narrow piece of colored cloth approximately twelve inches long. (The baby should not be left alone to play with the yarn or cloth.) Move the strip of yarn or cloth in a wiggly fashion and try to interest the baby to reach for it. Call the baby by name and continue to wiggle the strip. Encourage the baby to reach and attempt to grasp the moving strip. Observe the baby. Does he just ignore it, or does he try to reach and rake it toward him in an attempt to pick it up with the thumb and forefinger?

Allow the baby to touch and hold the strip. Gently withdraw the strip and lay it down in front of the baby. Give the baby an opportunity to reach for the strip. If there is no response, wiggle the strip again to encourage the baby to reach and attempt to grasp it.

At another time use a longer strip of yarn, cloth or string and tie a small object loosely to one end. Show the baby the attached object and allow him to hold and feel it. Lay the baby on his stomach. Place the attached object in front of him and within his reach. Gradually pull the strip away. Encourage the baby to watch as the attached object slowly is pulled away. Does the baby attempt to wiggle forward to grasp the attached object? Place the baby's hand on the object and slowly pull the strip away. Keep doing this until the baby gets the idea and is motivated to reach for the moving object. If the baby shows no interest at all, try this activity again at another time. This activity is designed to stimulate the baby to want to move forward. Body contact with the floor and the struggle to move toward an object should serve to initiate an interest in crawling in a rudimentary manner. Eventually the baby will discover that he can move forward and obtain an object with very little effort.

This activity develops

- eye-hand coordination
- eye contact and control on a moving object
- an interest in reaching and moving forward
- enhances the sense of touch

Age 0 – Week 24

Drop and Fall

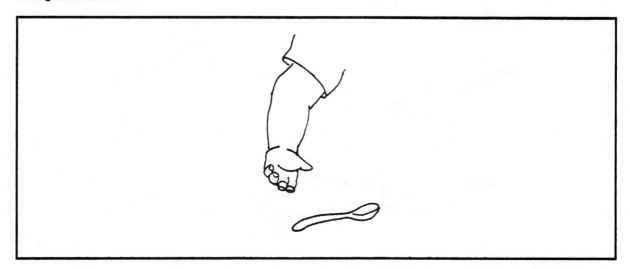

Obtain an object such as a spoon or a clothespin. Show it to the baby and allow him to hold and feel it. Place the baby in a sitting position on the floor. Hold the object slightly higher than the baby's eye view and encourage him to watch as you drop the object.

Does the baby attempt to reach for the object? Show the object to the baby again. Call it by name. Hold the object up and let it fall. Say the word, "down," as you drop the object. Repeat this several times emphasizing the word, "down."

Hand the object to the baby. Does he attempt to drop or throw it? Retrieve the object for the baby to drop or throw it again and again until the baby loses interest.

Choose some other objects for the baby to feel, hold, drop and watch as each object falls. As each object is dropped, use the word, "down," to stress the concept.

This activity develops

- eye-hand coordination
- an awareness of the concept, "down"
- the sense of touch
- the desire to become independent
- listening for the different sounds that objects make when they fall

Age 0 – Week 25

Listen to the Sounds

Obtain a coffee can such as the one used in week 17. Use a wooden spoon or a stick and tap on the plastic lid at the top of the can. Develop the rhythmic 1-2, 1-2 pattern as you tap on the can with the wooden spoon or stick.

Encourage the baby to use the wooden spoon or stick and copy your tapping pattern. It may be necessary for you to help the baby hold the spoon or stick to tap on the plastic lid of the coffee can. Count out the rhythmic pattern, "1-2" as you tap. Continue to do this until the baby loses interest. Repeat later at other times. Eventually the baby will be able to tap on the can independently, but not necessarily with the rhythmic pattern.

At another time during the week, assemble a shoe box, a stuffed paper bag, a magazine, a piece of wood and various other similar items for the baby to tap on and listen for the different sounds. Place them in a row and encourage the baby to explore each object. Then allow him to tap on each object with his hands. With your help, the baby can hold the wooden spoon or stick and tap on the various objects. The different sounds will serve to interest and entertain him briefly. Remember that a baby's attention span is very short. However, through this experience, he will learn to touch, hold, move and make sounds with the various objects. If the rhythmic pattern is repeated often enough, the baby will soon learn to tap out a rhythmic pattern.

This activity develops

- an awareness of a rhythmic pattern
- the feeling sensation of the vibrations
  produced when tapping on the various objects
- eye-hand coordination
- an awareness of different sounds
- free exploration

Age 0 – Week 26

The Sock Ball Throw

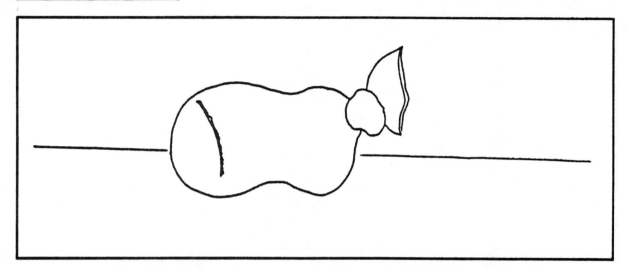

Locate the sock ball that was used in the week 6 activity or make a new one. Allow the baby to hold and feel the sock ball. Take the sock ball gently from the baby and throw it a short distance. Make sure that it is within the baby's eye view. Retrieve the sock ball and throw it again. Then give the sock ball to the baby and encourage him to throw it. Help him to try to aim and throw the ball. Praise the baby for any positive attempt that he makes. This will motivate him to want to continue. Repeat this activity at various times.

At another time during the week sit on the floor facing the baby and throw the sock ball gently to him. Does he reach and grab for the sock ball or does he just let it fall? Encourage him to get the ball and throw it to you. He may want to hold the ball, but try to encourage him to throw or give you the ball. Praise him for any attempt that he makes. Try to avoid saying, "No, no, watch Mother." You can say, "I throw the sock ball this way. Can you throw it like that to me?" Then give the baby the sock ball. He may just look at it or put it down. If this occurs, stop the activity and try again later. With practice, the baby will learn to coordinate and be able to throw the ball. However, the ability to aim accurately will come later. This activity is primarily designed to stimulate the baby to develop an interest in throwing for a purpose. At this age, babies enjoy throwing and dropping objects for no special reason.

This activity develops

- an awareness of throwing an object for a purpose
- eye control in focusing on a moving object
- enhancement of the sense of touch
- further development of eye-hand coordination

Age 0 – Week 27

Toss the Ball Up and Watch

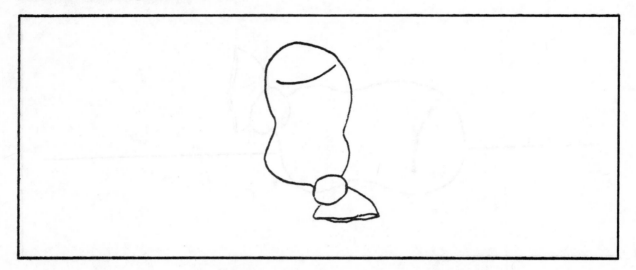

Use the sock ball again and with both hands toss the sock ball up in eye view of the baby. Talk to the baby as you do this. Encourage the baby to look up and watch the ball as it goes up. Use the word "up" as you say, "Watch the ball go up." This activity should be repeated, as well as the activity for week 24 when the concept "down" was stressed. The baby should be motivated to look up and watch the ball come down. Change your voice inflection each time the ball goes up as you say the word "up." Likewise, as the ball falls, use good voice inflection for the word "down."

Give the ball to the baby and encourage him to use both hands and toss the ball up. Call the child by name and praise him for any positive attempt that he makes. Help him if necessary and avoid negatives such as, "No, no, do it this way." With practice, the baby will enjoy tossing the ball while you say the words "up" and "down." Be sure to praise him for his efforts.

This activity should be repeated, as well as many of the previous activities. Doing an activity only once does not produce any mastered skills nor does it reinforce any spatial or basic concepts. Repetition is very necessary.

This activity develops

- eye-hand coordination
- an understanding of up and down
- eye contact with a moving object
- confidence through praise and encouragement

Age 0 – Week 28

Awareness of Feet

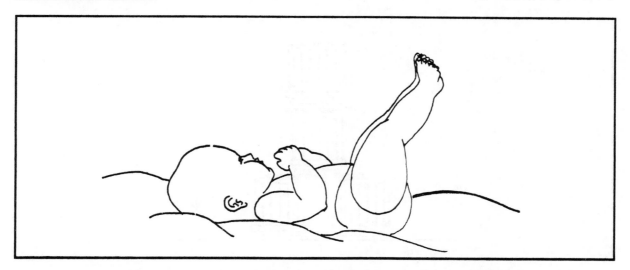

Lay the baby on his back and bring his left leg up so that he can grasp his left foot. Place his left leg back down and lift the right leg so that the baby can grasp his right foot. This activity will be more interesting if a jingle bell is attached to each shoe, bootie or sock that the baby is wearing. Do this several times and talk to the baby as you move the left and right legs. The sound of the jingle bell should serve to interest the baby. Allow the baby to play with his feet and the jingle bells. Then gently lay the left and right legs down. Does the baby repeat this activity independently? Which leg does he attempt to move first? Repeat this activity at various times and try to note which leg the baby moves first. Does he move the same leg first every time? If so, he may be showing a preference at an early age. However, it is desirable to continue to move the left leg first when you initiate this activity. This is suggested primarily to develop the concept of left and right through the sense of touch. The bells, if used, enhance the awareness of left and right through the use of sound.

Remove the baby's shoes and socks and encourage him to play with his feet and toes. The rhyme suggested in week 22 (This Little Piggy) can be used to motivate the baby to explore his feet and toes. Babies need to be aware of their body parts and should be stimulated to explore them through the sense of touch.

This activity develops

- further awareness of left and right
- further awareness of feet and toes
- free exploration
- grasping coordination
- enhancement of the sense of touch

Age 0 – Week 29

Stacking and Falling

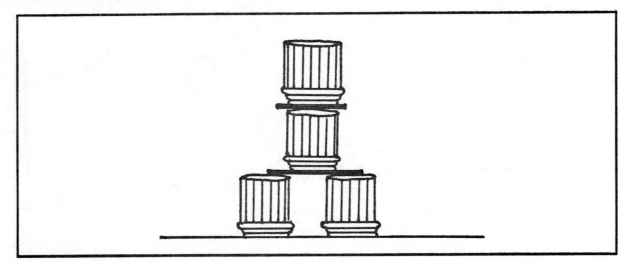

Use any three objects, such as large plastic laundry detergent caps, spools or wooden blocks, for this activity. Stack the three objects and knock them down while the baby is watching. Repeat this several times. If the baby wants to help, encourage him to do so. Then, both of you knock them down. Use the word "down" as the objects fall. Encourage the baby to stack the three objects without your help. However, if he shows signs of needing your help, by all means, help him. Be sure to praise the baby for any positive responses he may show. Continue to allow the baby to stack the three objects and knock them down. Each time the objects fall, use good voice inflection to stress the word "down."

Throughout the week, find other objects to stack or use the same ones. Avoid using objects that the baby can swallow. Three objects are sufficient at a given time. At this age, too many objects to stack may cause excessive stimulation.

At another time, cut several squares or rectangles from cardboard or Styrofoam meat trays which are large enough to support two or three detergent caps. Assemble additional detergent caps, spools or wooden blocks and use these to balance or stabilize a higher stack.

This activity develops

- eye-hand coordination
- an interest in copying or following directions
- a further understanding of the concept "down"
- enhancement of the sense of touch

Age 0 – Week 30

Paper Noise

Use any kind of paper that has been cut in squares approximately 12 x 12 inches. Newspaper may be used, but the ink smears. Take one of the squares of paper and show it to the baby. Ball it up in your hands and make as much noise with the paper as you possibly can. Use another square of paper and ball it up close to the baby's ear so that the baby can hear the crumpling sound better. Give the baby a piece of paper and encourage the baby to ball it up. If it is necessary, ball up a square of paper simultaneously to make sure that the baby understands what you want him to do. Repeat this activity as long as the baby remains interested. If there is no interest, try again later.

If the baby has been cooperative, encourage him to help you put the balls of paper in the waste can. Make a game of it by alternating with the baby in putting the balls in the can. Praise the baby for any positive attempt that he makes.

At another time, choose a large toy and show it to the baby. Place the toy inside a box that has been stuffed with crushed paper. Close the box and encourage the baby to open it and find the hidden toy inside. The noise of the crushed paper will interest the baby. However, he may need help at first in finding the hidden toy. Repeat this activity and allow the baby to attempt to find the hidden toy independently. Praise him for any positive response. This helps to develop confidence and a good self-image. For further interest, you can change the object that is to be hidden in the box.

This activity develops

- the small hand muscles
- enhances listening
- encourages the baby to copy or attempt a task independently
- an awareness of the concept "inside"

Age 0 – Week 31

Shake, Listen and Find

     Use a container such as a shoe box, coffee can, oatmeal box or something similar with a lid. Place a small toy, rattle or block inside the chosen container and close the lid. Shake the container to make a sound. Ask the baby what is inside. Stress the word "inside." Open the container and let the baby peek inside. Take the object out of the container and let the baby feel and look at it. Name the object and tell the baby to put it back in the container. Replace the lid and shake the container. Again ask the baby what is inside the box and allow him to peek, remove the lid and retrieve the object that is inside. Repeat this activity as long as there is interest.

     At another time, change the object that is to be placed inside the container. This will add interest and will assist the baby in learning the names of the different objects that are chosen to hide in the container. He will also discover that the different objects make different sounds when they are shaken in the container.

     This activity develops

- listening
- an understanding of the concept "inside"
- eye-hand coordination
- association skills

Age 0 – Week 32

Watch the Ball

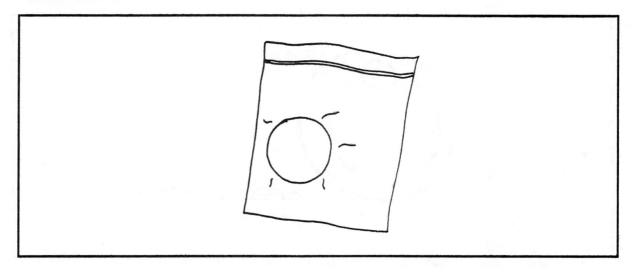

Show the baby a small ball and allow him to hold and feel it. Then place the ball in a zip-lock bag and fasten it securely. Use your finger and push the ball around inside the bag. Tell the baby that the ball is inside the bag and stress the word "inside."

Allow the baby to feel the ball and push it around. Encourage the baby to watch the ball as it moves around inside the bag. Show the baby how you can stop the ball with your hand, release it, and move the ball again. Encourage the baby to independently move the ball around inside the bag. This new experience will serve to entertain the baby briefly. However, this activity should be repeated at various times. Other objects can be placed inside the bag individually. The baby can push and explore the movement of each object that is placed inside the bag.

This activity develops

- the sense of touch
- eye-hand coordination
- free exploration
- skill in keeping the eye on a moving target

Age 0 – Week 33

Bowl and Ball Roll

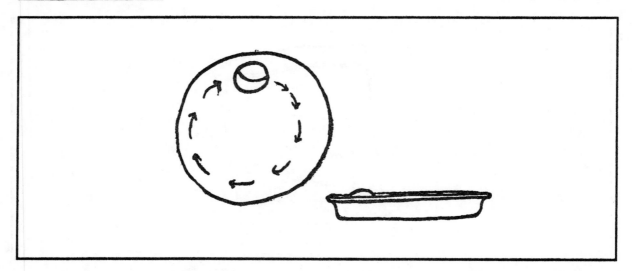

Use a large round plastic container, a large flat cake tin or a similar container without a lid. Place the ball that was used in the week 32 activity in the container. Push the ball around the edge with your finger. Allow it to roll freely but keep it in motion. Encourage the baby to watch as the ball moves around. Does the baby watch or try to stop the ball? If so, you know that the baby is paying attention.

Stop the ball and place the baby's hand on it. Help the baby get the ball in motion. Talk to the baby as both of you watch the ball move. Continue to keep the ball in motion and allow the baby to move the ball independently as much as possible with his hand.

At another time during the week, place the ball in the same container, tilt and move the container so that the ball moves around the edge of it in a circular motion as before. Repeat this activity several times so that the baby can watch the ball move. Help the baby hold the container and repeat the activity. Praise the baby for any positive response he makes.

If this activity is repeated often enough the baby will become aware of the restrictive movement of the ball in a boundary of a circle.

This activity develops

- enhancement of the sense of touch
- an awareness of a circle
- skill in keeping the eye on a moving target
- beginning independence and confidence
- eye-hand coordination

Age 0 – Week 34

Sizes

Obtain a set of unbreakable mixing bowls and a set of measuring cups. Place the mixing bowls in a row in clear view of the baby's reach. They should be arranged in a graduated order with the smallest one on the left. Place the smallest bowl inside the next to the smallest. Continue to nest the bowls until they are stacked according to size. Repeat this activity several times and encourage the baby to assist you. Use the words "large" and "small" as you stack and unstack the bowls. Continue doing this until the baby loses interest. Repeat this activity often and the baby will soon learn to do it independently.

At another time, use a set of unbreakable measuring cups and repeat this activity. In this way the baby will become aware of different sizes and the round shape of the objects. The child will discover this through seeing, feeling and doing.

This activity develops

- an awareness of size
- more of an awareness of the circular shape
- sense of touch
- more of an awareness of left and right
- independence

Age 0 – Week 35

Blowing Bubbles and Water Splash

You will need an empty sewing spool or a bubble pipe for this activity. In addition, buy a jar of bubble blowing solution or use soap or a liquid detergent solution. Wet the bottom of the spool to blow bubbles for the baby. This can be done outside, inside or at the baby's bath time. Whichever you choose, entertain the baby for a while by blowing and trying to catch the bubbles.

The bubbles are round and colorful, and the baby may watch and even try to catch and pop them. He will delight in watching them float and then disappear. When a bubble pops say, "The bubble popped." Keep saying the word "popped." The baby may repeat the word or make sounds in his attempt to say the word. You have probably noticed that the baby has been uttering sounds and can say some words. Repeating the sounds that the baby makes encourages him to practice and stimulates him to want to communicate verbally.

At bath time, make a splashing sound with the water. Exaggerating the sound will tend to capture the baby's attention and will encourage him to want to make the splashing sound. As you talk to the baby say, "Splish, splash" or something similar. Babies enjoy interesting sounds and are more attentive when good voice inflection is used.

Wring out a wet wash cloth and listen to the sound it makes. Use verbal sounds to imitate the sound that the water produces as it is squeezed from the wash cloth. Give the baby a small sponge and encourage him to listen for the water sounds. The unbreakable measuring cups used in the week 34 activity can also be used in the bath tub to make interesting sounds with the water.

This activity develops

* skill in watching a moving object (bubble)
* an awareness of the round shape of bubbles
* awareness of wetness
* listening for different sounds
* enhancement of the sense of touch

Age 0 – Week 36

Shoe Box House

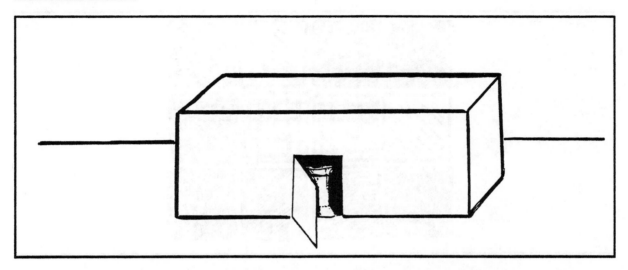

Take a shoe box and draw a doorway on one of the long sides. Cut on two of the lines of the doorway but leave the left side uncut so that the door can be opened and closed. Use a spool or a similar object that is just a little smaller than the door opening and place it in clear view of the baby.

Show the baby the shoe box house and call it by name. Tell the baby that you are going to open the door of the house. Open the door of the shoe box house and place the empty spool inside. Close the door and tell the baby that the spool is inside the house.

Open the door and take the spool out of the shoe box house and place it beside the baby. Tell the baby that the spool is outside of the house. Allow the baby to hold and examine the spool and observe the baby's reaction. Does the baby attempt to put the spool inside the house or does he show little or no interest? If there is no interest try again later.

However, if the baby does appear interested, open the door and repeat each step with the baby watching. Be sure to use the words "inside" and "outside" as you move the spool accordingly. Encourage the baby to do this independently and praise him for any positive response that he makes.

This activity develops

- an awareness of the concepts, "inside" and "outside"
- eye-hand coordination
- beginning steps in following directions
- independence
- an awareness of "open" and "close"

Age 0 – Week 37

Feely Squares

Use a piece of poster board or shirt cardboard and cut the board into 12 square pieces approximately 5 x 5 inches. Collect some scraps of different textured and colored fabrics. Cut two pieces of each scrap the same size as the squares and glue or staple them to the cardboard pieces. This activity will be more interesting if the chosen fabrics are made of corduroy, terry cloth, silk, dotted swiss, fake fur, suede, metallic, quilted material or any other textured cloth that will arouse the curiosity or hold the attention of the baby.

Allow the baby to feel each cloth square one at a time. After all of the squares have been examined, place the squares side by side to resemble a patch quilt and allow the baby to explore. Observe which squares attract the baby's attention. Encourage the baby to feel as you touch and talk about them. This is a good time to talk about colors and textures. For example, corduroy is bumpy and silk is smooth.

As an extension of this activity, the baby may benefit from seeing and feeling two identical squares of matching cloth. When the baby is more familiar with the squares, he may show an interest in matching them.

This activity develops

- an awareness of different colors
- an awareness of the square shape
- an awareness of different textures of cloth
- enhancement of the sense of touch
- an awareness of like textures

Age 0 – Week 38

The Magic Mirror

Use a piece of cardboard approximately 8 x 11 inches to draw an outline of a mirror with a handle. Cut a round hole where the glass mirror would ordinarily be in the frame. Look through the hole and pretend that it is a "magic" mirror. Look at the baby and say, " I see (call the baby by name)." The baby will delight in seeing your face peeping through the hole of the "magic" mirror. If other members of the family are present, pretend to see them in the "magic" mirror and call them by name. Use the "magic" mirror and name objects in the room that are in clear view of the baby. For example, "I see a table." Continue to do this as long as you have the baby's attention. Good voice inflection will serve to retain the baby's interest.

Put the "magic" mirror up to the baby's face. Make sure the baby is looking at you and say, "(call baby by name) sees Mommy." Encourage the baby to hold the "magic" mirror and look at different things that you call by name. If he does not understand, show by touching the object and repeat its name. This activity teaches the baby the names of different things. Although he may attempt to say some of the words, he will probably just listen.

This activity may seem ridiculous to you, but you are playing a game with your baby. The baby realizes that a face and other objects can be seen through the hole of the magic mirror, and this fascinates him.

As an extension of this activity, use the magic mirror at various times with the child up to age 5 or 6 to play the game "I Spy." It can be used when teaching a single color, shape, size, number, letter or word.

This activity develops

- an interest in playing a pretend game
- listening skills
- vocabulary
- visual skills
- association of the name and object of different things

42

Faces

Glue a baby's face that has been cut from a magazine on one side of a piece of cardboard. It will be more interesting if you use a picture of your baby in a frame. Place the picture of the baby face down on the floor. Slowly turn the picture over and say, "Peek-a-boo." Put the picture face down again and repeat the activity. Continue doing this until the baby tries to turn the picture over by himself. Change the inflection of your voice as you say the word "peek-a-boo" each time that the picture is turned over. Continue doing this until the baby loses interest.

At another time, place a picture of a family member's face down on the floor and play the peek-a-boo game again. As you slowly turn the picture over to reveal the face say, "Peek-a-boo, I see (use the family member's name)." Extend this activity by using pictures of other family members. In this way the baby will learn to associate the name with the correct picture. This will also help the baby learn to call the family members by name.

This activity develops

- interest in playing a game
- skill in identifying family members
- association skills
- listening skills

Age 0 – Week 40

Move and Roll

Place the baby on the floor where there is a wide empty space. Lay the baby on his back and gently roll his body from left to right several times in succession. As you do this, talk to the baby and as he is being rolled say, "Whee-ee," or some other words to make the rolling activity more interesting. When you stop rolling the baby's body, observe his reaction. Does he attempt to continue to roll himself, or does he appear to want to stop? If there is no further interest, try again later. This activity is important because it involves the coordination of many muscles. It also assists in reinforcing left and right laterality as the baby's entire body is placed in motion from left to right.

At another time, obtain a large ball that can be rolled easily to the baby. Sit on the floor and place the baby in a sitting position facing you. Roll the ball to the baby and encourage the baby to roll the ball back to you. Praise the baby for any positive response that he makes and continue with this activity as long as the baby appears interested. This is an activity that should be repeated often. It would also be beneficial for the baby to repeat some of the previous activities, especially those in which the baby showed little or no interest.

This activity develops

- a further awareness of left and right
- enhancement of the sense of touch when the baby's body is rolled, also when the ball is rolled
- eye-hand coordination
- motivation to increase attention span
- skill in playing a simple ball game with another person
- confidence

Age 0 – Week 41

Poking

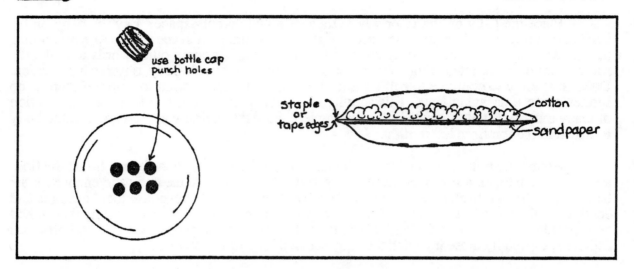

Obtain a small, smooth bottle cap about the size of a dime. Make six indentations on two Styrofoam picnic plates by pressing the cap firmly on the plates. Be sure to press hard and twist the cap to make smooth holes in the plates. If the holes are ragged, use small sharp fingernail scissors to make the holes neat. Cut a large sheet of sandpaper the size of one plate and lay it inside one of the inverted plates so that the rough side faces the holes in that plate. Pack loose cotton, cotton balls, or fiberfill on top of the smooth side of the sandpaper sheet. Place the other Styrofoam plate with the inverted side facing down on top of the other plate. Staple or tape the two plates containing the sandpaper and cotton together.

Poke your index finger in each of the holes on the sandpaper side. This is the rough side. Turn the connected plates over and poke your index finger at random in the holes on that side. This side feels soft. Encourage the baby to use his index finger to poke it in the holes at random. Show him both sides of the plates and allow him to feel and explore both sides independently.

The baby may be reluctant to poke his finger in the holes. He may just look at it and let it be. Therefore, he may need some encouragement to use his finger to poke in the holes of the plate. If you have a Chinese checker board, the baby will probably enjoy poking his finger in the holes of it. It makes no difference if the baby chooses another finger for poking. Encouragement, praise and good voice inflection will serve to increase the baby's interest. Use the words, "rough" and "soft" as you talk to the baby. This will increase his understanding of these concepts.

This activity develops

- eye-hand coordination
- free choice exploration
- enhances the sense of touch
- an awareness of "rough" and "soft" textures
- confidence

Age 0 – Week 42

Drop It In a Container

Take an empty coffee can with a plastic lid and remove the metal piece from the bottom end with a can opener. Place masking tape on any rough edges. Trace and then cut a hole in the plastic lid with a pair of kitchen scissors or a sharp pointed instrument. The hole should be circular and a little larger than a large empty sewing spool. One or more spools may be used for this activity. Colored spools are more appealing to the baby. Felt markers can be used to color neutral colored spools.

Place the plastic lid on one end of the can and place it on a flat surface. Take a spool and drop it in the hole of the plastic lid. Lift the can and find the spool. Repeat this activity several times. Give the baby a spool and encourage him to drop it in the hole of the plastic lid. He may need a little help coordinating at first, but with several attempts he should meet success. If you use several spools, they may all be dropped in the can through the hole in the plastic lid individually. The baby will enjoy lifting the can and finding the spools.

This activity can be used later for the baby to do independently. Encouragement and praise are necessary for motivation; therefore, remember to encourage and praise even though you may be busy elsewhere.

This activity develops

- eye-hand coordination
- enhances the sense of touch
- skill in following directions
- independence
- confidence

Age 0 – Week 43

Pull and Let Go

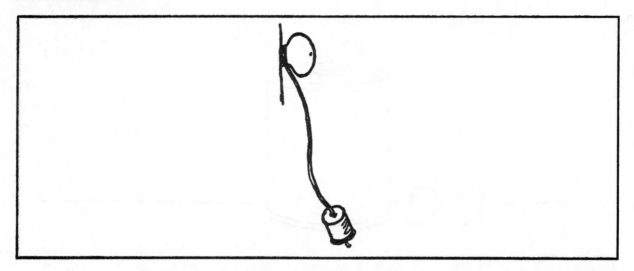

Use a large rubber band or a piece of elastic and fasten it securely to any small safe object such as a spool, a rattle, a plastic lid, etc. Tie this securely to a chair, table, play pen rail or a door knob so that the attached object will hang freely.

Show the baby how you can pull the object and let it go. The baby will see that the object returns to its original position. Pull the attached object several more times while the baby watches you. Does the baby attempt to help you or does he just watch? Encourage the baby to help you pull or allow the baby to pull the object independently. Continue doing this until the baby loses interest. Be sure and praise the baby for any positive response that he makes.

At another time, different objects can be used for this same activity. Babies of this age enjoy pulling, poking and pushing objects around, and will work independently if a few safe objects are made available to him.

This activity develops

- eye-hand coordination
- independence
- motivation to increase attention span
- confidence

Age 0 – Week 44

Name and Find

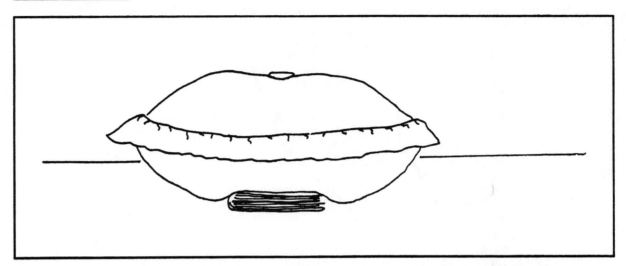

Give the baby a book to hold and allow him to examine it. Tell the baby that he is holding a book. Ask the baby to give the book back to you. Tell the baby to watch as you hide the book under a pillow or magazine. Tell the baby to go and find the book. Retrieve the book if the baby does not seem to understand. Show the book to the baby and hide it in the same place. Keep doing this until the baby gets the idea and can find the book independently. Praise the baby for any positive response. Repeat the word "book" as often as possible and eventually the baby will say the word "book."

Choose different familiar toys to hide from the baby. However, hide only one object at a given time. Call the object by name as you hide it. The baby will be more confident if you will hide it in the same place. However, if the baby can readily find the hidden object, try another hiding place, such as under the sofa or a table. Try to hide it under something each time so that the baby will understand the spatial concept, "under." Reinforcing the name of each item will stimulate the baby to listen, and eventually, he may begin to say the names of some of the objects. Much praise and encouragement are needed for the motivation of this type of activity.

This activity develops

- following directions
- listening
- language development (names of objects)
- visual perception in finding the correct objects
- confidence
- independence

Age 0 – Week 45

Which Hand?

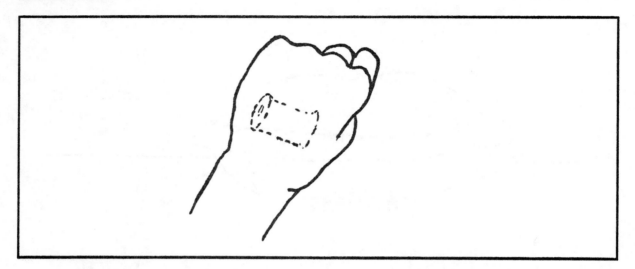

Choose an object that can be concealed in one hand. Show the small object to the baby as you identify the name of it. Retain the object in one hand and put both of your hands behind you. Clasp both of your hands as if both of them are holding the object and bring your hands back in clear view of the baby. Call the baby by name and ask him to point to the hand that has the object in it. Continue to do this several times. Use the same hand and object each time until the baby understands and can point correctly to the hand that is concealing the object. Praise the child for any positive response.

After the baby is comfortable with this activity, feel free to alternate hands. However, never change hands to conceal the object when your hands are behind you. The object of this activity is for the child to remember which hand he saw you hold the object before you clasped each hand behind you. Changing hands behind you may tend to confuse and frustrate the baby. It may also cause the baby to lose confidence and trust in you. Other objects may be used in the same manner once the baby is comfortable with this activity.

This activity develops

- memory recall
- association of object and the correct hand
- interest in playing a game

Age 0 – Week 46

Listen and Do More

Place three objects in a row in front of the baby. Some suggested objects are a rattle, a sock ball, a small stuffed animal, a spoon, or any similar item. Three items are suggested because too many objects may over stimulate and confuse the baby. Start on the left and name each object that has been placed in the row. Allow the baby to hold and touch the first one on the left. Replace that one and allow the baby to hold and feel the middle one. Replace that object and allow the baby to hold and feel the third one in the row. Replace that object to the row. Encourage the baby to name the three objects as you point to each one. If the baby just watches, repeat the name of each object several times as you move from left to right.

Ask the baby to hand you the first object. Call it by name, but do not touch or point to it. If the child does not understand, pick up the object, call it by name and replace it. Repeat the procedure and ask for the same object by name. Keep doing this until the baby understands and hands you the correct object. Be sure to praise the baby for any positive response that he makes.

Call the second object by name and instruct the child to hand the object to you. Once again, if the baby does not understand, pick up the object, call it by name and replace it. Continue doing this for the third object until the baby can respond correctly. If the baby appears to become frustrated stop this activity, and try again at another time.

If you repeat this activity often enough, the baby will gain more confidence and will welcome a change in the position of the three objects. Later the three objects may be exchanged for other items and used with the same procedure.

This activity develops

- more awareness of left and right progression
- eye-hand coordination
- further development of sensory perception
- vocabulary development
- skill in listening to and following directions

Age 0 – Week 47

Command and Do

Assemble a stuffed teddy bear, the coffee can with the plastic lid and spool that was used in the week 42 activity and a medium size ball. Place them in order from left to right. Show the baby how to hug the stuffed animal as you remove it from the left position. Say, "Mommy hugs Teddy." Tell the baby to hug the teddy bear. Say, "(baby's name) hugs Teddy." Praise the baby if he responds positively. If he just watches you, hug the bear again and encourage the baby to do likewise. Continue to do this until the baby responds correctly or loses interest.

Put the teddy bear back in place and pick up the spool and drop it in the hole of the plastic lid on the can. Say, "Mommy put the spool in the can." Since the baby has done this before, he may readily respond. If not, keep trying until he follows your command. Once the baby has responded correctly, clap your hands, praise him and say, "(Baby's name) put the spool in the can." Roll the ball a short distance and say, "Mommy rolled the ball." Encourage the baby to go and get the ball and roll it back to you. Help the baby if he has difficulty retrieving or rolling the ball back to you. Respond to him again by calling him by name and praising him for his positive actions. Continue to do this until the baby understands how to go and get the ball even though it was not rolled directly to him. Try to avoid rolling the ball a long way, because it will be difficult for the baby to retrieve and roll the ball to you.

This activity develops

- skill in following directions
- listening skills
- language development
- eye-hand coordination
- an understanding of affection by hugging the teddy bear
- confidence

Age 0 – Week 48

Where Does It Belong?

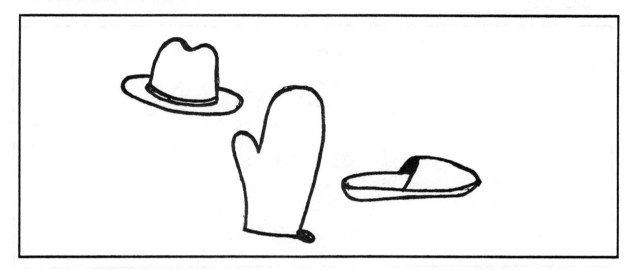

Obtain a mitten that is larger than the baby's hand. (An oven mitt will do.) Also, assemble a large bedroom slipper and a hat that is easy to put on the baby's head but is not too large.

Put the mitten or mitt on your hand and take it off. Encourage the baby to put the mitten or mitt on either one of his hands. (Do not be concerned about the thumb as long as the baby gets his hand inside.) Help the baby put the mitten on if it is necessary. Talk to the baby as you do this. Practice putting the mitten or mitt on and taking it off until the baby is confident in doing this.

Put the slipper on your foot and take it off. Then encourage the baby to try it on his foot. Allow him to choose either foot. Help him if necessary. Practice this as long as the baby is interested.

Place the hat on your head and encourage the baby to take it off of your head. Does he put the hat on his head? If not, encourage him to do so. Repeat the process if he does not seem to understand. Do this until the baby gets the idea.

Place the mitten or mitt, slipper and hat in a row. Tell the baby to put the mitten or mitt on. Does he put it on his hand or just watch you. Show him how, if he does not understand.

Then tell the baby to put on the slipper. Can he do that independently? Assist him if he does not quite understand. Point to the hat and tell him to put the hat on. Does he put it on his head or just watch? Help him if necessary. Continue doing this activity at various times and allow the child to play with the items independently. Be sure to praise him whenever he makes a positive response.

This activity develops

- listening to and following directions
- language enrichment
- association skills
- confidence and independence

Age 0 – Week 49

Point to It

Cut a picture of a baby's face from a magazine or draw a face and show it to the baby. Point to the left eye on the picture of the face and say, "Eye." Gently touch the baby's left eye and then touch your left eye and say the word eye again. Follow the same procedure for the right eye, the nose, the mouth, the left and right ears and the hair. Repeat this activity several times or until the baby loses interest.

Throughout the week and whenever possible, stress the parts of the face. If the baby seems confused, spend several days on the eyes, then progress and spend several days each on the nose, mouth, ears and hair. When the baby is confident, encourage him to point to or touch a part of the face on command. Clap your hands and use good voice inflection to motivate the baby's interest and give him confidence.

Point to pictures of faces in magazines and books whenever possible and allow the baby to point to the eyes, nose, mouth, ears and hair of each face. This will enable the baby to associate the facial parts in pictures, as well as those in real life.

This activity develops

- listening skills
- an awareness of the parts of the face
- skill in associating different parts of the face

Age 0 – Week 50

Home Sounds

Stress one familiar home sound each day throughout the week. For example, you may choose the washing machine sound. Exaggerate the sound verbally, and encourage the baby to imitate the sound that you make. Listed below are some suggestions that you can use in making some home sounds. Many other sounds may be added to this list.

- washing machine - "swish, swish"
- dryer - "mmmmmm"
- telephone - "ring, ring, ring"
- dishwasher - "squish, squish"
- vacuum cleaner - "zzzzzz"
- electric saw - "brr, brr"
- electric drill - "drr, drr"
- person walking - "clip, clop"
- door bell - "ding, dong"
- car - "brm, brm"

This activity develops

- an awareness of home sounds
- skill in associating home sounds with the correct object
- verbal stimulation to imitate the sounds of home objects
- listening for a purpose

Over

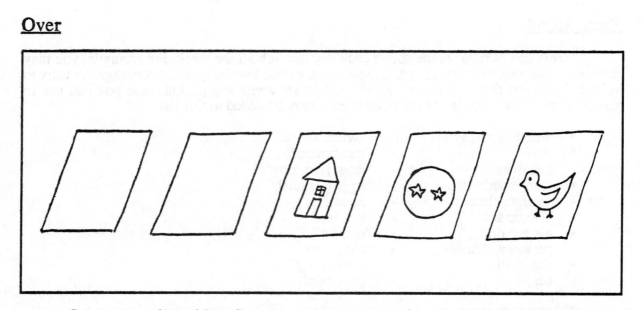

Cut some cardboard into five pieces that are approximately 3 x 5 inches or assemble five plastic lids to use for this activity. Select five simple, colorful pictures of things such as a ball, a house, a bird, a baby, and a dog. Glue the pictures to one side of each card or lid. Place them on a flat surface in a row with all of the pictures facing up. Begin on the left side and turn the first picture over. As you turn it over, say the word "over" and tell the baby the name of the picture that is on the card or lid. Do the same for the other four pictures keeping them in a row. Tell the baby that you have turned all of the pictures over. Then ask the baby to find the pictures. If the baby does not seem to understand, slowly turn the first picture on the left over and again say the word "over." Tell the baby that you have turned the card or lid over to find the picture. Encourage the baby to turn the second card over. Stress the word "over" and tell the baby the name of what is on that picture. Praise the baby for any positive response and encourage him to turn the others over to find the other pictures. Repeat this activity several times. Allow the baby to continue to do this activity alone, providing there is still some interest in this activity.

For additional interest, other pictures may be substituted for this activity. Choose simple, colorful pictures with little detail. Tell the baby the name of each picture before turning the pictures over. Use only a few pictures at a time to avoid confusing the baby. This will help to increase the baby's vocabulary, as well as teach him the spatial concept of "over."

This activity develops

- an awareness of the concept "over"
- eye-hand coordination
- association skills
- vocabulary enrichment
- independence
- confidence

Age 0 – Week 52

In and Out

Place five objects such as a block, a cup, a spoon, a small stuffed or plastic animal and a favorite small toy in front of the baby. Name the objects one at a time and allow the baby to hold and touch each one before you place it in a shoe box.

Remove the block from the box and hand it to the baby. Tell the baby that you took the block out of the box. Stress the word "out." Instruct the baby to put the block back in the box. Emphasize the word "in." Repeat this for the cup, spoon, animal and toy.

After all of the objects are back in the box, encourage the baby to find the block in the box and hand it to you. If he does not understand, pick up the block and hand it to the baby as you say the word "block." Tell the baby that the block is out of the box. Be sure to use the word "out." Ask the baby to say the word "block" if he can. Then instruct him to put the block back in the box. Next, tell the baby to take the cup out of the box and give it to you. (Give only one command at a time to avoid confusion. Two commands can be given when the child is more secure with this activity.) Continue to encourage the baby to take one of the objects out of the box, name it, and then instruct the baby to put it back in the box. Stress the words "in" and "out" and praise the baby for any positive response that he makes.

The baby can be encouraged to play independently with the objects in the box. For further interest, other objects may be used in the box. Remember to use only a few objects at a time. Too much clutter confuses babies.

This activity develops

- language development in naming objects
- enhances the sense of touch
- eye-hand coordination
- an awareness of the concepts "in" and "out"
- independence
- confidence

Part II

(One - Two Years)

Introduction

The child at age one is beginning to display signs of independence, but she still needs much supervision and guidance. It is important to capture the right moment to interject the suggested activities to stimulate the child. Planning an exact time each day is not recommended, because young children are not time clocks even though they may be on a general schedule. Your child may sense regimentation and display negative behavior.

Try to understand your child by observing her daily patterns of behavior. Notice when your child seems to be looking for something to do. It could be in the early morning or after a nap in the afternoon. It depends on when she wants to be stimulated with something special.

It is important to be aware that a child of this age has a very short attention span and may not be able to complete a suggested activity at a chosen time. These activities need to be repeated for further stimulation at various times over an extended period of time. The child will develop self-confidence and independence as she becomes aware of her immediate environment.

Books with large colorful pictures that have little detail appeal to this age child. The child will delight in hearing the books read over and over, even though she often may not sit still long enough for the books to be completed at a given time.

Songs, rhymes and rhythms will capture the child's interest. Continue to repeat them often, and the child will soon be reciting her favorite ones from memory.

The child at this age is curious and will readily explore her immediate environment by feeling, poking, digging, pulling, pushing, peeking and banging. She will also enjoy stacking and carrying objects, filling and emptying containers, and putting and taking off the lids of available containers.

Life is a very busy time for a one year old child. She is more aware of herself. She will show more affection and will use gestures or point to convey wishes. Gradually, she will begin to communicate more verbally with a limited vocabulary. The more you interact with her by talking, reading, showing and performing activities, the more comfortable your child will be with you. This will serve to instill trust and security which will help to motivate your child's learning.

Note: The author and publisher are not liable for any injury or death incurred due to the misuse of the suggested materials and directions. As with all child-related activities, materials should be selected with careful attention to child safety; adult supervision is essential.

Age 1 – Week 1

The Face and Head Game

Touch the child's head with your hand and slowly move your hand from the neck to the left side of her head, across the top and down the right side of her head to the neck. This will give the child the feeling of the outline of her head. Tell the child that you have moved your hand around her head.

Draw a large circle or oval on a blank piece of paper and tell the child that you are drawing a picture of her head. Gently touch the child's left eye and tell the child that you are going to draw a picture of her eye. Draw the left eye in the proper place on the drawn face. Touch the child's right eye and do the same as with the left eye. Touch the nose, name it and draw it on the paper face. Touch the mouth next and name it as you draw it in place; make the mouth smile. Tell the child that you have drawn a happy face on the paper. Then touch and draw the left and right ears, naming and talking about them as you draw. For realism, add some hair to the drawing.

If the child still appears to be interested, take her pointer finger and trace around the outline of the drawn head. Touch the left eye, then touch the right eye, naming them as you touch them. Touch and name the nose. Then touch the smiling mouth as you sweep your hand from left to right on the drawn smile. Next touch the left and right ears as you name them. Point to the drawn hair and touch the child's hair as you say the word, "hair."

Repeat this activity throughout the week. In addition, point to the faces of the family, as well as those found in books and magazines, and identify the parts of the head each time that you talk to the child about the parts of the head. Praise the child for any positive response.

At another time, use large buttons, spools, felt pieces, chips of paper or anything that can be used for markers. The markers should be easy for the child to pick up and hold. Do not leave the child alone with any markers that can be swallowed! Use the drawn picture of a face or any large face and instruct the child to put a marker on an eye. It is not advisable to use the words, left and right. Therefore, allow the child to place the marker on either eye. Then tell her to put a marker on the other eye. Repeat the procedure for the nose, mouth, ears and hair. Help the child, if necessary, and remember to praise her whenever possible.

Another activity that can be performed to reinforce the memory of the parts of the face, is to paste a picture of a large face on cardboard or construction paper. When the paste is dry, cut the face in two pieces (left and right). Tell the child to put the face together.

Throughout the week, repeat these activities with your child, especially when the child seems to need you. While you are doing housework, you can interact with your child by telling her to point to any one of the parts of the face. Politely help or correct the child if necessary and remember to praise her.

This activity develops

- the sense of touch
- eye-hand coordination
- association skills
- listening
- language development
- following directions
- confidence
- awareness of left and right

Age 1 – Week 2

Spools

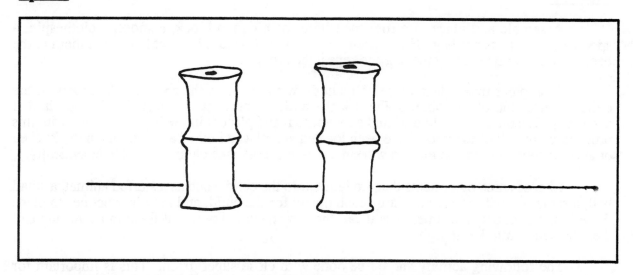

Select an assortment of spools and allow the child to explore with them. If the child does not show an interest in them, encourage her to look at, feel, push, roll, tap, or stack and knock them down. You may need to show the child how, but be sure to allow the child to play and explore before introducing any further activity.

At another time, encourage the child to bring two spools together and tap out the rhythm of 1-2, 1-2. Sing the words, "one-two, one-two" as you clap your hands together. Stand and tap your feet on the floor to the rhythm of 1-2, 1-2. Encourage the child to tap the spools while you clap or tap your feet. The child may lay the spools down and copy your actions. If this occurs, allow the child to do so.

Some time during the week, show the child how to stack the spools into sets of two. If the child stacks them higher than two, politely suggest that she make hers the same as yours. However, if she insists on stacking the spools her own way, allow her to do so and try again later.

You and your child can have fun rolling a spool back and forth to each other. The child may also be interested in stringing the spools. They can be strung with string or yarn. A pipe cleaner can be twisted to make a needle. Thread the string or yarn through the eye of the needle and secure the first spool for the child with a large knot or a piece of tape. Show the child how to string the spools and encourage her to try it independently. Help her whenever it is necessary. Remember to give praise for any positive actions.

This activity develops

- free exploration
- rhythm and awareness of the pattern 1-2
- awareness of sets of two
- eye-hand coordination
- independence

Age 1 – Week 3

Pick Up

Assemble and place in a row such items as a cup, a block, a spool, a clothespin, a spoon and a large paper bag. Name each item for the child and instruct her to put them in the bag. Tell the child to empty the bag and repeat the process.

At another time, place these items in different areas in the room in clear view of the child. Name one of the objects and ask the child to place it in a bag. Help the child if necessary. Encourage the child to find another item and place it in the bag. Continue with this procedure until all of the items have been located and placed in the bag. Do this in the kitchen or another room where you may be working, and encourage the child to work independently.

Choose some other items that are familiar to the child, such as a stuffed animal, a small ball, a rattle, a small book, etc. Name each object for the child, and then instruct her to place these in the bag, one at a time, as you call them by name. Try to put them in a row and call them by name from left to right.

The following activity should be done with close supervision. This is important for awareness of detail and eye-hand coordination. Assemble in a row, a raisin, a button, a piece of yarn, a paper clip and a key, and instruct the child to pick up these items, one at a time from left to right, as you call them by name in that order. They should be placed in a small container as the child picks them up. It is not necessary to use the words left and right, even though at this age, left and right awareness is important. Repeat this activity only with close supervision to prevent the child from swallowing or choking on these small items.

This activity develops

- left to right awareness and eye training
- listening
- following directions
- language enrichment
- awareness of "in" and "out," such as in the bag or container

Age 1 – Week 4

Containers and Lids

Assemble a plastic jar and lid, a pan with a matching lid, a shoe box and lid and several other things with matching lids. Make certain that the lids will be easy for the child to take off and replace. If the task is too difficult, the child will become frustrated and lose interest.

Once the materials are assembled, present three of these containers to the child and allow her to remove and replace the lids. The child may need some assistance in putting the correct lids on the containers, but be sure and allow the child the privilege of trial and error. Nevertheless, assist the child whenever necessary to avoid frustration.

Change the type of containers throughout the week and try to let the child work independently whenever possible. Use a maximum of three containers at a time. Too many containers will confuse the child. Use the words "on" and "off" as the lids are put on and taken off.

Throughout the week, call your child's attention to other things that have lids. It may be in the bedroom, kitchen, bathroom or other places. This will serve to expand your child's awareness of things in her immediate environment.

This activity develops

- problem solving through free exploration
- awareness of "on" and "off"
- awareness of matching lids
- enhancement of the sense of touch

Age 1 – Week 5

Let's Play Ball

Obtain a nerf ball if possible, although a rubber ball will suffice for this activity. The ball should be about six inches in diameter. This size is recommended so that the child can easily hold the ball with both hands. The nerf ball is soft and is easier for a child to grab and control.

Sit with the child on a smooth non-carpeted area and roll the ball a short distance to the child. Observe to see if the child watches the ball or does she attempt to stop the ball? Talk to the child and encourage her to catch the ball as it is rolled to her. Continue to do this until the child loses interest. Repeat this activity often to develop skill in watching and receiving a ball. Praise the child whenever she responds positively.

Once the child is comfortable in watching and receiving a ball, encourage the child to roll the ball back to you. Much practice is needed to ensure a straight aim or roll. To accomplish this, place books on each side of the ball's path, or use long blocks, a broom or a mop for boundaries. At first, encourage the child to use both hands to roll the ball. Gradually, the child will develop skill and will be able to roll a ball successfully with one hand.

A homemade tunnel can easily be made with a corrugated box by cutting an opening on opposite sides of the box. A table, chair or building block tunnel may also be used for the child to roll the ball under. After the child is better coordinated, line up an empty plastic detergent bottle at the end of a controlled narrow path and encourage the child to use the ball to knock down the plastic bottle. Be sure to praise and encourage the child in a positive manner.

During a given week, be sure and repeat many of the activities that have been suggested in previous weeks. In this way, you help your child to develop confidence, security and also independence. Remember that young children need to repeat activities in order to build a sound foundation for learning.

This activity develops

- eye-hand coordination
- tactile sensation (feel of the ball)
- following directions
- associating different uses for one object, the ball
- language development by listening to words
  used during the activity

Age 1 – Week 6

Let's Go Walking

The lines on a tiled floor, masking tape, yarn or string placed in a straight line on the floor can be used for this activity. The line space should be approximately five feet long.

Walk on the designated straight line while the child watches you. Then encourage the child to walk on the straight line. To make this activity more interesting, tell the child to pretend that the line is a bridge that goes across some water. Explain that a bridge allows people to go across a body of water without getting wet. Make sure that the child understands that this is like a game and if she steps off the line, then she will get wet. If the child still does not understand, walk across the pretend bridge again. Talk to the child as you do this and deliberately pretend to lose your balance and step in the pretend water. Laugh and tell the child that you got wet, because you were not careful and you fell in the water.

Instruct the child to put one foot in front of the other so that the heel of one foot touches the toe of the other foot. Also suggest that the child hold both arms out straight to help her maintain her balance. Praise the child even if she seems to find this activity difficult.

Repeat this activity often throughout the week. The child will soon become confident in crossing the pretend bridge. You may even observe the child doing this activity independently, and chances are that the child will not use the designated line where you first introduced this activity. She may even find another line to practice her line walking.

Since a child of this age may spontaneously enjoy walking backwards at various times allow her to do so. If she does not initiate this on her own, show her how to walk backwards on a given line. Point out that she should keep her eyes on the line as she walks backwards.

Next, the child can be requested to straddle the line as she walks forward. Later, the child can try walking backwards in this manner. It may be difficult for her, but watching the line as she walks backwards involves much concentration and coordination. Try this at a later date if the child appears to encounter any difficulty.

This activity develops

- leg, foot and eye coordination
- language interaction
- concentration
- following directions
- independence

Age 1 – Week 7

Look at Me

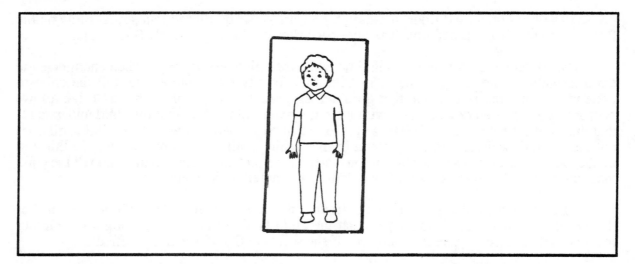

Lay the child down on a large sheet of brown or white blank paper. Use a crayon and quickly trace around the child's body. Tell the child to get up and look at the shape of her body on the paper. Say to the child, "Look how big you are!"

Use a crayon or felt marker and draw a left eye on the paper. Then draw a right eye. Ask the child what they are. As you draw the nose and smiling mouth, ask the child to name them also. Help the child if necessary. Point to the position where the left ear should be, and ask the child what should be drawn there. Praise the child if she responds correctly. If not, identify the ears as you draw them in place.

Call the child by name, and instruct her to find the eyes, nose, mouth and ears. Does the child point to the eyes on the paper or her own eyes? Whichever the child points to, make a point of letting the child know that the face on the paper represents her face. Use the word "picture" to identify the face in the drawing.

Look at the child's clothing and name the main color that the child is wearing. Ask the child to find that one color among the crayons or felt markers that you have been using. If the child needs help, repeat the question and direct the child to look more closely. Emphasize that the color chosen is the same color that is found on her clothing. Use only one color at this time. If you use several colors, a child of this age will become confused. Introduce only one color at a time, and delay adding another color until the child is very comfortable in identifying a specific color.

Sketch in the clothing with a marker on the outline. Show the child how to hold a crayon or marker. Make a mark on the paper to show the child how to color the clothes on the outline model of the child. The child should be allowed to hold the crayon the way she feels most comfortable, even though you may have shown her the correct way. Observe the child's hand preference, if any. A child at this age may switch hands to color. It is best to allow free movement of the crayon irrespective of the line boundaries of the clothing.

The scribbling stage of writing or drawing will take place during this activity. Observe the child. The arms, legs and body will probably all be scribbled on. Note that most of the scribbling is up and down or round and round. Ignore any scribbling outside the lines, and praise the child for the nice coloring.

You may want to hang this " masterpiece" on the refrigerator or somewhere else, and throughout the week allow the child to scribble some more on the outline picture to fill in with more color. Be sure to use the same color and repeat the color name often. Cut the outline out if it is still visible after the child finishes coloring. The child will enjoy watching you cut it out.

This is an opportune time to point out the body parts for association. Name the neck, arms, hands, chest, stomach (tummy), legs, feet and toes. Leave out the word "toes" if the child is wearing closed shoes.

This activity develops

- an awareness of the body shape
- skill in associating the outline with herself
- awareness of a specific color and its name
- more awareness of the body parts
- language enrichment
- eye-hand coordination
- matching a specific color

Age 1 – Week 8

What Made That Sound?

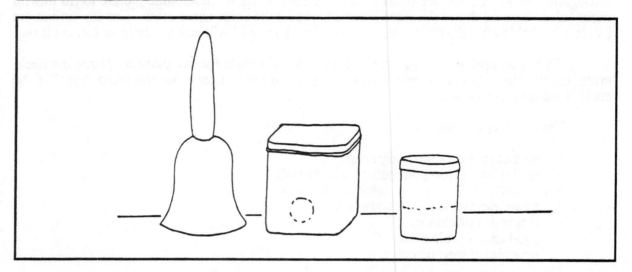

Assemble a bell or timer, a marble that is in a closed metal container, water in a small closed plastic container that is not full, or any three different sound makers of your choice.

Ring the bell or timer and say its name. Roll the marble around in the container and say its name. Swish the water around in the closed plastic container and say, "Water." Do this several times and encourage the child to say the name of each thing as you make the respective sound. The child may just watch what you do, but continue to make the sounds until the child loses interest.

At another time, put the containers behind the sofa, a chair or something that will hide the three containers. The hiding place must be where the child can easily go and retrieve one of the three things.

Choose one and make a noise with it. Ask the child to find the one that made the sound. Help the child if she seems confused. Continue to play the game and praise the child whenever you can. If the child makes a mistake, keep working with the same noise maker until the child successfully finds the correct one.

Choose three other different things and tell the child to close her eyes or turn around while you make a sound with one of the materials. The child can then be instructed to point to the correct one. Continue to make the child aware of specific sounds throughout the house and outside.

This activity develops

- listening skills
- association skills
- following directions
- vocabulary enrichment
- confidence

Age 1 – Week 9

What's Outside?

Borrow several books from the early childhood section of the library. The books should have some pictures of trees, flowers, birds and houses. Read and talk about the pictures and tell the child some things that are found outside. It will be beneficial if you can take the child outside after you read one of the books and point out some things that are found outside that you read about in that book.

Walk outside with your child on another occasion and go near a tree. Touch the tree and talk about how tall and big it is. If possible, pluck a green leaf from the tree and let the child feel it. Tell the child that the leaf is green. If it is autumn try to find a green leaf.

Look at the grass and tell the child that grass is green also. Allow the child to feel some blades of grass, and make the child aware that the tree is much taller than the grass. Look up and down at the tree so that the child will understand what you mean by the word "tall."

Show the child some flowers if they are in bloom. The child should be allowed to touch and smell the flowers, but she should also be told not to pick flowers without permission. Make the child aware that trees, grass and flowers all have green leaves.

Go to a place outside where some soil is visible. Take a stick and dig a little to loosen it. Let the child dig too if she wishes. Encourage the child to feel the soil and tell the child that trees, grass and flowers live in the soil.

Show the child the roots of some weeds if possible. Let the child feel the roots and observe the root hairs. Tell the child that roots soak up water and minerals for the trees, grass and flowers to help them to grow, and that roots also hold the plants in the ground. Make the child aware that trees, grass and flowers are living things.

Pick up a rock and tell the child that a rock is not living. Also say, "Soil helps living things to grow, but it is not a living thing." Do not expect the child to understand all of this. You are making the child aware of her environment. This should stimulate the child to think. You can subdivide this activity and talk about one new thing outside every day or you can combine two things and talk about them.

At another time during the week, read and look at a book about trees, grass and flowers. Can your child recall anything that you saw, felt or talked about outside? Does the child recognize and recall the color green?

Observe the birds outside. Naturally, the child will not be able to feel them; however, you may find a feather and allow the child to feel it. Talk about birds and tell the child that birds are different colors. Explain where they live and describe their nests, eggs, habits and how they move. Your discussion will depend on the child's interest.

Continue your discussion of things outside only when the child appears receptive. Point out the yellow sun, the blue sky and the white clouds. Caution the child about looking directly at the sun. She should know that this can damage the eyes. At night you can talk about the moon and stars. Do not expect her to be an authority of what is outside. At this age it is for awareness and children are curious about their natural surroundings.

This activity develops

- an awareness of the outside world
- an awareness of the colors green, yellow, blue and white
- vocabulary enrichment
- enhancement of the sense of touch
- skill in associating what is found outside and in a book

Age 1 – Week 10

What is Moving?

Assemble a stuffed animal, a plastic cup and a ball or three similar things. Name each object for the child. Tie a string or piece of yarn around each of the three objects leaving approximately twelve inches free. Cover the three objects with a cloth, receiving blanket or a large towel, but leave the three strings visible from the cover.

Pull the string that is attached to the stuffed animal and instruct the child to watch. Be sure that you do not expose the objects that are covered. Ask the child to name the object that is moving. Tell the child to look at the shape of the covered moving object. If the child has difficulty naming the object, retrieve it for the child and identify it again. Cover the stuffed animal again and repeat the process. Do this until the child is secure in naming the moving stuffed animal. Continue with this procedure until the child can readily identify all three covered objects when they are moved.

Play this game as long as the child appears to be interested. Vary the game at another time by changing the three objects and wiggling the string "snake fashion" as you pull the strings one at a time. It is important to work with only a few things at a time. Too many items may excessively stimulate the child and cause confusion.

Encourage the child to work independently by covering the objects and pulling the strings one at a time. The child will delight in watching the objects move. She will realize that she is causing the motion and will find it challenging to cover the objects completely. This will encourage her to solve the problem to accomplish the task.

Remember to repeat some of the activities from the previous weeks, especially those that seemed difficult for the child at that time. Children enjoy and need the repetition.

This activity develops

- language interaction
- visual discrimination
- eye-hand coordination
- independence
- problem solving

Age 1 – Week 11

What Can I Smell?

Assemble some vanilla, a little cold coffee and some apple juice. Pour a little of each on separate pieces of cotton. Show the child the original container for each liquid. Allow the child to sniff and smell each of the liquids. Name them but do not expect the child to recall their names.

Allow the child to smell the vanilla and ask her to point to the correct container. If the child fails, allow her to smell each liquid again and identify each container again. Continue to repeat this activity until the child is successful or loses interest. Praise the child for any positive response.

At another time, use orange juice, tomato juice and vinegar and repeat the procedure. Other liquids or spices may be introduced when you feel the child is ready for some new things to smell.

This is a good time to tell the child that some things can hurt us if we smell them too closely. Emphasize that adults will tell her what is safe to smell. She should be told that she should never smell from any bottle or container without permission because it could be dangerous.

As you work in the kitchen, encourage your child to smell the different foods that you cook. Make the child aware of the common smells of the baking of bread, cake and cookies. The smell of fish is distinct, and the child will have little difficulty recognizing that smell. Some children are curious about the different smells of spices, especially cinnamon. With supervision, your child can sniff and smell the many different odors of spices.

Perfumes, lotion, after shave, deodorant, powder and soap are other smells that interest children. Make the child aware that some things smell good and others do not. Talk about the nose and its location. Make the child aware that the nose is used for breathing and smelling. The child may enjoy chanting this jingle:

> "Nose, nose, nose,
> It can smell a rose"

This activity develops

- an awareness of the sense of smell
- skill in matching and associating different smells
- free exploration of safe smells
- an awareness of the danger of some smells
- more of an awareness of the nose and its purpose
- language enrichment

Age 1 – Week 12

Let's Go Fishing

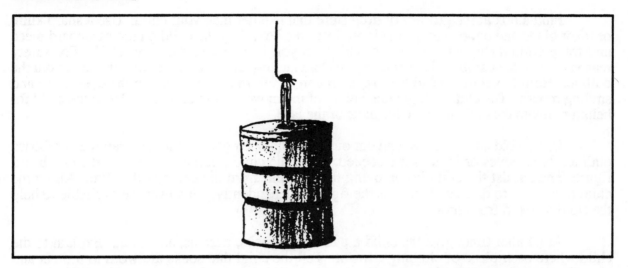

Obtain a coffee can with a plastic lid. Attach a twelve inch string to a clothespin. Cut a hole in the plastic lid, a little larger than the clothespin. Place the lid on the can.

Lower the attached clothespin through the hole of the plastic lid and hold on to the string. Hand the child the string with the attached clothespin, and tell the child to pull the string and lift the clothespin up through the hole. Allow the child to solve the problem. If she has difficulty, assist her in lifting the clothespin through the hole. Be sure to praise the child for trying.

Different objects of similar size may be substituted and lifted through the hole in the same manner. A different lid may be used if some of the objects are too large for the present hole. The child should be encouraged to work independently.

To make the activity more interesting, you can tell the child that the object is a pretend fish in the sea. While the child is "fishing" she may enjoy chanting this jingle:

"Fish, fish, fish in the sea,
Come on up and look at me"

This activity develops

- eye-hand coordination
- skill in problem solving
- an awareness of the different materials used for"fish"
- an awareness of the rhyming words "sea" and "me"

Age 1 — Week 13

Can I Dress Myself?

Find a box at the grocery or drug store that is taller than your child. Use a sharp knife or razor blade and cut one long side loose from the box. Lay the child on the cardboard piece and trace around the child's outline with a crayon just as you did in week 7. For safety reasons, move the cardboard away from the child and use the razor cutter or knife to cut out the outline. Hold the child's hand and use a crayon or felt marker to draw in the eyes, nose and smiling mouth. The child will get the feeling of the movement in drawing. Praise the child for helping. Invite the child to name the parts of the face.

Use an old shirt or sheet and cut out a simple open garment larger than the cardboard outline. No sleeves or buttons are needed. Help the child put the garment on the cardboard figure. Then assist the child in removing the garment from the cardboard figure. Allow the child to attempt to dress and undress the figure independently. However, be available to help the child to avoid frustration.

At another time, give the child a pair of big socks, mittens, and a hat. Explain to the child where each piece of clothing is worn. Tell the child that socks are worn to protect and keep the feet warm. Mittens are worn when it is cold to keep the hands warm. A hat is also worn to keep the head warm.

Hug the child and say, "I love (child's name)." Observe the child. Does the child copy you by hugging the cardboard figure? Kiss the child and once again say, "I love (child's name)." Observe the child's response. Your child will become aware of love and affection for others. Love and affection are very necessary for a child's self-image and confidence.

The child can be allowed to work with the cardboard figure independently. In fact, she may even be interested in giving the figure a name. The body parts may also be reviewed.

This activity develops

- an awareness of the shape of the body
- an awareness of the body parts
- language interaction
- problem solving in dressing and undressing the figure
- an awareness of the purpose of clothing
- an awareness of giving affection to others

Age 1 – Week 14

Exploring With Dirt, Sand or Rice

This activity can be controlled inside, but can be done more easily outside. If this activity is to be done inside, obtain a dishpan and fill it half full of dirt, sand or rice. Place an old shower curtain underneath the dishpan to catch any spills. A sand box or non-grassy area can be used for this activity outside.

Use a mixing bowl or sand pail, a large wooden spoon or shovel and assorted sizes of plastic containers or measuring cups for this activity. Let the child feel the dirt, sand or rice and encourage her to pick some up and let it fall back into the container. Allow the child to freely explore the dirt, sand or rice, but make certain that the child does not eat or throw it. Ask the child to tell how the dirt, sand or rice feels. If there is no response, talk to the child about the feel of whichever one of the three you are using. For further enrichment of this activity, all three kinds of materials can be used on separate occasions.

Later, show the child how to fill the containers by using her hands, the spoon or shovel. Then show her how to empty it out and start over again. Make the child aware that it takes several handfuls, spoonfuls or shovelfuls to fill a container.

If the child would rather just play with the dirt, sand or rice allow her to do so. Skill in filling and emptying containers can be encouraged at another time.

Large beans may also be used for this activity. In this way the child can either pour the beans or pick them up in handsful or individually to put them in a container. This is also a good activity for older preschoolers.

This activity develops

- enhancement of the sense of touch
- eye-hand coordination
- an awareness of different sizes of containers,
  especially large and small
- free exploration
- skill in associating what can be used to fill the containers
- language interaction

Age 1 – Week 15

My New House

Obtain a large box at a furniture or appliance store suitable for making a cardboard house. Draw and cut a door large enough for the child to go in and out of easily. If you want the door to open and close, leave the left side of the drawn door intact. A doorknob can be made with a spool fastened with a long bolt and nut that will fit through the spool and the cardboard. Alternatively, cut a round hole a little larger than the child's finger so that the hole will be a substitute for a doorknob. Use masking tape to tape over any rough edges. Draw and cut out two or more windows, and encourage the child to help you decorate the outside of the house with felt markers.

Invite the child to move in her new house. Once the child becomes familiar with the house she will enjoy going in and out of the house. She can be taught to wave " bye-bye" each time she goes in the house. She may begin to carry objects back and forth to her new house, since children of this age enjoy carrying objects around from place to place. If she gets tired, she may even take a nap in her house.

This activity develops

- language interaction
- fine and gross motor coordination
- an awareness of "outside" and "inside" the cardboard house
- security or a feeling of possessing something of her own
- an awareness of "open and close"

Age 1 – Week 16

Rhythm Band Music

Assemble an empty oatmeal box or a coffee can and replace the lid to make a pretend drum. Give the child a wooden spoon or stick and encourage her to tap on the drum. Allow her to do this until she loses interest.

At another time, sing or chant, "Rum, tum, tum, beat the drum." Repeat the chant until the child attempts to repeat what you say. This chanting instills the awareness of 1-2-3, 1-2-3, but use the chant instead of numbers for a while with the child. Then use the pretend drum and tap on it to the rhythm of "rum, tum, tum." Tell the child to tap on the drum while you say the chant. The child may say the chant with you as she attempts to tap out the rhythm. Allow the child to continue as long as she is interested.

Later in the week, a few small rocks can be placed inside a closed plastic or metal container such as a small coffee or cake tin. Let the child shake and rattle the container and listen to the new sound. While the child shakes the rocks in the container you could tap out the 1-2-3 rhythm with the pretend drum. Observe the child. Does she want the drum or does she continue to shake the rocks? If she insists on taking the drum, exchange with her and shake out the 1-2-3 rhythm with the rock shaker. Any response will show that the child is aware of the difference in the two sounds.

Two spoons can be tapped together to produce a "joyful noise." Also two wooden blocks tapped or rubbed back and forth together will produce different sounds. A bunch of keys on a ring can produce an interesting jingle when they are shaken. The child may also enjoy placing dried beans in a tightly closed container to make sounds. All of these materials can be used to emphasize the rhythmical pattern of 1-2, as well as the rhythm 1-2-3.

This activity develops

- auditory discrimination
- an awareness of different rhythmical patterns
- eye-hand coordination
- language interaction
- independence
- free exploration

Age 1 – Week 17

Exploring With Water

Assemble a sponge, wash cloth, cotton ball, paper towel, a piece of celery and anything else that you wish to use to show the child how something can absorb water. Use a dishpan, plastic tub or something similar and fill it half full of water. Allow the child to hold and feel the dry sponge. Dip the edge of the sponge in the water and let the sponge absorb the water to its saturation point. Once again allow the child to hold the sponge. The child will become aware of the change in the feel and weight of the sponge and will sense the moisture caused by the water.

Wring out the sponge and allow the child to play with the sponge and dabble with her hands in the water. Encourage the child to listen for the sounds that the water produces when it is disturbed.

At bath time, give the child a dry wash cloth and tell her to put the cloth in the water of the bath tub. Ask the child how the cloth feels. If there is no response, discuss the wetness of water and explain that the wash cloth soaked up all the water that it could hold, making the cloth heavier. Hold the cloth up and allow the child to observe the water as it drips down from the cloth.

Place a small transparent container of water in the kitchen sink. Add a little food coloring to the water. The child may enjoy choosing the color to use. Identify the chosen color by name. Encourage the child to feel a cotton ball. At this time you can say, "This is soft dry cotton." Allow the child to hold and feel the cotton. Instruct the child to slowly dip the cotton in the colored water. The child will delight in seeing the white cotton change color. The child's hands can attempt to wring out the cotton. The child may notice that the cotton increases in size (swells). You can make the child aware of this by saying, " Look, the (name the color) cotton is wet and it got bigger." The child will enjoy repeating this activity. Repeat the same activity with a paper towel, but encourage the child to choose a different color of food coloring.

Give the child a stalk of celery at another time and encourage her to smell, feel and taste it. Tap the celery on the side of the kitchen sink and make a sound with it. Tap out a 1-2 or a 1-2-3 rhythm several times to maintain the child's attention. Place a transparent container of water in front of the child and allow her to choose a color to add to the water. Try to discourage yellow because it is too pale of a color. Place the stalk of celery in the colored water, and from time to time, let the child observe how it absorbs water and changes color.

This activity develops

- further awareness of the sense of touch
- eye-hand coordination
- free exploration
- more awareness of different colors
- an awareness of wetness, weight, absorption
- observational skills

Age 1 – Week 18

Put It Through the Slit or Hole

Assemble at least five keys that are approximately the same size. Cut a slit from a plastic container or coffee can lid. The slit should be large enough so that the keys can be pushed through the hole with little resistance. Place the lid on the container and encourage the child to pick up a key and push it through the slit in the lid of the container. The key will make more of a sound if you use a metal coffee can. Emphasize the sound that the key makes as it hits the bottom of the container. Allow the child to continue until all of the keys have been pushed through the slit. Remove the lid, empty out the keys and repeat the process until the child loses interest.

Other materials may be selected for pushing through the slit such as circles cut from Styrofoam meat trays, buttons, pennies, metal baggie ties, plastic bread tabs, washers, etc. These materials will not only add variation, but they will enhance the experiences for the child.

This activity develops

- fine motor control
- problem solving
- following directions
- eye-hand coordination
- independence and confidence
- enhances the sense of touch

Age 1 – Week 19

Finger Painting Can Be Fun

Take two tablespoons of flour and add a little water at a time until you have made a thin paste. Add a few drops of food coloring. Use a spoon and place a blob of this mixture on a large piece of wax paper that has been taped to the kitchen counter or table. Protect the child's clothing with an old shirt or use a large bib before allowing the child to finger paint.

Show the child how to move and slide the fingers and hands across the wax paper. Use the word "slippery" and "wet" in your conversation with the child. Encourage the child to move her hands up and down, back and forth and around and around. Use the pointer finger to make some dots across the paper and allow the child to explore with the wet, slippery mixture on the paper.

Avoid drawing pictures for the child, because this activity is for free movement and exploration. Drawing pictures for the child may inhibit creativity.

At the conclusion of this activity, if the child made an interesting creative design or picture that you would like to save, press a piece of construction or typing paper firmly over the picture. Carefully lift the top edge of the paper and pull it away from the wax paper. You will then have the picture printed on the paper. Praise the child and hang the picture on the refrigerator with tape or a small magnet. When the picture is dry, allow the child to feel it. Tell the child that the water evaporated from the picture.

For larger quantities of finger paint, mix 3 tablespoons of sugar, 1/2 teaspoon of salt, 1/2 cup of cornstarch and 2 cups of water. Cook on low heat until smooth and thick. Cool, then pour into small jars and add a different food coloring to each jar.

The child may enjoy repeating this activity at another time. Remember to review and repeat some of the activities that were introduced earlier in the year.

This activity develops

- free exploration
- creativity
- fine motor control
- more awareness of "wet," dry" and "slippery"
- independence and confidence

Age 1 – Week 20

Painting With a Brush

Use a large sheet of paper or an old newspaper. Tape the paper to a table, counter or something stationary. Mix a little food coloring with water and use an old or new regular paint brush that is approximately two inches wide. Place the colored water in a heavy skillet or a pan to avoid tipping or spilling.

Place the brush in the colored water and show the child how to wring out the excess water on the edge of the pan. Then instruct the child to brush over the paper gently. Allow the child to explore with the brush and colored water. Assist the child only when it seems necessary and praise the child for trying. The child may lay the brush down and prefer to hand paint. Allow the child to explore and create. When the child is finished, hang the picture on the refrigerator for the other family members to see.

Daily painting with a new color may serve to motivate the child. With continuity, progress will be noted. When the child shows some dexterity, purchase a set of children's water colors or tempera paints. The colors are more vivid and will have greater appeal to the child.

This activity develops

- eye-hand coordination
- free exploration and creativity
- more awareness of different colors

Age 1 – Week 21

Inside-Outside

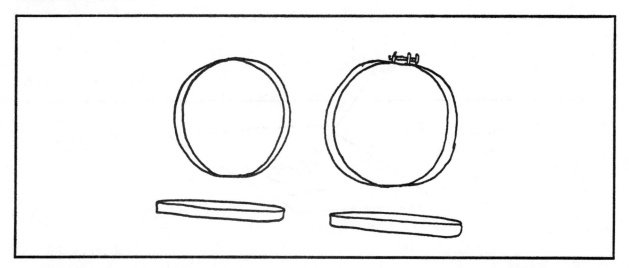

Obtain two embroidery hoops (one large and one small) or cut two circles from cardboard or paper plates. The circles should fit inside of one another. If they are colored different colors with felt markers they will have more appeal to the child.

Place the smaller circle on the left and the larger one on the right of a flat surface. Pick up the smaller one and show the child how it fits inside of the larger one. As you do this, tell the child that you have placed the smaller circle inside of the larger one. Emphasize the word "inside." Then take the smaller circle and place it on the left of the larger circle and tell the child that you took the smaller circle outside of the larger circle. Emphasize the word "outside."

Perform this activity several times and encourage the child to work independently. If the child does not work from left to right, avoid correcting her. However, each time that you perform this activity, try to work from left to right. In this way, you are training the child's eyes to move for left to right progression.

Use a hoola hoop and encourage the child to jump inside and outside of the circle. The hoola hoop may also be used for the child to throw a bean bag, yarn ball, a sock ball or any safe object "inside" the boundary of the hoola hoop. Then tell the child to take the object(s) "outside" of the hoola hoop. The child may enjoy repeating this and the other suggested activities. The spatial concepts of "inside" and "outside" should be emphasized so that the child will understand.

This activity develops

- an awareness of "inside" and "outside"
- an awareness of "large" and "small"
- further awareness of left and right progression
- gross motor coordination
- eye-hand coordination
- following directions

Age 1 – Week 22

Upstairs and Downstairs

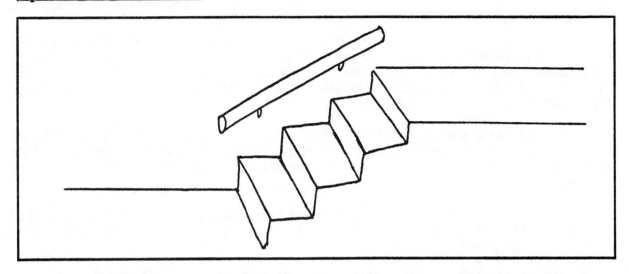

Now is a good time for the child to practice going upstairs and downstairs. Three stairs should be sufficient for a child on which to practice. If you do not have stairs in your home, you can use three boxes that are weighted inside for stability. Cinder blocks or bricks may also be used to make temporary stairs. If you use imitation stairs, place them against the wall. This will give the illusion of real stairs. Emphasize the words, "up" and "down" to ensure that the child comprehends the meaning of these concepts.

As the child is encouraged to go up and down the stairs, it will be more interesting for her if you will say a jingle or a chant such as:

> "(child's name) goes up, up, up.
> (child's name) comes down, down, down."

The child will enjoy going up and down the stairs over and over again. With much practice, the child will soon gain enough confidence to want to go higher on the stairs. For safety reasons, three stairs should be sufficient for a child of this age without supervision.

This is a good time to talk about safety on the stairs. The child should be made aware of the consequences if she is not careful when climbing and descending the stairs. The child should also be told not to leave toys on the stairs, because they may cause someone to fall.

This activity develops

- an awareness of "up" and "down"
- self-confidence
- independence
- gross motor coordination
- listening

Age 1 – Week 23

Home Clay Exploration

To make a quick clay, mix two cups of flour, a half cup of salt, and gradually add one cup of water. Add a little food coloring and knead this mixture until it is well blended. Peppermint or some other pleasant flavoring may be added for interest. However, tell the child that the clay is not food and should not be eaten. This mixture will keep for several days in the refrigerator if it is kept in a closed plastic bag.

To make a more stable clay, mix 1 cup of flour, 1 tablespoon of oil, 1 cup of water, 1/2 cup of salt, 2 teaspoons of cream of tartar and food coloring. Cook over medium heat until the mixture forms a ball. Knead until smooth. This mixture will keep indefinitely in a plastic bag or sealed container.

Tape wax paper to a counter or table top. An old plastic place mat may used instead of the wax paper for the protection of the work area. Either will make it easier to clean up when the activity is completed.

Give the child a piece of clay that can be held comfortably in her hands. Show the child how to squeeze, roll and pat the clay. Then allow the child to explore with the clay until she loses interest.

If the child needs some motivation, roll a small piece into a ball and pat it flat. Does the child attempt to copy you? For further interest and motivation, roll the clay into a long roll and join the two ends together to make a circle or some other shape. Talk to the child about each shape that you make.

Encourage the child to squeeze, roll and pat the clay as you talk about how it feels. Ask the child to smell it. Talk about the odor of the clay. Is it a pleasant odor? Then encourage the child to poke, pull, roll and break the clay into pieces and allow her to continue to explore with the clay.

This activity develops

- fine motor coordination
- enhancement of the sense of touch
- free exploration
- language enrichment through conversation
- creativity
- independence

Age 1 – Week 24

Cardboard Puzzles

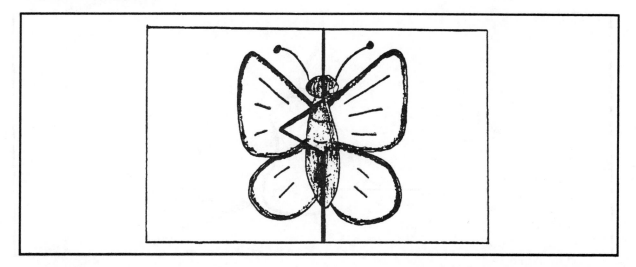

Cut or draw three large 8 1/2 x 11 inch pictures with bright colors. The pictures should have very little detail. The pictures could be of a house, a tree and a butterfly. Show the child each picture and identify it by name. Glue the pictures on heavy cardboard and allow them to dry. Then cut each picture in half from the top to the bottom with only one irregularity in the cut.

Mix the pieces and place them on the floor or a table. Encourage the child to put the house together. Then suggest that the child put the tree together and then the butterfly. Help the child if she does not seem to understand and talk about each picture. For example, you could say, "The house is red. We live in a house."

These puzzles can be used over and over. The child will become more confident, and perhaps she will talk about the pictures by using one word or a phrase.

Three more pictures with more detail may be cut from a magazine or newspaper and be used in the same manner. These pictures may be cut in either two or three pieces each. The child will be more successful if the picture images are large, colorful and have little detail. It is advisable to use only three puzzles at a time. Too many pieces tend to confuse young children.

This activity develops

- an awareness that two or more parts make a whole
- more awareness of color
- language enrichment through conversation
- eye-hand coordination

Age 1 – Week 25

Drop Small Objects in a Bottle

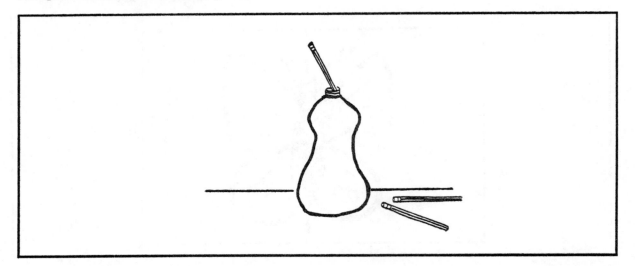

Use any large plastic non-breakable bottle with a narrow opening for this activity. Assemble a small rock, a popsicle stick, a pencil with no point, a clothespin or any safe object that will easily go through the small opening of the plastic bottle. You may choose to use a set of 4 similar objects instead of different ones. A face or flower may be drawn on the bottle with a felt marker to add interest to this activity.

Encourage the child to choose an object and drop it in the narrow opening of the bottle. Assist the child if necessary.

Listen for the sound of each object as it is dropped into the bottle. Exaggerate the sound as you try to imitate the sound in some manner. Words such as "ping," "thud" or "plop" will serve to make the child listen more closely as each object is dropped into the bottle.

When all of the objects have been dropped into the bottle, turn the bottle upside down and allow the child to use both hands and shake the objects out of the inverted bottle. Repeat this activity and encourage the child to work independently. Assist the child only when she appears to need help.

This activity develops

- eye-hand coordination
- problem solving
- listening for a purpose
- self-confidence
- following directions
- language interaction

Age 1 – Week 26

I Can Carry a Tray

Children of this age love to pick up tiny pieces of thread, lint or paper and show them to an adult. Encourage the child to look on the floor for tiny pieces to pick up and place in a container. Commend the child for any positive response.

At another time, use a Styrofoam or cardboard meat tray and place several lightweight, non-breakable objects on it. Select a small block, spool, clothespin, spoon or something similar that is lightweight and will be easy for the child to carry.

Encourage the child to balance the tray and carry it a short distance. Then instruct the child to bring the tray back without dropping any of the items. If one falls off the tray say, "Oops." Tell the child to pick up the object that fell and place it on the tray. If the child has any difficulty, be ready to assist, but allow the child to do as much independently as possible.

More small lightweight items may be added to the tray until a sensible capacity load has been reached. Praise the child for being able to carry so many things on a tray.

At another time, place a small rubber/plastic ball on the tray. Instruct the child to walk very carefully with the tray and watch the ball as she carries the tray. Observe the way the child balances the tray and make positive suggestions for the child to maintain the ball on the tray. If the ball falls off, tell the child to retrieve the ball and to try again. Remind the child to walk slowly, very carefully and to watch the ball. With patience and guidance your child will succeed. Praise will motivate her to try to do her best.

This activity develops

- skill with the sense of balance
- coordination using both hands
- an awareness of "light" and "heavy"
- skill in manipulation and observation of different objects on the tray
- an awareness of stationary objects and the effect that the moving ball had on balance

86

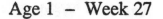
Put the Fish in the Boat

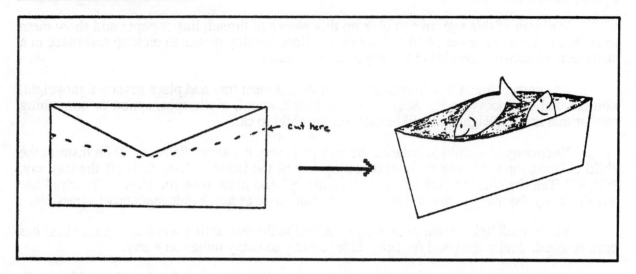

Cut three or four fish from construction paper, index cards or light-weight cardboard. The fish should be approximately 3 x 4 inches. Color each fish a different color and add an eye and a mouth to each one. This will add interest for the child and will help to motivate her to participate in this activity.

Use a large business envelope or a folded piece of paper for the boat. Cut the envelope or paper to resemble a boat. Leave the top slit open and tape or staple any other open sides. This makes a flat boat. Decorate the boat with different colors.

Encourage the child to pick up a fish and put it in the boat. This will require the child to separate the two top sides in order for her to slip the fish in the boat. Call the fish by color when the child picks up the fish to put it in the boat. When all the fish have been "caught" and are in the flat boat, take the fish out and start again.

At another time you may repeat this activity using numbers and counting. For example, write a number on each of the fish from one to four and instruct the child to find the fish with a specific number on it to put in the envelope (boat). Count the fish several items to ensure that the child understands counting one to four before proceeding any further. As the child is picking designated fish, ask her how many fish are in the "boat" and how many are not.

This activity develops

- skill in picking up a flat object
- eye-hand coordination
- problem solving
- confidence
- independence
- language interaction

Age 1 – Week 28

Where Is the Room?

Take the child by the hand and walk with her to her room. Tell the child that this is her room. Walk with the child to your room and tell the child that this is your room. Then walk to the bathroom and identify it. Make sure that the child knows the names of these three rooms.

Call the child by name and tell her to show you her room. Praise the child if she follows this command correctly. If the child seems confused, take her to her room once again and tell her that you are in her room. Repeat this until the child can show you to her room.

Continue this activity with your room and the bathroom. If the child still seems to be confused, try again at another time. However, if the child is successful and appears to be enjoying this activity, choose three other rooms and repeat the process.

It may take several days for the child to go to the correct room when requested, but much praise and encouragement are keys to motivation and success.

This activity develops

- an awareness of rooms and their positions
- following directions
- language interaction
- confidence

Age 1 – Week 29

Big and Little

Assemble a big and a little spoon, a big and a little lid, an empty toilet tissue roll and an empty paper towel roll, a big and a little shoe, or select several similar items of big and little things.

Pick up the big spoon and tell the child that it is bigger than the other spoon. Tell the child that the other spoon is little. Say the word, "big" and "little" several times as you continue to show the child the big and little objects of each kind. Place the big and little items of the same set together, preferably in a row.

Tell the child to pick up the big spoon. If the child does it correctly, praise her and instruct her to put it back in place. If the child picks up the incorrect item, tell the child what it is, identify its size, and tell the child to put it back in place.

Continue working only with the concept of "big" until the child is confident in choosing the bigger item correctly. Avoid using the word "large." Interchanging words at this age may confuse the child.

Introduce the "little" concept when you feel that the child is secure in choosing the bigger object each time a big and little object are compared. Changing the commands for the child to choose between "big" and "little" during one sitting of this activity may be too difficult and confusing for her. Introduce this concept with caution if you feel your child is ready. It is better to be secure in doing an activity than to be confused and frustrated with one that is too difficult.

This activity develops

- an awareness of the concepts, "big" and "little"
- vocabulary enrichment in naming the objects
- following directions
- skill in making a choice
- an awareness of comparison
- eye-hand coordination

Age 1 – Week 30

Stepping Stones

Cut a big and a little square from a piece of carpet. The pieces should be small enough so that the child can lift and move the squares to a different position, but large enough so that the child can easily step on them. If you cannot obtain two scrap pieces of carpet, use two rubber mats or something else that is not slippery.

Lay the big carpet piece on the floor and place the little carpet square right in front of it. Leave a small space between the two squares, so that the child can distinctly see the two carpet pieces. Nevertheless, they should be close enough so that the child can stretch her legs slightly when she steps from one carpet square to the next.

The child should be instructed to step on the big carpet piece first, and then to step forward on the little carpet piece. The child should turn around, pick up the big carpet piece and place it in front of the little carpet piece. The child should continue to step forward on the squares and remember to place the next square in front of the other one each time she takes a step forward.

The child should be encouraged to walk to a specified distance stepping only on the big and little squares to get to that point. For interest and motivation, an object such as a toy fish or crab may be placed at the end of the given point as an incentive for the child to move forward. The squares can be referred to as stepping stones for the child to use in crossing a river. The child should be reminded to be careful, so that she does not lose her balance and fall in the river. If she does, she will get her feet wet. Increasing the distance each time the child does the activity should challenge her to try harder to be careful.

This activity develops

- better coordination of large and small muscles
- an increased awareness of "big" and "little"
- independence
- confidence
- an awareness of distance
- following directions
- enhancement of the sense of touch in moving the square pieces
- language interaction

Age 1 – Week 31

Stencil Up and Down

Obtain a piece of cardboard approximately 8 1/2 x 11 inches. Cut a rectangle 2 x 6 inches from the center of the cardboard with a single edge razor blade or some other sharp cutter.

Place a piece of newspaper or some other kind of paper under the cardboard. Tape the corners of the 8 1/2 x 11 inch cardboard to the paper with the longer sides of the cut out rectangle in a vertical position. Tape the paper to a table or some other smooth working area to prevent it from slipping.

Move your hand up and down to feel the cut out area of the cardboard piece. Encourage the child to also feel the cut out area.

Allow the child to choose a crayon. Name the color and tell the child to move the crayon up and down inside the cutout area. As the child's hand moves up and down say a chant such as: "Up, down, up down. I am drawing up and down." Allow the child to color the cut out area with the crayon until she loses interest. However, if the child is still interested, the cardboard piece may be moved and taped in another place on the paper. The child may wish to choose another color crayon. If so, name the color and permit her to continue with this activity.

At another time, follow the same procedure as before, except turn the cut out rectangle so that the longer sides are in a horizontal position. Let the child feel the cut out section by moving her hand or finger from left to right. Once again, allow the child to choose a crayon to use. Name the color and encourage the child to move the crayon back and forth on the paper that is underneath the cardboard stencil. As the child moves the crayon back and forth chant this chant, "Back and forth and across you go. Where you will stop, I don't know." The child may prefer to just scribble back and forth for awhile with a crayon. Continue with the chant and allow her to do so.

This activity develops

- an awareness of vertical and horizontal direction
- an awareness of boundaries with the cut out piece
- eye-hand coordination
- freedom of choice
- an awareness of different colors
- language interaction with the chants
- listening

Age 1 – Week 32

Vegetable Printing

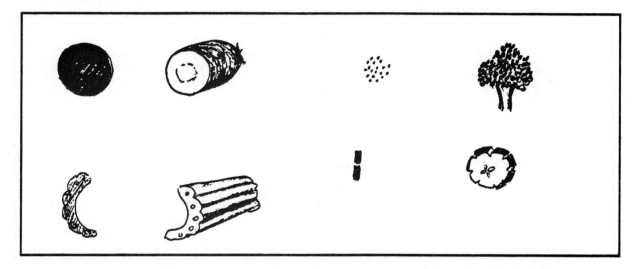

Cut off one end of a carrot. Assemble some newspaper or blank paper and tempera paint. Leftover water base paint from a home project may be used instead of the tempera paint. Pour a little of the paint into a Styrofoam meat tray or plate. Tape the paper to a suitable flat work area. Put an old shirt or a large bib on the child before you begin this activity.

Dip the cut end of the carrot in the paint. If the paint seems too thick, add a little water and stir. Lift the carrot and press the end with the paint on it to the paper. The shape of the cut end of the carrot will then be printed on the paper. Allow the child to hold the carrot and place the cut end in the paint. Assist her in pressing firmly to print the shape on the paper. Then allow her to print independently while you supervise. The experience of using a food to print should prove to be of interest to the child. Make sure that the child is aware that the carrot is orange.

A celery stalk can be used for printing at another time. Tell the child to note its color and shape. Broccoli flowerets, as well as many other vegetables, make interesting designs when they are used for printing. The child can make interesting pictures with a combination of different vegetables and colors. However, make only two or three vegetables available at one time to prevent over stimulation.

This activity develops

- creativity
- an appreciation of the beauty of color and shape
- eye-hand coordination
- free exploration when printing
- more of an awareness of different colors
- a new sensation with the sense of touch in printing with the different vegetables

---

Age 1 — Week 33

This Side, That Side

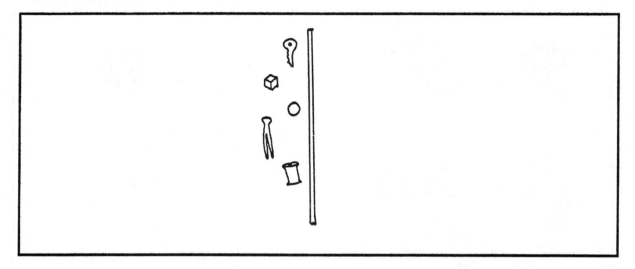

Assemble about ten small objects. They can be toys or safe household items. Use masking tape or a piece of yarn to divide an area into left and right sides. Avoid using the words left and right.

Pick up an object and say, "This side," as you place that object on the left side of the boundary formed by the yarn or tape. Pick up another object and say, "That side," as you place the second object on the right side of the boundary.

Encourage the child to play with you. At first you can place your items on the left side, one at a time, as you say, "This side," while the child places an object on the right side, one at a time, as the child says, "That side." If the child does not talk, but places the objects on the correct side at the right time, praise her and disregard the fact that she does not talk. However, be sure to continue to emphasize, "This side, that side," as the objects are placed alternately in the correct position.

At another time, play the game and change sides. As the child progresses with this skill of alternate positions to enhance left and right laterality, she can be encouraged to play the game independently. Be certain and encourage the child to say, "This side, that side."

This activity develops

- listening skills
- eye-hand coordination
- further awareness of left and right
- enhancement of the sense of touch of the different objects
- verbal skills
- confidence
- independence

Age 1 – Week 34

On and Off

Use about ten narrow elastic pieces fastened together or rubber bands for this activity. The bands should be large enough to fit easily over a doorknob. This activity will be more challenging if the bands are of various sizes. Place the bands in a small plastic container or basket.

Show the child how to put a stretchable band on a doorknob. Then allow the child to try to put one on the doorknob. If the child is successful, allow her to put the remainder of the bands on the door independently.

When all of the bands are on the doorknob, show the child how to take them off and place them in the container again. Encourage the child to repeat this activity until she loses interest.

At another time, the child can place a stretchable band on every doorknob in the house. She will delight in having you see that she can do this. The child should be instructed to remove all of the bands from the doorknobs and place them in the container before repeating this activity. If she does not wish to continue with this activity she should still be encouraged to remove all of the bands from the doorknobs before stopping.

This activity develops

- skill in following directions
- an awareness of stretchable materials
- an awareness of "on" and "off"
- problem solving
- independence
- one to one matching
- eye-hand coordination

Age 1 – Week 35

Straw and Spool Stack

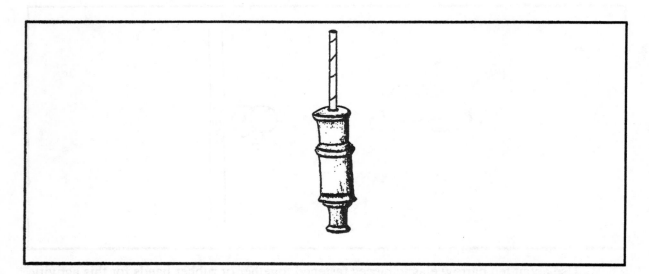

Assemble several long straws that will fit easily in the center of sewing spools. Ten or more spools will make this activity more meaningful. The spools may be of different sizes and colors. The neutral colored spools may be colored with felt markers for added interest. Stack several spools on top of each other. Gently knock the stack of spools down. Stack the spools again, but this time place a straw in the center of the stack. Attempt to knock the stack down as you did before. Point out to the child that the stack of spools did not fall down. Stack several other spools on top of each other, but do not place another straw in the center of the stack. Ask the child to knock the two stacks down. The child will note that one stack will stay in place, providing the child does not knock it too hard, while the other stack can be readily knocked down.

Allow the child to stack the spools without using any straws. Encourage her to stack the spools as high as she can. Tell the child to be very careful so that the spools will not fall. If the stack falls, encourage the child to continue and help her if necessary. Then carefully insert a straw in the center of the stacked spools. If the stack is high enough, two straws may be needed. The child may just enjoy exploring with the spools in stacks. However, she may still need your guidance and help when she attempts to insert the straws.

You may count the spools with the child for added interest. If a spool falls off of a stack say, "Look, one spool fell off." Continue to stack the spools and count them. Insert a straw for stability as you stack. Place a spool on the top of the stack when there is no longer a support from the straw. Gently tap the stack and cause the top spool to fall. Make the child aware that the other spools did not fall, because they were supported by the straw. The child may not understand the word, "support," therefore use the phrase, "held up" for clarity.

Allow the child to explore with the spools and straws at another time with no interaction from you. Observe the child. Does she discover that the spools can be rolled back and forth? Does she begin to stack and use straws for the support of the stacks, or does she just enjoy watching them fall down when she stacks a few? She may also discover that the spools have holes at each end and will become aware, subconsciously, that materials have different uses.

This activity develops

- eye-hand coordination
- an awareness of sizes if different size spools are used
- an enhancement of the sense of touch when stacking
- visual skills through observation of the spools
- an awareness of more than one
- an awareness of support to prevent the spools from falling

Age 1 – Week 36

Stuff It in the Box

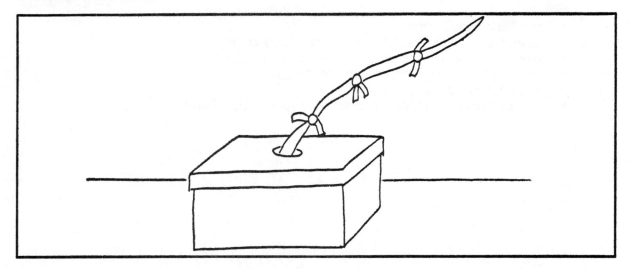

Use a long strip of a cloth remnant, several narrow strips of different textured cloth or wide yarn. The strip should be approximately a yard long after knots have been tied at 3-4 inch intervals. The textured cloth strips and knots are suggested for tactile variation and interest.

Take a shoe box with a lid and make a hole about an inch in diameter in the center of the lid. Stuff the cloth or yarn strip through the hole in the lid with your hands. Continue until all of the cloth strip is in the box. Make the child aware that the cloth strip is all in the box. Say, "It is all gone."

Lift the lid and push a small part of the cloth or yarn strip up through the underside of the lid hole. With your hands, begin to pull the cloth or yarn strip out of the box through the hole. When it is all out of the box say, "Look, it came back."

Repeating this activity at different time intervals will serve to entertain the child, as well as develop basic eye-hand coordination skills. It may be necessary for you to help insert the strip in the hole of the box.

This activity develops

- more awareness of "in" and "out"
- skill in manipulating the strip
- tactile enhancement
- skill in visual observation

Age 1 – Week 37

Clothespin Snap

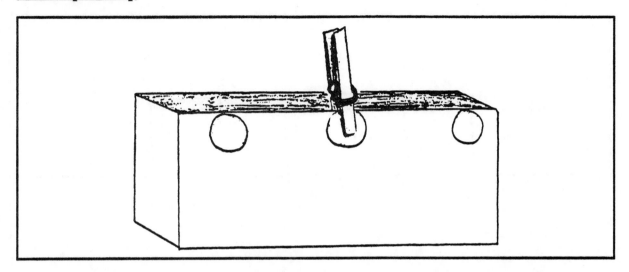

Use the same shoe box that was used previously or select another box of similar size without a lid. Make dots around the top edge of the box approximately 3 inches apart. Assemble 12 clothespins. The slip-on type clothespins may be used and will be easier for the child to manipulate. However, the spring type clothespin will offer more of a challenge to the child. If you use the spring type clothespin, it will be easier for the child to succeed by turning the clothespin upside down before placing it on a red dot. As the child progresses, encourage her to place the spring type clothespins on the red dots in the upright position.

Place a clothespin on one of the red dots on the top edge of the box. Encourage the child to try to put the clothespin on the next red dot. Continue with this activity until all of the clothespins are used. Assist the child if necessary. Say to the child, "The clothespins are all on the box. Now let us take the clothespins off the box." Emphasize the words, "on" and "off." Count the clothespins with the child for number awareness.

This activity may be repeated many times and will be more interesting if the clothespins are colored or painted, and the shoe box is decorated with bright colors. As the child progresses, stickers, shapes, numbers or letters may be used instead of the red dots.

This activity develops

- eye-hand coordination
- an awareness of "on" and "off"
- tactile enhancement
- matching one to one
- skill in visual observation

Age 1 – Week 38

<u>Shake and Find</u>

Assemble three to five plastic film containers and a jingle bell that is to be used to make a noise inside one of the containers. Put the bell inside one of the film containers and cap it. Place all of the containers in a row.

Shake each container and encourage the child to listen for a sound from one of the containers. By listening, the child should be able to choose the container that has the bell inside after all of them have been shaken. If she is unable to identify the correct container, repeat the activity until she is successful. The idea is for memory recall of the object and its position in the row.

Change the positions of the containers and repeat the activity. If the child has difficulty again in finding the correct one, try again. Continue with this procedure as long as the child appears to be interested. If there is no interest, try again at another time.

A paper clip, a marble, a button, a small rock, a teaspoon of rice or beans are some suggested materials that can be used to vary this activity. Use only one item in a container to compare with the other empty containers at a given time until the child is confident. Then two containers can be used with objects. The child can later sort the ones that make a sound and play the game "This Side, That Side" as in week 33.

This activity develops

- skill in auditory discrimination
- listening for a purpose
- skill in making a logical choice
- an awareness of a change in positions of the containers
- memory recall

Age 1 – Week 39

Flowers in the Basket

Use a piece of Styrofoam that has been wedged into a plastic cup, a grocery berry basket or a similar container. Assemble five flowers. The flowers may be real, plastic, silk or homemade with pipe cleaners and paper. Punch five small holes in the Styrofoam, and dot each hole with a red felt marker so that the holes will be clearly visible.

Encourage the child to place a flower stem in each of the five holes of the Styrofoam. Direct the child to remove the flowers and then place them back in the holes several times.

Talk to the child about pretty flowers. Make the child aware that it is the stem that holds a flower up when it is in the soil or a container.

If it is possible, take the child outside and show her a stem of a plant, preferably a flower. Remove a weed and show the child the root of the plant. Tell the child that a root is connected to the stem and holds the plant in the ground. Allow the child to feel and examine the root of the weed. Talk more about roots if the child appears interested. Be sure to instruct the child not to pick flowers without permission.

This activity develops

- skill in looking for detail (the holes in the Styrofoam)
- matching one to one (flower to hole in the Styrofoam)
- an awareness of pretty flowers, stems and roots
- language interaction

Age 1 – Week 40

Poke and Print

Use a large Styrofoam meat tray, tempera paint, a two inch regular paint brush, paper for printing and a tapered blunt pencil for this activity.

Tell the child to hold the blunt pencil and poke holes in the Styrofoam tray. Encourage the child to be gentle, and press firmly to make good indentations in the tray.

Brush a thin coating of paint over the inside of the tray with the poked holes. Lay a piece of paper about the size of the tray on the painted area of the tray. Press firmly and remove the paper carefully. You should now have a printing of the child's poked holes. If the printing is too faint, brush more paint on the poked surface and try to print again.

Allow the child to poke indentations on another Styrofoam tray for free exploration. She may also wish to spread the paint and print independently on the tray. Assist her if necessary. She may also enjoy just poking holes on another Styrofoam tray, or painting independently on a piece of paper that has been taped to a flat smooth surface.

If the child chooses to paint independently observe the movement of her painting strokes. Are they up and down? Are the strokes from left to right? Are they in a circular motion? All of these arm movements are developmental. A child's first paintings are called scribbling. Through practice the arm movements will soon create rudimentary forms of objects that will have meaning to the child. As the child develops skill in painting, you will be able to recognize some of the forms.

This activity develops

- creativity
- free exploration
- eye-hand coordination
- more of an awareness of color
- an awareness of printing
- confidence and independence

Age 1 – Week 41

Collect and Return

Assemble a shopping or tote bag with a comfortable handle, so that it will be easy for the child to carry. Plan three rooms for the child to visit. You may wish to choose three safe objects and place one in each of the rooms before you begin this activity with the child. Or you may allow the child to chose a safe object from each of the three rooms. Some objects which may be placed in the rooms are a baby shoe, a button, a spool, a bell, or something similar. Give the child the bag and go with her to the first room and instruct her to put the safe object in the bag. Name the object for the child and tell her to put it in the bag. Likewise, go to the second and third rooms. The child will then have three objects in the bag.

Go to a fourth room and take each object out of the bag. Ask the child to name each object. If she needs help, repeat the names of the objects. Talk about each of the objects and instruct the child to return each object to the correct room. Go with the child and assist if necessary.

This activity can be varied with other rooms and different objects. The child should be able to identify each room by name or identify to whom the room belongs. This activity can also be repeated outside using trees, flower beds, light poles and other stationary objects for boundaries.

This activity develops

- skill in memory recall
- association of positions in space
- following directions
- language interaction
- skill in observation and in differentiating objects
- confidence and independence

Age 1 – Week 42

Rip It

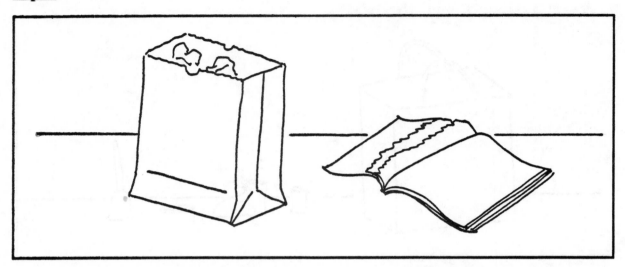

Assemble an old magazine and a large paper bag. Give the child the magazine and show her how to rip out the pages. Remind the child that all magazines are not for ripping, and that she may only rip old magazines with permission.

Encourage the child to rip out a page from the magazine and put it in the opened paper bag. Allow the child to continue to rip and put the pages in the bag. Emphasize the sound that the paper makes when the pages are ripped out.

This activity may last for a while, or the child may quickly lose interest. If this occurs, tell the child to look at the pictures in the magazine and show you her favorite picture.

Ripping paper is a good activity for this age child. It should be encouraged often. Other activities that have been introduced earlier should not be forgotten. Many of these activities should be repeated. Not only will they be beneficial, but the child will derive many new skills by repeating them.

This activity develops

- an awareness that paper can be changed by ripping
- listening for a purpose (paper ripping)
- an awareness of how to clean up a mess
  (putting paper in the bag)
- confidence and independence

Age 1 – Week 43

Pans and Lids

Assemble three pans with matching lids. Mix the lids and the pans and allow the child to explore with the pans. Observe the child. Does she match the lids correctly with the pans, or does she just bang them to make noise? After a period of free play, encourage the child to put the lids on the matching pans. Help the child if necessary.

Later the child may choose three small objects to place in each of the three pans. Be sure that the child knows the names of the three objects. Tell the child to put the lids on the matching pans. Again assist the child if necessary. Instruct the child to find a specific object in one of the pans. Continue with this activity until all three objects have been located correctly.

At another time, the child can be instructed to put all of the lids on the left side of a given boundary and all of the pans on the right side. This activity was introduced in week 33. The boundary can be made with string, tape or an object. The child should enjoy playing "This Side, That Side" again. Also, the child can help you put the pans away when the activity is completed.

This activity develops

- free exploration
- problem solving
- matching
- sorting
- independence and confidence

Age 1 – Week 44

Funnel Fun

Assemble a funnel and several different sized plastic bottles. Water, sand or rice may be used to fill the bottles. Store each of these in a plastic container or pitcher. Each material should be used separately during this activity, even though the same procedure will be similar for each one. However, you may choose to use all three at different times for interest and enrichment.

The water activity should be done in the bathroom, kitchen or outside. The sand and rice activity should be done outside, but if it is done inside, a large plastic cloth or old shower curtain can be used to catch the spills. A large plastic tub can also be used to catch the spills.

Show the child how to use the funnel and use one of the materials to pour and fill the plastic bottles. After the brief instruction period, allow the child to work independently while you supervise. Dump the material from the bottles back into the original container and repeat this activity as long as there is interest. The child should be allowed to feel each material while she is working with it, and be free to make other suggestions as to how the material can be used.

At another time, fill a small jar three-quarters full with white rice, add a few drops of food coloring and two tablespoons of denatured alcohol. Cover and shake well. The child will delight in seeing the rice change color. Combine other colors for interest.

This activity develops

- an awareness of how to pour and fill a container
- an awareness of "empty" through free exploration
- eye-hand coordination
- tactile enhancement

Age 1 – Week 45

The Big Button

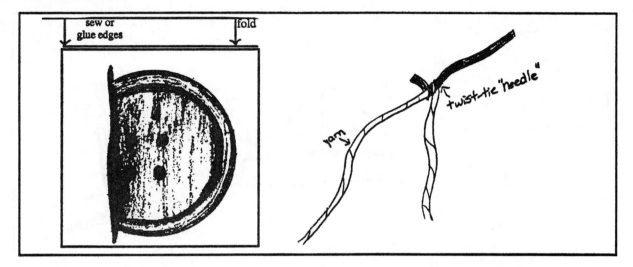

Use a plastic lid and trim the rim away with a pair of kitchen scissors. This will be used as an imitation button. Assemble a piece of cloth that is more than twice the size of the newly made plastic button. Fold and sew or glue around the edges to secure the open edges of the folded cloth. Cut a slit in the cloth a little larger than the large plastic lid. Show the child how to button and unbutton using the cloth and the imitation button. Allow the child to button and unbutton as long as she appears interested.

Punch four evenly spaced holes with a hole puncher in the large plastic lid to resemble a button with four holes. Cut a piece of yarn, approximately 24 inches long, and tie it to a plastic covered baggie tie. Twist the baggy tie several times to make a needle. Thread the yarn through the needle and join the ends together and tie a large oversized knot. Show the child how to use the needle to go in and out of the holes of the imitation button. Encourage the child to follow your directions, but if she resists, allow her to go in and out of the holes at random. Unthread it when the child has used all of the thread and let the child continue to thread the yarn in and out of the holes of the imitation button. A child of this age is too young to attach a button to another material. To attempt to do this at this point may cause frustration.

An old garment with a large button and button hole can be given to the child so that she can practice buttoning and unbuttoning. Buttoning will probably be easier for the child, but with much practice she will soon develop more skill in unbuttoning a garment. When the child shows enough skill, a garment with smaller buttons and button holes may be introduced.

This activity develops

- problem solving
- eye-hand coordination
- tactile enhancement
- following directions

Age 1 – Week 46

Fold It

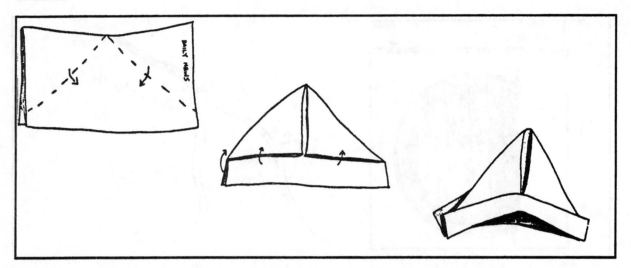

Assemble an old magazine with colorful pages. Show the child how to fold the pages in half while the pages are still intact. Allow the child to fold the pages until she loses interest. Remember that the period of interest at this age is very brief. Use the word, "half" in talking with the child at various times throughout each day and throughout the week to emphasize the concept.

At a later time, use the same magazine or a different one and show the child how to fold the top right edge of the page down. A new shape (triangle) will be formed in the fold. Use the word, "top" in your conversation with the child.

Later, show the child how to fold the bottom right edge up to form a shape like the one formed at the top fold. Use the words, "top" and "bottom" with the child whenever possible to ensure that the child has a working knowledge of these concepts.

As an extension of this activity, fold an old newspaper's top edges down diagonally to form two triangles. Then fold each half of the opened bottom up to form a paper hat brim. Place the hat on your head. Make another hat on a smaller scale for the child. Encourage the child to participate in helping you make the hat for her. The child should be able to help fold the newspaper. However, newsprint ink smears, so work in an area where it will be easy for you to clean up.

This activity develops

- tactile sensitivity in feeling and folding paper
- eye-hand coordination
- an awareness of "half" and "whole"
- an awareness of "top" and "bottom"
- an awareness that paper has more than one use
- confidence and independence in folding

Age 1 – Week 47

Find and Touch

Use a small sock ball, yarn ball or bean bag for this activity. Tell the child to find one of the following body parts at a time and touch it with the sock ball, yarn ball or bean bag.

• head	• arm
• eye	• hand
• nose	• leg
• ear	• foot
• mouth	• stomach (tummy)

If the child has difficulty, review the body parts and repeat this procedure by asking the child to touch a body part. The more you repeat this activity, the more confident the child will become. This is a three-step activity in which the child must listen, locate and then touch a specific body part.

As an extension of this activity, the child can be instructed to touch a body part of a doll. Then the child can use the sock ball, yarn ball or bean bag and touch a named body part of the doll.

Instead of touching, the child may wish to point. Touching of the identified body parts and pointing to the identified body parts are two different concepts. The child should be encouraged to do one or the other when you are doing this activity with her. Holding an object and using it to touch something is more advanced than just pointing.

This activity develops

- following directions
- further enhancement of the sense of touch
- an awareness of the commands, "point" and "touch"
- hand coordination
- further awareness of body parts

Age 1 – Week 48

The Medicine Dropper

Assemble an old medicine dropper and two clear plastic containers. Allow the child to choose a color from the food coloring assortment and place a drop or two in one of the containers that has been filled with water. Show and tell the child that one of the containers is "empty" and the other one is "full."

Hold the medicine dropper and place the bottom of it in the colored water in the container. Squeeze the bulb and call the child's attention to any air bubbles that escape when the bulb is squeezed. Release the pressure on the bulb of the medicine dropper and show the child that the medicine dropper has lifted (sucked up) some of the colored water.

While still holding the medicine dropper, place it in the empty container. Squeeze the bulb and release the pressure. A little colored water should now be in the empty container. To speed up the process, you may assist the child by using a large meat baster, preferably transparent so the child can see the liquid.

Encourage the child to work independently while she tries to fill the empty container with the colored water. The child may lose interest quickly. However, this is an activity that the child can be encouraged to do a little at a time. Eventually she will have a reasonable amount of colored water in the container.

Show the child empty and full containers whenever the opportunity arises. This will serve to enrich the child's awareness of these two concepts.

This activity develops

- observational skills
- following directions
- an awareness of "empty" and "full"
- eye-hand coordination
- freedom of choice (choosing a food color)
- an awareness of air and air bubbles
- confidence and independence

Age 1 – Week 49

Button, Zip, Snap, Velcro

Obtain an old coat, dress or some other garment with a large button and buttonhole, or use a folded piece of cloth with a large button sewed on it. Use another piece of folded cloth to make a buttonhole or slit that is the size of the button on the folded piece of cloth. Allow the child to button and unbutton using the same procedure as in week 45.

At another time, obtain a jacket, slacks or a skirt with a zipper. Allow the child to practice zipping the zipper up and down. Emphasize the sound that the zipper makes when the child moves the tab up and down.

Sew large snaps on a folded piece of cloth or use an old garment with several snaps on it and encourage the child to snap the snaps and take them apart. This will fascinate the child momentarily, but the activity may be difficult for her. Be sure to assist her if necessary. Praise her for trying, even if you do most of the snapping. Emphasize the sound that the snaps make when the two pieces snap together.

Use a tennis shoe with a velcro fastener or sew or glue your own velcro pieces on a folded piece of cloth. Allow the child to open and fasten with the velcro. Encourage her to listen for the sound that is produced when the two pieces of velcro are separated.

The child should be free to feel and explore the materials containing the button and buttonhole, the zipper, the snaps and the velcro. Hook and eye fasteners may be introduced if you feel the child can manipulate them. Try to make the child aware of the many things that are used for fastening materials together.

This activity develops

- an awareness of different materials used for fastening clothing
- problem solving
- listening for the different sounds of the fasteners
- confidence and independence
- eye-hand coordination

Age 1 – Week 50

Listen and Draw

Assemble several sheets of blank scrap paper, crayons and a tape recorder or record player. Allow the child to choose a color from the crayon selection. Call the chosen color by name and ask the child to repeat the color's name.

Play a soft or slow song on a tape recorder or record player, and encourage the child to listen to the music. As the child listens, determine the beat and count and clap out the beats. Encourage the child to draw on the paper with the timing of the music. It may be necessary for you to guide the child's hand to give her the idea. Once she seems to understand, allow her to move the crayon freely around on the paper. Avoid correcting the child's movements. Continue to count and clap out the beat of the music to motivate the child to continue to move the crayon. When the music stops, praise the child for making such a beautiful "musical" picture.

Hang the picture on the refrigerator or place it somewhere else to show the child that you appreciate her art work. The child may be interested in producing another "musical" picture for a special person in the family. To conserve paper, the child can be encouraged to use both sides of the paper when making a picture. The child may also wish to change colors. This is a good time to ask the child to name the color when she chooses a different color for her picture.

At another time, a faster song can be played on the tape recorder or record player. Help the child to clap out the beat of the music. Then encourage her to try to keep up with the music as she draws a fast "musical" picture with a crayon on paper. Observe your child's rhythm and continue to count and clap as she draws. Be sure to praise her for any positive response that she makes.

This activity develops

- free expression
- an awareness of rhythm
- listening skills
- large and small muscles of the arm and hand
- an appreciation of creative art
- independence and confidence

Age 1 – Week 51

Open and Close

Take the child by the hand and walk to a room where the door opens and closes easily, and the doorknob is easily accessible. Hold the doorknob and gently open and close the door. Allow the child to practice turning the doorknob, because she may find it difficult once the door is closed securely.

Talk about which way the doorknob is turned to open the door and explain that when the door is closed the striker on the side of the door hits the striker plate. The striker is pushed in and snaps back in place when the door is closed. The word, "spring" may be used in explaining this door function, but it may confuse the child. It may be better to just show the child the striker and striker plate and allow her to experiment with it as she turns the doorknob. The child will be interested in watching it and may enjoy exploring it independently.

At another time, allow the child to open and close a door in another room. Use the words, "open" and "close" and tell the child that there are some doors without knobs that can be opened and closed. Some examples are sliding doors, swinging doors and kitchen cabinet doors without visible hardware. The child should be allowed to open and close different kinds of doors whenever possible.

Talk about safety in the kitchen when opening and closing doors of the cabinets. Emphasize that the child should not open and close these cabinet doors without permission. Explain what the word "permission" means. Tell her that some of the cabinets contain materials that a child should not bother. Open each cabinet and allow her to peep inside, so that she will not be curious about the contents of each.

This activity develops

- an awareness of the concepts, "open" and "close"
- free exploration
- skill in turning knobs to open and close a door
- independence and confidence
- eye-hand coordination
- language enrichment when discussing knobs, doors and safety

---
Age 1 – Week 52

Find Me

Tell the child that you are going to hide behind a door or a piece of furniture. Encourage the child to cover her eyes with her hands. When you are hidden say, "Find me." Hopefully, the child will be listening and can find you. Do this several times and hide in the same place. When you think the child is secure with the game, hide in a different place that is close to the first hiding place. Continue to do this until the child loses interest.

At another time, encourage the child to hide. Tell her that you will try to find her. Does the child hide in one of the places where you previously hid or does she find a new hiding place? Finding a new hiding place denotes that the child understands the game. If the child hides in the same place, she may need encouragement to find a different place to hide. This is a game that very young children can play together with the guidance of an adult.

This activity develops

- listening for a purpose ("find me")
- skill in tracing the sound of a person's voice
- an awareness of "out of sight" and "in sight"
- more of an awareness of a position in space
- independence and confidence

Part III

(Two - Three Years)

Introduction

The child of two needs much to do! He is more inquisitive and active, because he is far more aware of the environment. Size, color and shapes are meaningful to him and he delights in using this knowledge to further enrich his experiences.

He is more verbal and can readily recite short poems, nursery rhymes and songs. His vocabulary has increased, and he interacts more in conversation and is able to recall a sequence of events. Some children of this age may tend to stutter because they think faster than they can speak. It will benefit the child if you will be patient and listen if he struggles to express himself.

The child will enjoy scribbling in up and down strokes whenever a pencil, crayon or other kind of marker is offered to him for use. These up and down strokes soon develop into back and forth and circular strokes. This is the beginning of a child's creative art expression. Much praise and encouragement is needed as the child expresses his "view" of his immediate surroundings. Negative criticism at this age can have a detrimental effect on the child's freedom of creativity.

Most children of this age prefer large muscle activities such as running, jumping, kicking, dancing, pedaling, pushing, pulling, throwing a ball and participating in simple active games. This strong desire for gross motor activity is present because the child has developed better coordination. Fine and gross motor activities should be encouraged to ensure the refinement of coordination in both areas.

Size differences are apparent to a two year old. He can identify the members of the family and realize that they are larger than he is because he is very much aware of himself. He may even know his name, age and sex.

Real and fantasy stories are of interest to the child, especially animal stories. His period of interest is very short, but he may listen attentively to brief stories and rhymes. Many words and sounds that he hears are often imitated. He may pretend to be in his own world of fantasy. This is very much a part of a child's need to sort out his feelings as he adjusts properly to the real world.

Note: The author and publisher are not liable for any injury or death incurred due to the misuse of the suggested materials and directions. As with all child-related activities, materials should be selected with careful attention to child safety; adult supervision is essential.

Age 2 – Week 1

Humpty Dumpty

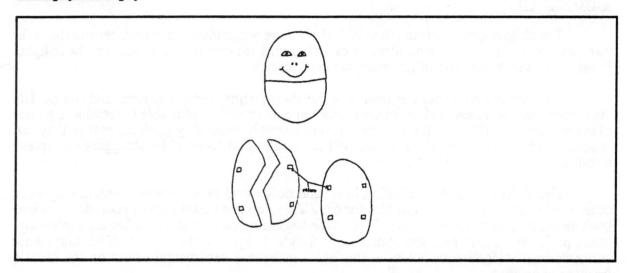

Use two pieces of white cardboard or poster board that are approximately 8 1/2 x 11 inches. Draw and cut out two large ovals. Draw a line across the middle of each oval with a black felt marker. Also use the marker to add two eyes, two dots for a nose and a smiling mouth to the top half of one of the ovals.

Color the lower oval half a bright color. Cut the front oval in half from top to bottom so that it resembles a broken egg. Do not cut the other oval. Cut four small pieces of velcro and glue these pieces to the top and bottom of the back (reverse) side of the piece that is cut. Two pieces should be on the left and two on the right side. Glue the matching velcro pieces to the back side of the other piece, so that when the front and the back are matched together evenly they will be fastened with the velcro. In this way, Humpty Dumpty can be put back together once he is broken apart. Paper strips may be added for arms and legs, if desired. However, the puzzle will be easier for the child to manipulate without the arms and legs.

Read the following rhyme to the child:

> "Humpty Dumpty sat on a wall
> Humpty Dumpty had a great fall
> All the king's horses and all the king's men
> Could not put Humpty Dumpty together again."

After reading the rhyme several times to the child show the cardboard Humpty Dumpty to the child. Point out the "front" and the "back" of Humpty Dumpty. Emphasize the words by using good voice inflection. Tell the child that things have a "front" and a "back." Ask the child to find a "front" and a "back" of something other than Humpty Dumpty. The child may realize that he has a "front" and a "back" side. If not, point this out to the child. Continue to look for other things and discover the "front" and the "back" of each.

Allow the child to explore the Humpty Dumpty that you made. After a brief period, show the child how to take Humpty Dumpty apart, if he has not already discovered this.

Repeat the rhyme and show the child how to put Humpty Dumpty back together. Encourage the child to say the rhyme with you. Repeat this activity several times until the child can successfully take Humpty Dumpty apart, and then put him back together independently.

As an extension of this activity, let the child pretend to be Humpty Dumpty. The child can sit on a pillow to represent the wall. As the rhyme is being recited, the child can pretend to "fall off" the wall at the precise moment that the words, "great fall" are said in the rhyme.

This activity develops

- an awareness of words that rhyme
- an awareness of "front" and "back"
- an awareness that when something breaks it can be repaired
- freedom for dramatization

Age 2 – Week 2

Jack in the Box

Obtain a box that is large enough to contain the child in either a standing or squatting position. If the top has flaps, tape them together to form a lid. Cut around three edges of the lid with a razor cutter or sharp knife so that the lid will open and close easily.

Show the child that the lid of the box will "open" and "close." Discuss what the words "open" and "close" mean. This concept was introduced in the age 1, week 51 activity.

Squat down, put your hands on your head and ask the child to do the same. Tell the child to pretend that he is in a box with the lid closed. Tell him to pretend that his name is Jack.

Say the following action rhyme and tell the child to listen and jump up from the squatting position when you say the word, "pops."

> "Jack in the box all shut up tight.
> Not a breath of air, not a ray of light.
> How dark it must be, you cannot see.
> Open the lid and out "pops" he."

Repeat this action several times. Then invite the child to climb into the box. Tell the child that you are going to close the lid so that it will be dark inside until he opens the lid. Remind the child to listen and jump up when you say the word, "pops." Repeat the action rhyme. If the child seems to enjoy it, continue until the child loses interest. Later, the child can be allowed to do this independently and will find it fun to "pop up" out of the box.

At another time, introduce the action song, "Pop Goes the Weasel." Invite the child to walk around something that can be used as a pretend vinegar jar. As you and the child walk around the pretend vinegar jar say or sing the action rhyme.

"Round and round the vinegar jar,
The monkey chased the weasel.
The monkey thought 'twas all in fun.
"Pop" goes the weasel."

On the word, "pop," clap your hands. Make the child aware that he should listen for the word "pop" and also clap his hands with you.

For further enrichment, show the child a picture of a monkey and a weasel. Tell the child that they are animals with fur and any other facts that you feel will be of interest to the child. For example, they have two eyes, a nose, two ears, a mouth, four legs, a tail, as well as other features and habits.

This activity develops

- listening for a specific word and then reacting
- more awareness of "open" and "close"
- listening for sequence in the action rhymes
- memory recall of the rhymes
- gross motor skills
- independence and confidence

Age 2 – Week 3

Top and Bottom

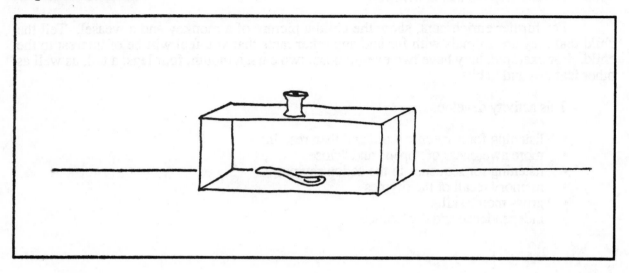

Assemble a shoe box and two small familiar items such as a toy, a rattle, a spool or a block. Turn the shoe box on one of its long sides. Show the child the top and the bottom. These will represent top and bottom shelves.

Tell the child to put one of the small items on the "top" shelf. Be sure to call the item by name. Instruct the child to take the same item and place it on the "bottom" shelf. Redirect the child if it is necessary. Repeat this activity using the other small item. Continue to use the two items interchangeably for placement on the "top" and "bottom" shelves.

Two objects for this activity is enough at a given time. This activity involves two steps; listening for the name and the place. Too many objects may tend to confuse and frustrate the child. Varying any two small items will enrich the child's experiences with the concepts of "top" and "bottom."

From time to time, show the child the "top" and "bottom" shelves throughout the house or ask the child to show you which shelf is the "top" and "bottom" as you point or touch it.

This activity develops

- an awareness of "top" and "bottom"
- eye-hand coordination
- tactile sensitivity in handling various items
- listening skills

Age 2 – Week 4

Big and Little

Make a batch of clay dough. Mix 1 cup of flour, 1 tablespoon of oil, 1 cup of water, 1/2 cup of salt, 2 teaspoons of cream of tartar and food coloring. Cook over medium heat until the mixture forms a ball. Knead until smooth. This mixture will keep indefinitely in a plastic bag or sealed container.

Use an old tray or placemat, tape some wax paper to a work area or use a cardboard piece that has been sealed with contact paper. Put the clay dough on the work area and use both hands to show the child how to pat, squeeze and pull the clay. Allow the child to feel, pat, squeeze, pull, and explore with the clay.

Take a long piece of the clay and make a circle by joining the two ends of the long piece together. Encourage the child to make one too. Tell the child this shape is called a circle. Encourage the child to make another circle. If the child previously made a big circle, tell him to make a little circle. If he made a little circle, tell him to make a circle that is bigger. Emphasize the words, "big" and "little" to make sure that the child understands these concepts.

Roll out some more of the clay and make a square. Point out to the child that the square does not have a curve or bent line. It has corners. You can show the child how a clay circle can be pinched at four equidistant points to make four corners to form a square. Encourage free exploration of the clay at various times and review the concepts, "big" and "little" using the clay. Other materials may also be used to emphasize the concepts of "big," "little," "circle" and "square."

As an extension of this activity, the child may enjoy playing the game, "I Spy." The child can "spy" something "big," something "little" or, at another time, "spy" something that is a "circle" or a "square." These things can be found in the house, outside, in a store or elsewhere.

The child may also enjoy making a big circle by clasping both hands overhead and making a little circle with the thumb and forefinger of one hand. You can tell the child to make one or the other with his hands for additional interest.

This activity develops

- eye-hand coordination
- an awareness of a "circle" and a "square"
- further awareness of the concepts, "big" and "little"
- free exploration to create with clay
- independence and confidence
- enhancement of the sense of touch with the clay

Toss in the Can

Assemble a sock ball, a bean bag or a yarn ball and an empty trash can or tub. Place the can or tub close to the child.

Show the child how to toss the ball or bean bag into the trash can or tub. Encourage the child to use one hand, but accept either under- or overhand tosses. Insisting on one or the other at this age may confuse or frustrate the child. The child may even prefer to use both hands. The object is to aim for the target with the ball or bean bag.

This is a simple activity and should interest the child. However, make it clear to the child that he should aim for the trash can or tub and not the furniture, lamps, tables, etc.

When the child has gained confidence in tossing the ball a short distance, the trash can or tub can be moved farther away from the child. This will offer more of a challenge to the child and will increase his skill and confidence.

This activity develops

- eye-hand coordination
- gross motor coordination
- interest in a game
- following directions
- an awareness of distance and time in relation
  to when the ball is first tossed and when it stopped

Age 2 – Week 6

Let's Make a Necklace

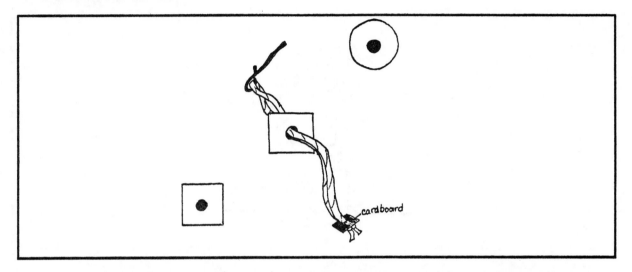

Use several pieces of construction paper and cut them into ten circles and ten squares that are approximately two inches in size. Punch a hole in each circle and square with a hole puncher or something round and sharp. Use a bent and twisted pipe cleaner or baggie tie to form a needle. Thread a piece of yarn approximately thirty-six inches long through the needle that was made. Join the two ends of the yarn and tie a small square of cardboard to this to act as a knot. If you only tie a knot at the two ends of the yarn, the circle and square pieces will slip off.

Show the child how to thread the yarn through the holes of the circles and squares. Because the child is too young to introduce a pattern with circles and squares, allow the child to string the circles and squares in any order. The child should be encouraged to finish this activity even though it may not be completed the same day. A few shapes can be threaded on at a time, depending on the interest of the child. When the child completes the necklace, remove the cardboard square and tie the two ends together. This will form a necklace for the child to wear. Tell the child how pretty it is as you place it around his neck. Invite the child to tell you which shapes are "circles" and which are "squares." The colors that are used for the necklace may also be identified.

If the child has enjoyed this activity, a necklace can be made for the other members of the family. Different colored circles and squares may be used for variety and interest.

This activity develops

- eye-hand coordination
- an awareness of different colors
- an awareness that a task should be completed
- a further awareness of "circles" and "squares"
- an appreciation of something created
- confidence

Age 2 – Week 7

The Box Walk

Obtain two shoe boxes that will fit the child's feet. Establish a finish line by choosing a piece of furniture, some object or place a piece of tape on the floor as the boundary.

The child should be instructed to place each foot in one of the two boxes. Tell the child to go to the finish line by sliding the boxes forward as he walks. Show the child what you mean if he seems to have difficulty. Encourage him to go to the finish line and return to the starting place.

Play or hum "The Skaters Waltz," if you have the record or know the song. As the child moves along with the sliding boxes, he will enjoy it more if there is a tune to make the activity more interesting. He can pretend to be ice skating on a frozen pond. The child may also enjoy sliding the boxes as he walks around the house, providing it is safe for him to do so.

This activity develops

- an awareness of completing a task (finish line)
- gross motor coordination
- an awareness of something different to do with the feet
- an awareness of left and right laterality
- independence and confidence

Age 2 – Week 8

My Name

Teach the child to say this rhyme as a chant:

> "My name is (child's name)
> I am two
> I am a (girl) (boy)
> And I love you."

As you practice this chant, hold up two fingers when "I am two" is said. When "And I love you" is said, hug the child.

If the child is reluctant to say the rhyme, repeat the chant and pause at the last word of each line. Encourage the child to listen and "fill in" the missing words.

After practicing this rhyme several times, tell the child that you are going to look for pictures of two things. Hold up two fingers again and ask the child to count the fingers that are up. Count, 1-2. Use two of the child's fingers and count, 1-2.

Sit with the child and look at a book and count objects in pictures of things that you see in the book. Avoid counting higher than two, because the idea is to teach the concept of two.

The child may also enjoy arranging blocks, toys, books, buttons, rocks, shells, keys or similar objects into sets of "two." This is a simple but very important activity.

This activity develops

- an awareness of name, sex, and age
- an awareness of the concept, "two"
- an awareness of the rhyming words "two" and "you"
- an interest in memory recall of the rhyme

Age 2 – Week 9

What Color Am I Wearing?

Look at the child's clothing and point to one color. Call the color by name. Tell the child to look for something else in the room that is the same color. If you cannot find something of the same color, look in a book or magazine to find the color.

Repeat this activity for every color that the child is wearing. This need not be done all at one time but can be done throughout the day. You can spend a "special" time with each color. In this way, you will help to reinforce the child's skill in recognizing and naming that color.

Chanting a nonsensical rhyme as you stress a color may motivate the child to more readily respond. For example:

"Red, red, rhymes with head."
"Yellow, yellow, meet a fellow."
"Blue, blue, touch my shoe."
"Orange, orange, eat an orange."
"Green, green, what's between"?
"Purple, purple, dance with murple."
"Brown, brown, make a frown."
"Black, black, where is Mack"?

Keep doing this as a game each day and eventually the child will learn to recognize and name the colors. If your child already knows the colors, play "I spy a certain color" to improve the child's listening and observational skills. Recognizing, matching and naming colors are important concepts for a child of this age to master.

This activity develops

- an awareness of colors
- skill in color matching
- skill in naming the colors
- an awareness of clothing and detail
- listening and observational skills

Age 2 – Week 10

Moving Hands and Fingers

Place a cup of flour in a mixing bowl, and encourage the child to help you add a little water at a time to make a thin paste. If the mixture seems too liquid, add a little more flour. Let the child choose the color of food coloring to be used. Add a few drops of food coloring to the mixture and pour it into a large zip-lock plastic bag, or use a plastic bag heat sealer, if you have one. Make sure that the bag is sealed with very little air trapped inside. To control any leakage that may occur, put the sealed bag inside another plastic bag and seal it. Place the mixture that is in the sealed bags on a flat work area.

Allow the child to move his hands gently over the surface of the plastic bag. The thin paste inside will move according to the movement of the child's hands or fingers. Free exploration should be encouraged as long as the child shows an interest. When the child is finished working, this bag of thin paste may be stored in the refrigerator for a few days without spoiling.

The bag of mixture may be given to the child at another time. He will become aware of the cool feeling of the plastic bag that contains the thin paste, and will probably make a comment. Explain to him that the refrigerator made it cool to keep it from spoiling. Encourage the child to use his index (pointer) finger and gently move his finger from left to right. It is not necessary to use the words, "left" and "right." By showing the child the movement of the left and right progression, the child's eyes and finger movement are being trained for future reading and writing skills. The child may enjoy watching and copying you as you make straight lines, curvy lines and zigzag lines from left to right. Each of these kinds of lines should be emphasized one at a time. If the child insists on moving the finger or hand from top to bottom or from bottom to top, allow him to feel free to do so.

For further enrichment of this activity, the child may be encouraged to make circles and squares. Some may be big and some little. Talk to the child about the shapes and sizes that he may form.

This activity develops

- a tactile approach to hand movement (feeling)
- more of an awareness of "left" and "right"
- free exploration and creativity
- an awareness of the line variations
- visual skills (copying)

Age 2 – Week 11

Jump and Hop

Assemble two pieces of yarn or string. Cut one length approximately two yards long and the other length one yard long. On the floor or outside, make a big circle with the longer piece of yarn or string and a little circle with the shorter piece. Talk to the child about the big and little circles.

Show the child how to jump up and down on two feet inside the bigger circle. Then do the same for the little circle. Counting each complete jump or chanting "jump, jump, thump," will motivate the child to want to jump. The child may soon tire and lose interest. This activity should be repeated so that the child will develop skill in jumping with two feet in a given space.

Show the child how to hop on one foot inside the big and little circles. It may help the child to balance better if he holds one foot up in back with his hand while he hops on the other foot. The child should practice balancing on each foot, one at a time, before attempting to hop inside the designated circle. As the child hops, count or chant, "hop, hop, stop" or use other words that rhyme to maintain the child's interest.

As an extension of this activity, the child can toss a bean bag or some other object inside one of the circles and then jump inside the circle, pick up the object and jump or hop while holding the object. You should designate the circle (big or little) and the activity (jump or hop) that he should use to perform this task.

This activity develops

- gross motor coordination
- awareness of "big" and "little" circles
- awareness of the difference in jumping and hopping
- awareness of "inside" and "outside" a boundary
- listening and following directions
- awareness of counting sequence or rhyme

Age 2 – Week 12

My Family

Use a photograph of the family or individual pictures of each member. Point and name each family member and allow the child to point to and name each member also.

Talk about the family members. Say something special about each member. Some special characteristics of each member can be: size, boy or girl, place at the eating table, something they like to do, color of hair, type of shoes and various other characteristics that may be meaningful to the child. Use the words, father (daddy), mother (mama), sister, brother and baby to ensure that the child can make the proper relationships to the family members. To enhance this discussion, point to each finger as you say this finger play:

(point to thumb)	"This is Mother
(point to index finger)	This is Father
(Point to middle finger)	This is Brother Tall
(Point to ring finger)	This is Sister
(point to little finger)	This is Baby
(use the other hand to embrace	
all of the fingers mentioned above)	Oh, how I love them all."

Repeat and encourage the child to copy your finger actions and words. Eventually the child will be able to recite this finger play rhyme.

At another time, look through old magazines and choose a picture of a man, woman, boy, girl and baby. Cut the pictures out while the child watches. Place the pictures on the floor and instruct the child to select the picture that he thinks should be the father of this family. Help the child with the selection if necessary. Then tell the child to find which picture should be the mother, brother, sister and baby. Praise the child for any positive response. The child should realize that the pictures are not really members of his immediate family, but in a game, these pictures can be used to represent the family.

These same pictures can be pasted on a piece of paper, construction paper or cardboard and stapled together to form a Family Book. For interest, the pages can be cut in the shape of a house.

This activity develops

- more awareness of family members
- awareness of love and affection in the family
- awareness of various sizes of family members
- visual observation of cutting and awareness of pasting
- awareness of pictures to represent real people
- listening and identifying skills

Age 2 – Week 13

I Can Paint

Tape a large piece of newspaper to a flat work area. With a felt marker, draw a square or rectangle around the edges. This will be the frame or the boundary for the child's picture. Protect the child's clothing with an old shirt. This should be placed on the child with the buttons in the back. The shirt will fit better if the sleeves are cut off. Allow the child to use a regular paint brush that is approximately two inches wide to paint a picture. Assemble some leftover water base paint or tempera paint and use one color at a time. For convenience, a small amount can be placed in a juice or soup can. The container can be placed inside a dishpan or another container to minimize the spilling of paint. Wash the brush if you change color and allow the first color to dry before using another to prevent the blending of colors. Food coloring and water can be used for paint if you prefer not to use tempera. The color will not be as vivid, but the child will be exposed to the same painting skills.

Show the child how to dip and rub the brush against the sides of the can to eliminate excess paint. With the wet brush, instruct the child to brush the paint on the paper within the frame boundary that was drawn. Encourage the child to paint a picture of whatever he wishes and fill in as much of the area as possible. Observe the child's strokes. Are they up and down, back and forth, or does he make circular brush strokes? All of these movements are developmental for later control in painting a recognizable object in a picture.

Invite the child to tell you a story about his picture when he finishes painting. Accept whatever he says about his picture. Praise and encouragement are needed, therefore it is important to avoid negative criticism. You may want to hang this "masterpiece" up for the other family members to praise.

This activity develops

- free exploration with paint
- creativity
- further awareness of a boundary
- eye-hand and arm coordination
- imagination and language in describing his picture

Age 2 – Week 14

Farm Animals

Buy a child's farm animal picture book, borrow one from the library or collect pictures of farm animals to use with this activity. The pictures should be colorful with little detail other than the specific animal in the picture. Some suggested animal pictures are: a dog, cat, pig, horse, donkey, lamb, duck, hen, rooster, turkey and cow.

At first, use the pictures to name each animal. Practice the animal names with the child until you feel the child can name the animal successfully as each picture is shown.

After the child is confident with the animals' names, try to make the sound of each animal. This will help the child learn to associate different animal sounds with the pictures. Some suggested sounds for animals are:

(dog)	bow, wow
(horse)	neigh, neigh
(cat)	meow, meow
(donkey)	hee, haw
(rooster)	cock-a-doodle-do
(cow)	moo, moo
(lamb)	baa, baa
(pig)	oink, oink
(duck)	quack, quack
(turkey)	gobble, gobble

Assist the child in recalling and reproducing each animal sound and repeat this activity often. The animal sounds will serve to interest the child, as well as amuse him.

As an extension of this activity, make a tape recording of the animals' names and their sounds. Play the tape often for the child. He will delight in attempting to make these animal sounds and in return he will be learning to articulate his tongue for future speech patterns.

The song "Old MacDonald" can be sung for enrichment. As it is sung, the child can fill in the animal names and sounds that he has learned. You may need to help him recall some of the animal names, but with practice he will soon learn to name them without your help.

This activity develops

- listening skills
- skill in naming animals using visual and auditory clues
- memory recall
- language enrichment
- confidence

Age 2 – Week 15

Put It in a Line

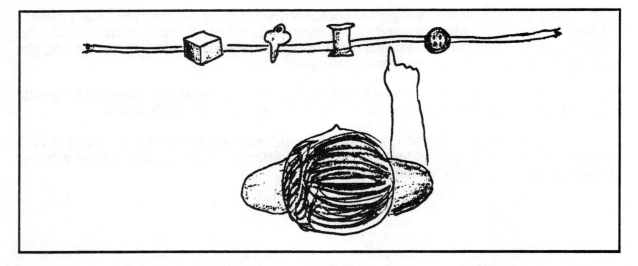

Use a piece of yarn or tape approximately one yard long. Lay it in a straight line so that it is facing the child from left to right. Give the child a paper bag containing assorted items such as a block, key, sponge, clothespin, large button, rock, spool, small toy, spoon, cup, etc.

Start on the left and place one of the items from the bag on the yarn or tape. Show the child left and right movement that he can follow by sweeping your hand across the yarn in this direction. Encourage the child to continue moving from left to right, placing the objects that are chosen from the bag on the yarn or tape until the bag is empty.

Next, encourage the child to pick up each item one at a time, from left to right, until all of the objects are back in the bag. The words, "left" and "right" need not be emphasized; just the movement with the hand is sufficient to enable the child to understand direction.

Repeat this activity on different occasions and substitute other items to place in the bag. Repeat some of the previous activities, because the child needs much repetition in order to master basic concepts and skills.

This activity develops

- awareness of "left" and "right" progression
- enhancement of the sense of touch in handling the objects in the bag
- eye-hand coordination
- skill in following directions and completing a task
- further awareness of the concept "empty" and "on"
- awareness of "one" object to place at a time

Age 2 – Week 16

Jack Be Nimble

Read the nursery rhyme, "Jack Be Nimble." The words are as follows:

"Jack be nimble, Jack be quick
Jack jumped over the candlestick."

Repeat the rhyme and emphasize that the words, "quick" and "stick" sound alike. Try to add more rhyming words by saying lick, click, tick, chick, hick, Dick, pick, Nick, Rick, sick, and kick. Encourage the child to say the rhyme with you several times. If there is enough interest, try to motivate the child to recall some of the words that rhyme with "quick" and "stick."

Invite the child to pretend to be Jack. Assemble a short candlestick or use a cup turned upside down for a pretend candle holder. Say the rhyme and encourage the child to jump over the candlestick when you say the word, "jump" in the rhyme. The child should practice jumping with his feet close together. Be sure to emphasize the word, "over."

At another time, encourage the child to jump as far as possible. Place an object to show how far the child jumped from a given point. Tell the child to jump again and see if he can jump to a greater distance. The child will delight in seeing his progress in distance. This should serve to motivate him to continue to practice his jumping.

This activity develops

- skill in listening and recall
- further awareness of rhyme
- role playing
- language enrichment
- gross motor coordination
- confidence
- awareness of the concept, "over"

Age 2 – Week 17

Feely Bag Fun

Assemble two lunch bags or two old socks. Place identical items in each of the two bags or socks. Some suggested items to use are: two spools, bottle caps, cotton balls, small sponge pieces, keys, large buttons, etc.

Show the child the two bags and match each set of two items one to one. In this way, the child will see and understand that there are two identical items of each kind. Refill the two bags or socks and give one of the bags containing identical objects to the child.

Take one of the objects out of the bag and show it to the child. Tell the child to feel in his bag for an object that is just like the one that you took out of your bag. Remind the child to "feel" not look. Help the child if necessary. Put the matched objects back into the respective bags or socks. Choose another item and continue until the child loses interest.

Items in the bags or socks may be changed, but the child should be aware of this to avoid confusion, distrust or frustration.

This activity develops

- further awareness and use of the sense of touch
- matching skills
- hand coordination
- following directions

Age 2 – Week 18

The Three Bears

Read the story of The Three Bears and ask the child the following questions. Where did the bears go? Who came to visit them while they were gone? Whose food did Goldilocks like best? Whose food was too hot? Whose food was too cold? Whose chair did Goldilocks like best? Whose bed did she sleep in first? Did I forget something in the story that you would like to tell me about? This leaves the discussion open for any recall or comment the child might have. If the child cannot answer the questions, read the story again and point out the answers to the child.

Invite the child to find a big chair in which to sit and call it Papa Bear's chair. Ask the child to find a middle size chair and call it Mama Bear's chair. Then look around for Baby Bear's chair. If you do not have a small (wee) chair, try to find a stool or turn a large bowl upside down and invite the child to sit in Baby Bear's chair. Ask the child which chair he likes best.

At another time, invite the child to retell the story of The Three Bears. Help the child by using picture clues in the story book. Count the characters in the story, 1-2-3 bears and Goldilocks is 1 more. Count 1-2-3-4.

Other simple stories should be read to the child often. Asking meaningful questions and role playing enhance the understanding and true meaning of stories.

This activity develops

- listening and memory recall skills
- skill in following a sequence
- role playing
- language enrichment
- more awareness of counting 1-2-3-4
- skill in using visual skills for recall

Age 2 – Week 19

Sock Match

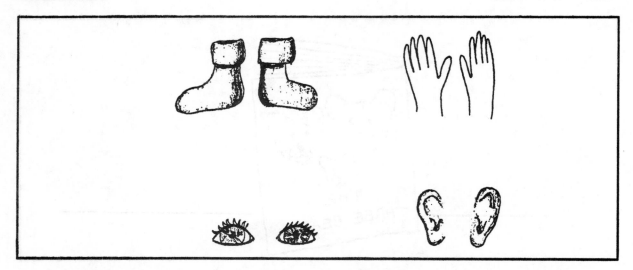

    Assemble several pairs of socks. Some of the socks can belong to the child, a brother, sister, mother or father. You may prefer to use swatches of cloth instead of socks. In this case, cut two pieces of the same kind of material in the shape of a pair of socks. A variety of colors and designs will make this activity more interesting.

    Show the child that there are two of each kind of sock. Mix the socks and display them on a flat surface in front of the child. Pick up one of the socks and tell the child to find its mate. Assist the child if necessary.

    Once all of the socks have been matched, tell the child that each matched set is called a pair; a pair is two. Then count each set 1-2, 1-2 to help the child to understand the concept of two.

    This activity can be repeated each time you are sorting clean laundry. The child should have some knowledge of matching socks and may show an interest in helping you with this task. It will be beneficial to the child if you will allow him to help, even if it takes you longer to sort and fold the clean laundry. In this way, the child will develop a sense of responsibility and also feel more of a part of the family.

    At another time, talk about what else comes in pairs. Hands, feet, ears, eyes, shoes, gloves and stockings are just a few of the many things that come in pairs. Pictures of these sets of pairs may be cut from old magazines, pasted on paper and assembled in a booklet. The booklet can be named, Pairs. The child will delight in looking through his new booklet and naming the things that come in pairs.

This activity develops

- eye-hand coordination
- awareness of a pair
- confidence
- a feeling of helping
- awareness of counting 1-2
- vocabulary enrichment

Age 2 – Week 20

Outline the Shape

Draw a circle about the size of a paper plate on a piece of paper with a wide red felt tip marker. Draw a 6 inch square with a wide blue felt marker on another piece of paper. Cut a piece of wide yarn, the size of the circumference of the circle. Cut several straws in 3 inch lengths so that you have at least 8 pieces. Identify the colors, red and blue.

Show the child how to use the yarn and lay it on the line that was drawn to form the circle. Lay the straw pieces on the lines of the square.

Identify the circle and the square. Emphasize the names so that the child can recall the name of each when you point to that shape. Talk about curved lines. Tell the child, he curved the yarn to form a circle. Hold the child's hand and make a pretend circle in the air. Then tell the child to make a pretend circle in the air by himself. Assist the child if necessary.

Point to the square and ask the child to recall its name. Tell the child that the square is made up of straight lines. Talk to the child about the corners of the square. The corners may also be called points. Ask the child how many straw pieces were used to form a side of the square. Since the pieces were cut in three inch lengths, it will take two of these to form one side of a 6 inch square. This should help to reinforce the concept of two. The child may enjoy forming a pretend square in the air.

As an extension of this activity, the child can form circles and squares using cooked colored (food coloring) spaghetti. This can be done on a flat surface or the spaghetti can be glued on paper to form a circle and a square.

The child may also be allowed to scribble with a crayon on paper in an attempt to form a circle and a square. Accept whatever the child draws and praise him for his efforts.

This activity develops

- further awareness of the circle and square
- eye-hand coordination
- awareness of curved and straight lines
- following directions
- further awareness of the colors red and blue

Age 2 – Week 21

Up and Down

Assemble at least 10 to 20 paper, Styrofoam or plastic cups. Present them to the child in a stack or several stacks. Allow the child to explore with the cups by unstacking and restacking them. The child may enjoy knocking the stacks over and watching to see what happens. Talk to the child about building the cups up, and then talk about taking the cups down. Emphasize the words, "up" and "down." Encourage the child to continue stacking and unstacking as long as he appears interested. If you help and motivate him, he will stay with the task longer.

As an extension of this activity, lay a long piece of yarn or string on the floor. Encourage the child to place the cups "up" and "down" in a row using the yarn or string as a guide. Move your hand from left to right to show the child left and right progression. Begin by placing the first two cups; one facing "up" and one facing "down," and encourage the child to use the other cups and continue to place them in a row with one cup "up" and one cup "down." When the child finishes suggest that he stack the cups and repeat the process.

To further emphasize the concepts of "up" and "down," play the game "Simon Says" with the child. The child is to follow a special command that Simon gives. You will pretend to be Simon and give the commands. Simon should say, "Simon says" before every command. However, if Simon commands the child to "stand up" or "sit down" without saying, "Simon says " before the command, the child is to remain in his present position and should only move when "Simon says" precedes a command. For example, Simon says, "Stand up." The child should stand up if he is in a sitting position. If he is in a standing position he should remain standing. Likewise, if Simon says, "Stand up" without saying, "Simon says" first, and the child stands if he is in a sitting position, then he did not listen carefully. This is a good game to teach your child to listen and respond correctly. At the same time, you can teach the concepts of "up" and "down."

When the child understands the game of "Simon Says," different commands may be introduced. Some other commands can be to turn around, raise hands above head, touch toes, wiggle fingers, jump up and down and clap hands. Interjecting too many commands for this age child at one time may tend to confuse and frustrate the child. Therefore, try changing the commands one at a time to ensure that your child understands the command and can perform it successfully.

This activity develops

- free exploration and problem solving
- awareness of "up" and "down"
- awareness of a pattern of "up" and "down"
- listening to directions carefully
- awareness of left and right progression
- fine and gross motor coordination

Age 2 – Week 22

What Belongs in the Drawer?

Select two empty drawers from the kitchen, bedroom or elsewhere for this activity. If this is not convenient, use two shoe boxes and tell the child to pretend that the shoe boxes are drawers. Make the child aware that we have special things that we keep in each drawer. Assemble any two sets of safe materials such as spoons and lids, socks and underwear, paper and crayons, and clothespins and spools. Mix the two kinds of materials that were chosen and point to a drawer and say for example, "This is the spoon drawer. Put all of the spoons in here." Point to the other drawer and say, "This is the drawer where I keep the lids. Put all of the lids in here." Repeat this procedure with any two sets of materials. Continue with this activity until you feel that the child understands that drawers keep special items.

Talk about keeping things in special places. Tell the child that this is the way we keep things in order and remember where things are kept. Invite the child to go with you to observe what is kept in different drawers. Talk about privacy, and that some drawers keep a person's personal things and other people should not bother those drawers. Also make the child aware, that some drawers may contain dangerous things such as knives. Therefore, children should not go in drawers without permission.

Emphasize the need for order in the home. Suggest a special drawer for the child to keep small items that belong to him. Provide a toy box, another large container or a shelf for the child to keep his larger toys or stuffed animals. In this way, the child should soon learn to keep his room in order, that is, the toys picked up. A room will stay neater if a child is allowed to choose only a few toys at a time to use. He should be trained to put those toys away before choosing others with which to play. Too many toys that are available at one time may tend to confuse the child.

This activity develops

- awareness of orderliness
- awareness of sorting items
- awareness of same and different kinds of items
- a desire to help
- confidence
- enhances the sense of touch when sorting different items

Age 2 – Week 23

Rub-A-Dub-Dub

Read the nursery rhyme,

"Rub-a-dub-dub,
Three men in a tub.
And who do you think they be?
The butcher, the baker, the candlestick maker
Turn them out, knaves all three."

Tell the child to imagine three men in a tub floating on the water, rocking back and forth. Briefly, tell the child that a butcher prepares meat, a baker makes bread, cakes and pies and a candlestick maker makes candles. A knave is a servant or a worker. Emphasize "three" men. Name them again and count 1-2-3.

Select a round plastic tub or a cardboard box that is big enough for the child to get in. Invite the child to get in the tub or box and to pretend to be one of the "three" men. Let the child choose which one he would like to be.

Say the rhyme again and encourage the child to move around in the tub or box and pretend to be floating and rocking back and forth on the high waves of the water. Emphasize safety but allow the child to rock back and forth and proceed with a chant of rhyming words such as rub, dub, tub, lub, nub, hub, sub, pub, cub and bub. The child will enjoy hearing the rhyme repeated, as well as the other words that rhyme with tub. Perhaps you and the child can think of some other words that rhyme with tub to add to the game.

Encourage the child to chant the rhyme with you while he is in the tub or box. With repetition, the child should soon learn to say the rhyme from memory and may recall rhyming words at random. Accept any nonsensical words the child may develop. This type of response will denote that the child is very much aware of words that sound alike at the end (rhyme).

This activity develops

- listening for a purpose (rhymes)
- memory recall
- role playing
- language enrichment
- freedom in making a choice (which man to role play)

Age 2 – Week 24

I Spy Red, I Spy Blue

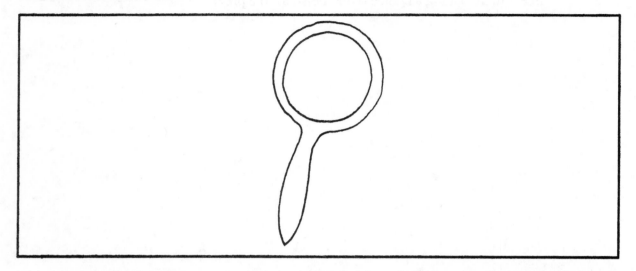

Find something that is all red and something that is all blue to use for this activity. It could be a sweater, shirt, felt marker, paper, crayons or yarn. If the child does not know the color "red," say, "This is red" as you show the child the red object. Do the same for the color "blue."

Play the game "I Spy" with the child. Look around the room and find something that has the color red in it. Then tell the child that you spy something "red." Allow the child to look around the room for something red and ask him to tell you when he has spied it. Continue playing the game until you cannot find anything else that has some red in it. Then play "I Spy" with the color blue in the same way.

To make the game more interesting, cut out a cardboard-shaped mirror with a hole where the glass should be. Look through the hole when you look at something red or blue. This will give the child a clue as to the direction of the red or blue object that you spy.

Encourage the child to go and point to something red or blue. Help the child if necessary. If the child is close to the object say, "You are getting warm." If the child is going in the wrong direction say, "You are cold." Avoid teasing the child. Security and success in finding red and blue objects are essential. Be sure to use only one color at a time. Interchanging the colors will tend to confuse a child of this age. This type of direction involves listening for the color and finding it in a certain place. The child must feel secure with the color to find its location.

This activity develops

- more awareness of the colors, "red" and "blue"
- skill in using clues for problem solving
- confidence
- language enrichment
- matching skills (finding something else the same color)

Age 2 – Week 25

The Washing Machine

Cut out a picture of a washing machine and a dryer from an old magazine, newspaper or catalog. Show the child the picture of the washing machine and allow him to observe its features. Ask the child if he can make the sound that a washing machine makes when it is filling with water. If he just looks at you, take him to the washing machine area and turn on the machine. Encourage the child to listen to water as it fills the tub. Exaggerate the noise the water makes "sssss" to motivate the child to listen and imitate the sound of the water as it fills the tub of the washing machine. Praise the child for any positive response.

Place some dirty clothes in the machine and tell the child to listen as the washing machine begins the washing cycle. Allow the child to observe the clothes moving around and around if your machine works with the lid open. Once again, exaggerate the sound "swish, swish" to motivate the child to listen and imitate the washing cycle sound.

With practice, the child will soon be able to respond fairly accurately to produce the washing machine's sounds. This involves mouth noises which may stimulate the child to move his body up and down and around and around as he imitates the washing cycle.

As the washing machine moves into the spinning cycle, encourage the child to listen again for the new sound "mmmmmm." Then review the three basic steps of washing. First, the water fills the machine. Second, the machine washes the clothes. Third, the water is removed from the clothes. Therefore, the child should be aware of the filling, washing and spinning cycles. Review the three sounds "sssss," "swish, swish" and "mmmmm."

Talk to the child and explain what happens first, second and third when clothes are washed? The child may even notice that on a long washing cycle there are several water fillings, washings and spinnings.

After the washing machine has stopped, ask the child what you should do with the clothes in the washing machine. Accept whatever the child says, but make the child aware that the wet clothes must be dried before they can be worn again.

If you have a dryer, put the clothes in it and tell the child to make the sound of the dryer. This time do not exaggerate the sound, allow the child to create his own dryer sound. If you do not have a dryer, invite the child to hand you the clothespins as you hang the clothes up to dry.

Ask the child what happens to the water in wet clothes. Make the child aware that heat and moving air help the water evaporate into the air. If clouds are visible, tell the child that the water outside evaporated and helped form the clouds.

As an extension of this activity, moisten a facial tissue and allow the child to blow it until it dries. Help the child if necessary.

The child may enjoy imitating other sounds in the home such as a telephone, mixer, dishwasher or garbage disposal. Outside, the child can imitate the sound of a car, bus, truck, train, plane, or lawn mower.

This activity develops

- awareness of different sounds
- listening for a purpose
- skill in associating washing machine sounds
- skill in imitating sounds
- awareness of the sequence in washing clothes

Age 2 – Week 26

Slide and Roll

Assemble a small box or block and a coffee or juice can. Use two pieces of yarn that have been placed parallel to each other, but wide enough apart for the child to move through the space. At the end of the yarn pieces, establish a finish line by placing an object there.

Tell the child to hold the block in his hand and slide it between the two pieces of yarn without touching the yarn pieces until he reaches the finish line. Remove the block from the child's hand and tell him to go back to the starting line.

This time the child should be instructed to roll the can between the two pieces of yarn. Remind him that he must start over if the can touches either of the yarn pieces. Therefore, he must be very careful and roll the can so that he can control it. The child may need some assistance. Once the child has reached the finish line by rolling the can, place the can beside the block at the starting point.

Ask the child which object got to the finish line faster. If the child cannot answer the question repeat the activity. Emphasize to the child that one of them is easier to move. He should be encouraged to watch so that he can answer your question. Which object moves faster through the space? Make the child aware that the block was slower, because it did not move as easily. The child had to work harder to make it move.

At another time, allow the child to slide the block from the start to the finish line without holding on to it. Then allow him to roll the can without holding on to it. Encourage him to try to stay in the boundaries, but if the block or the can touch and go past the yarn pieces, simply tell the child they went faster than before, because he was not controlling them.

This activity develops

- awareness of fast and slow
- more awareness of boundaries (left and right)
- awareness that it is easier to roll than slide an object
- skill in following directions
- awareness of start and finish

Age 2 – Week 27

I Can Dress Myself

Find a large piece of cardboard that is as long and as wide as the child. Lay the child on the cardboard. Trace around the child's body with his arms slightly away from his body and his legs apart. Use a felt marker and allow the child to help you add the eyes, nose, ears, smiling mouth and hair. Review the body parts and instruct the child to point to the respective parts of the body on command.

Assemble a complete outfit that the child is familiar with such as a T-shirt, shorts or slacks, socks and shoes. Encourage the child to lay the clothes on the outline of himself in the proper places. Discuss what should be first, then next and so on until the child has placed the clothing correctly. Avoid using the words "second" and "third" until the child has placed the clothes properly in sequence several times. Repeat the activity and then use the words, "first," "second," "third" until the clothing pieces are placed. It is important to mention the ordinals but emphasize only the word, "first."

If the child can place the clothes correctly, tell him that tomorrow he can dress himself. Let the child dress himself the following morning. You may need to assist him, but allow him to do as much as possible on his own. (Naturally, the undershirt and diapers are to be put on by you first.)

This activity develops

- further awareness of the body parts
- awareness of body size and shape
- skill in associating the placement of clothing
- awareness of the ordinals "first," "second" and "third"
- confidence and independence

Age 2 – Week 28

Clapping Hands

Clap your hands once in front of your waist. Ask the child to clap his hands just as you did. Next, clap your hands over your head once and encourage the child to do the same. Bend and clap your hands once below your knees and tell the child to do likewise.

Tell the child that this time you are going to clap two times. Count as you clap twice with the hands at waist level. Instruct the child to do the same. Count as you clap twice above your head and encourage the child to copy you. Count as you clap twice below the knees and instruct the child to do likewise.

Tell the child to watch, listen and clap. Do not speak as you clap once above your head. Did the child copy and clap correctly? Assist the child if necessary so that he understands what you want him to do. Again, do not speak as you clap once below the knees. Did the child respond correctly? Assist the child if necessary. Do the same at waist level.

Progress to two claps in the different positions. Once the child is secure in watching, listening and clapping, progress to varying the activity by using one or two claps interchangeably. However, be sure and do this only when the child has become competent in following the one clap activity and then the two clap activity. This will depend on the child.

This activity develops

- listening for a purpose
- watching for a purpose
- awareness of the change in body position
- further awareness of the concepts, "one" and "two"
- following directions

148

Spool Roll

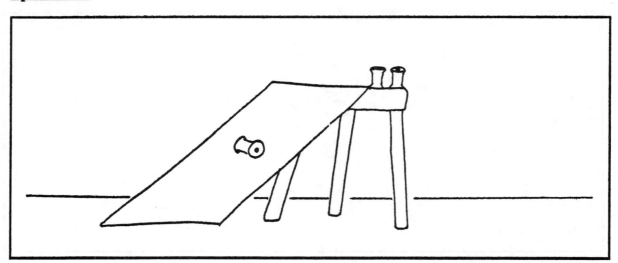

Assemble three spools that are the same size. Use a felt marker to color one red, one blue and one yellow. These are the primary colors. All other colors can be made from a combination of two or more of these three colors. Obtain a sturdy piece of cardboard that can placed against something stationary to form an incline plane. Position this in a long open area.

Identify the three colors of the spools. Place the red spool at the top of the incline plane and let it roll down hill until it stops. Do the same for the blue and yellow spools.

Ask the child which spool went the farthest? Which spool went the shortest distance or did they all come to rest at about the same place? Repeat the activity and note if there is any change. Which color spool went the farthest? Which color spool went the shortest distance? During this activity be sure to emphasize the three primary colors and the concept of distance.

Continue this activity and observe and note the color and distance of each spool every time the spool is rolled down the incline plane. Does one spool go farther more times than the others? For interest, use three spools of different sizes and note if there is any change in the distance that each spool rolls.

This activity develops

- more awareness of the three primary colors
- awareness of distance
- skill in comparing distance
- awareness of an incline plane
- awareness of change and position in space

Age 2 – Week 30

The Coat Hanger Hoop

Take a metal coat hanger and put tape around the hook and the area where it is fastened together. Do this for safety and to protect the door and doorknob from being scratched. Bend the hook and hold the neck of the coat hanger so that it is secure around the knob of a door where you plan to do this activity. Bend the metal of the rest of the coat hanger out until the part where it is fastened together is flush with the door. The metal can then be adjusted to be a round hoop.

Use a yarn ball, sock ball or nerf ball for this activity. Show the child how to toss and aim the ball to get it through the hoop. Pick the ball up and try again.

Begin to count each time the ball goes through the hoop. Encourage the child to continue by suggesting a number of times for the child to toss the ball successfully through the hoop. Continue with this activity until the child loses interest. However, leave the hoop on the doorknob for the child to use at other times independently.

Previous activities should be reviewed, and those that need further skill development or enrichment should be noted. Choose the appropriate time to re-introduce these previous activities that need reinforcement. You should feel free to vary the activity in any way as long as it teaches the basic concept that is intended in each activity.

This activity develops

- gross motor coordination
- more awareness of aiming at a target
- persistence to complete a task
- more awareness of counting
- independence and confidence

Age 2 – Week 31

Ladder Walk

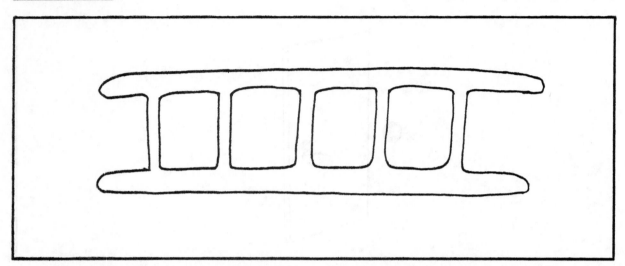

A wooden or metal extension ladder can be laid flat on the floor. This activity can be done in the basement, garage or outside. If this is not possible, lay long strips of yarn on the floor of a large area to resemble a ladder. Two pieces of yarn can be cut into six foot lengths to represent the long sides of the ladder. Six or more paper towel rolls with a piece of yarn pulled through each one can be used to make the cross bars (rungs) of the imitation ladder. The ends of the yarn of each towel roll should be tied to the long side pieces of yarn. After tying the rolls in place, stuff each roll with newspaper to prevent the rolls from being crushed completely flat.

Show the child how to walk "between" each rung without touching the rungs and the sides. Tell the child to turn around and come back to the starting point in the same manner. Be sure to emphasize the word, "between."

Next, instruct the child to walk "on" the rungs, being very careful to balance and not walk between the rungs this time. Once again, instruct the child to turn around and return the same way to the starting place. At this time emphasize the word, "on."

As an extension of this activity, encourage the child to walk forward again "between" the rungs, pick up an object at the end of the ladder and return to the starting place with the object. This can also be done with the child walking "on" the rungs.

This activity develops

- awareness of the concept, "between"
- awareness of the concept, "on"
- gross motor coordination
- body balance
- listening and following directions
- language enrichment

Age 2 – Week 32

Eggs in the Carton 1-2-3

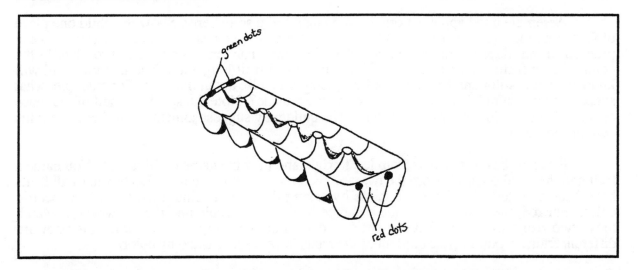

Assemble an empty egg carton and some raisins, beans or small buttons. Use a green felt marker and make a large green dot beside the left hand cup of the top and bottom rows. Use a felt marker and make a large red dot at the end of the right top and bottom cups of the egg carton. Tell the child that green means "go" and will be the starting signal. Similarly, red means "stop" and will be the ending signal.

Tell the child to put one raisin in each cup of the top row. Make certain that the child starts at the top left at the "green light" and stops at the "red light" in the top row. Then instruct the child to return the "green light" in the second row and place a raisin in each cup until he comes to the last cup at the "red light" of that row. Check to see if the child did this correctly and assist the child if necessary. Then empty the raisins from the carton.

Follow the same procedure by placing two raisins in each cup. If the child is interested go to the placement of three raisins in each cup. Remember to empty all of the raisins from the carton cups before beginning with a new number concept.

At this age, the concept of three is sufficient. Counting past three is fine, but making sets of objects higher than three can be overwhelming for the child. It is advisable to make sets of one, two and three with a variety of materials. This will help to build a good foundation for understanding numbers. Too much too soon can frustrate and confuse the child. Some children have been known to refuse to do activities, because they are challenged before they are ready for a basic concept. Slow and steady is the key to success.

This activity develops

- an understanding of sets of one, two and three
- more of an awareness of left and right progression
- awareness of the signals to start and stop
- more of an awareness of rows
- independence and confidence

Age 2 — Week 33

Fruits to See, Feel, Smell and Taste

Assemble a red apple, an orange, a banana and a strawberry. Show the child one piece of fruit at a time and tell the child its name. Ask the child to repeat the name of the fruit. Then proceed to introduce the other three fruits in the same manner. Ask the child to identify the color of each fruit. Be sure to stay with an individual fruit long enough so that the child will know its name, color and be able to tell you something else about the fruit. For example, what shape does it resemble? How does it feel on the outside? Note the specific smell of the piece of fruit. Is its outside bumpy or smooth? The child may suggest something different from his own observation.

Place each fruit in a row from left to right and play the game of "Find It." You name a fruit and the child selects it from the row and then replaces it in the row. Do this until all fruits have been selected. Continue the game by asking the child to find a fruit that is a specific color. For red, the child must make a choice between the apple and the strawberry. Match these two fruits to ensure that the child understands that they are the same color but are different fruits. Continue this until all of the fruits have been selected by color.

Place each fruit in a separate brown lunch bag and close the bag so that the child cannot see inside the bags. Play the "Find Me" game again, but this time the child must select the fruit by smelling it. You can play the game two ways. You name the fruit and the child finds the correct one by smelling, or you could allow the child to select a closed bag with a fruit in it and name the fruit from the smell he detects. For additional interest, change the positions of the bags.

Repeat these activities several times and later introduce other fruits in the same way. The child will learn to improve his sense of sight and smell.

At another time, introduce the sense of taste. Cut each piece of fruit in half and allow the child to smell each again. This is a good time for memory recall of the names of the fruits. Give the child a piece of each fruit one at a time and talk about how each fruit tastes.

Tell the child to close his eyes and open his mouth. Place a small piece of a fruit in his mouth. Tell the child to chew the piece of fruit and tell you its name and how it tastes. You can also ask the child to tell you what color the outside of that fruit is. In this way, the child is using his sense of taste to identify the fruit. Repeat this activity substituting other fruits. This will enhance the child's awareness of color, smell and taste. At meal time, when one of these fruits is a part of the meal, review the name, color and taste of it. In this way, you will be able to reinforce the child's knowledge of the fruit.

This activity should be done many times not only with fruits but with other meats and vegetables. The child's senses will be greatly refined if this activity is consistently done. However, it should be reinforced in a casual manner.

This activity develops

- an awareness of the sense of smell, touch and taste
- problem solving skills
- listening skills
- freedom of choice
- language enrichment
- confidence and independence

Age 2 – Week 34

The One-Two Walk

Use a long piece of cardboard approximately forty-eight inches (four feet) long or tape two shorter pieces together to make one this long. An old window shade, sheet or carpet remnant may also be used instead of the cardboard for this activity. If none of these are available, use three pieces of yarn placed parallel to each other to mark off a four foot space that is at least a yard wide. This will leave a foot between each piece of yarn. Five short pieces of yarn should be cut in two foot lengths and placed a foot apart from left to right to form boxes from the top to the bottom of the four foot configuration.

Assuming that you plan to use cardboard, draw a line with a felt marker in the center from the top to the bottom. Then draw lines from left to right approximately a foot apart to form boxes. Write the number 1 in each box on the left and the number 2 in each box on the right. Tape this to the floor to secure and prevent the child from slipping on the cardboard. If you use the yarn, write numbers on small cards and place each one in the top left of each box.

Encourage the child to step on the first set of the 1 and 2 boxes beginning with the left foot on 1 and the right foot on 2. Direct the child to put the left foot in the next box that is marked 1 and the right foot in the next box that is marked 2. Instead of saying left-right as the child walks forward, count 1-2, 1-2, 1-2, 1-2.

When the child gets to the end, direct him to come back to the starting point. This is done to avoid counting backwards if the child turns around and returns on the numbered boxes. Likewise, he would see the numbers upside down. This activity should be repeated often to reinforce the left and right movement of the feet.

As an extension of this activity, the child can place four like objects on all the 1's and choose another set of like objects to place on the 2's. He can then be directed to carry a shopping bag or something similar and walk forward in the spaces (1) left and (2) right. When he steps in the 1 box he should pick up the object in that box standing only on the left foot. As he places his right foot down in the 2 box he should put the first object in the bag and pick up the object in the 2 box and place it also in the bag. Again he will proceed to the next box with a 1 and pick up the next object in that box while he balances briefly on the one (left) foot before standing on both feet as his right foot is placed in the next 2 box. He will then place the first object in the bag and pick up the next object in the 2 box and continue until he reaches the end. At that point, he should replace the objects before beginning again at the starting place.

This activity of 1-2, 1-2, can be also done outside by drawing lines and writing numbers with a stick in the soil. You can also do this same activity using the sand at the beach.

This activity develops

- left and right awareness and movement
- listening and following directions
- gross motor coordination
- 1-2 rhythm
- visual recognition of the numbers 1 and 2
- confidence and independence

156

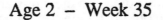

Tall and Short

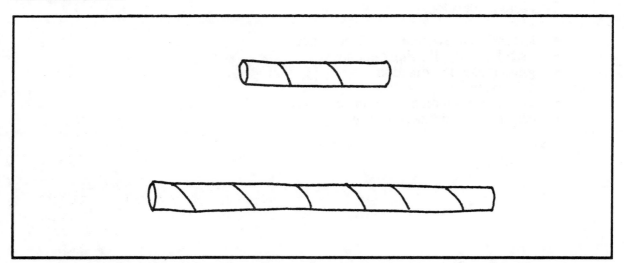

Obtain eighteen straws. Cut six of the straws in-half so that you have twelve tall straws and twelve short straws. Mix the straws.

Hold one tall straw up and tell the child that the straw is tall. Hold a short straw up and tell the child that the straw is short. Hold them side by side and compare them so that the child can see the difference in lengths.

Instruct the child to find a tall straw. Assist the child if necessary. Tell the child to find a short straw and help the child again if necessary. Lay the tall straw on the left of the child and the short straw on the right. Tell the child to put all of the tall straws in one pile and all of the short straws in another pile. Point to the tall straw and the short straw that you placed on the left and right of the child. Tell the child to use these as a guide. Help the child to sort the tall and short straws and say, "Tall straw or short straw" each time that the child picks up one of these to sort.

When all of the straws have been sorted, repeat the activity and continue until the child appears to be losing interest. This is an activity that the child can be encouraged to do independently.

At another time, the child can create a simple pattern with the straws by placing a tall straw, then a short straw and continuing to place them this way in a row until all of the straws have been placed in a line.

This activity develops

- an awareness of tall and short
- an awareness of many straws
- an awareness of sorting for a purpose
- an awareness of a pattern
- confidence and independence

Age 2 – Week 36

Is it Hot or Cold?

If possible, cut out pictures of the following items from a magazine: coffee, soup, hot chocolate, hot dogs, milk, popsicles, ice cream and kool aid. If you cannot find the pictures that have been suggested, choose any four items that are served hot and any four items that are served cold. Follow the same procedure that will be used with the items that have been suggested.

Talk about the coffee and allow the child to smell unbrewed coffee. Prepare a cup of coffee and allow the child to see the steam that escapes from the hot coffee. Be careful, but allow the child to feel the outside of the hot cup, so that he understands what the concept,"hot" means.

Pour a little milk for the child to drink. If the child is allergic to milk use a cold fruit drink. Tell the child the drink is cold and allow the child to feel the outside surface of the glass. Make the child aware that some foods and beverages are served hot and some are served cold.

Show the child a picture of a bowl of hot soup. Ask the child if soup is served hot or cold. Follow the same procedure with each hot and cold picture that you have selected to use. You may prefer to look in a magazine that advertises food products and share these pictures with the child instead of cutting individual pictures. Whichever you decide, the experience should serve to make the child aware of the concepts, "hot" and "cold."

At each meal, discuss which foods are hot and which are cold. Emphasize "hot" and "cold" until you feel certain that the child thoroughly understands and can quickly identify hot and cold foods.

As an extension of this activity, talk about the hot cooking stove, the cold refrigerator, the cold freezer and the hot furnace to emphasize these concepts further.

This activity develops

- awareness of "hot" and "cold"
- skill in distinguishing "hot" and "cold"
- awareness that pictures can be used to represent foods
- listening skills

158

Through the Tunnel

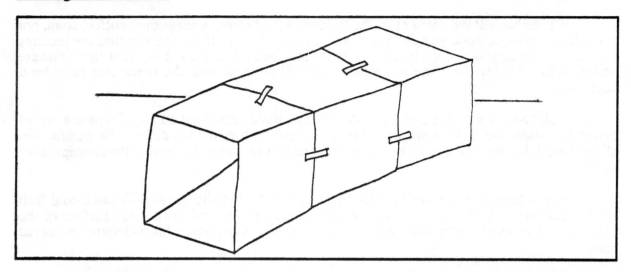

Assemble several cardboard boxes that are large enough for the child to crawl or wiggle through when the top and bottom are removed. Try to use the same size boxes for this activity and remove the top and bottom with a sharp knife or razor cutter.

Allow the child to crawl through each individual box. Then place the boxes together to form a long tunnel. Use masking tape to hold them together. Invite the child to crawl through the tunnel. The child should enjoy this and will want to continue crawling through the tunnel for a brief time.

Emphasize the word, "through" each time that the child goes through the tunnel. Tell the child what a tunnel is and that one can be made through rock and soil and even under the water.

As an extension of this activity, assist the child in making a sand or dirt tunnel. A coffee or juice can with both ends removed can be used for support. The child can then drive a small car or truck through his tunnel.

The child should be allowed to play with and explore the cardboard box tunnel until he loses interest. He may also enjoy using the dirt or sand tunnel at various times. Through this type of play the child will better understand the concept, "through" and the word"tunnel."

This activity develops

- awareness of tunnels
- awareness of the word "through"
- language enrichment
- gross motor coordination
- free exploration
- independence and confidence

Age 2 – Week 38

Little and Big

Buy a package of animal crackers or bake some little cookies. In addition, buy or bake five big cookies. Count the five big cookies and place them in a row. Tell the child to place a little cookie on each big cookie. When the child is finished, ask him how many little cookies he used. Praise the child if he responds correctly. If he does not respond correctly, count the big cookies again and repeat the question. Make sure that the child is aware that there are just as many little cookies as there are big cookies. Repeat the activity again if necessary.

Take all ten cookies and mix them up. Use a big bowl to hold the big cookies and a cup to hold the little cookies. Tell the child to put the big cookies in the big bowl and the little cookies in the little cup. Encourage the child to do this activity at different times. Choose a time when you think the child will be receptive.

At another time, suggest that the child put the cookies in a row, beginning with the big cookie on the left. Sweep your hand from left to right to emphasize left and right progression. Tell the child to place a big cookie in the row and then a little cookie and continue across with a pattern of big and little cookies until all ten cookies are in a row. Help the child if necessary.

This activity develops

- awareness of "big" and "little"
- more of an awareness of a pattern
- more of an awareness of sorting
- listening and following directions
- more of an awareness of left and right progression
- confidence and independence
- awareness of the concept "five"
- more of an awareness of one to one matching

Age 2 – Week 39

Bowling

Assemble several empty plastic dish detergent bottles or any similar tall narrow bottles. Line them up so that they are very close together. Some should be behind the others. They can be placed like regular bowling pins or in a similar shape. Use a tennis ball or a ball slightly larger. It should be a ball that the child can manage easily. Instruct the child to aim and try to knock the bottles down.

Direct the child to use both hands to roll the ball if he seems to have difficulty in managing the ball. If the ball does not roll far enough to reach the bottles, change the boundary line so that the child can succeed in rolling the ball to make contact with the bottles. This will build the child's confidence. Count the bottles that are knocked down each time. Set the bottles back in place and encourage the child to roll the ball again. If the child knocks all of them down, count the bottles and say, "All the bottles were knocked down." Praise the child for his efforts.

When he is secure, change the boundary and move the bottles farther apart to offer more of a challenge to the child. Also, make bowling lane boundaries with blocks, mop handles or something similar.

As the child gains skill and confidence, he will probably notice and comment that some of the bottles were not knocked down. This is an appropriate time for you to build an awareness of addition. For example, suppose you have six bottles and four of them were knocked down. Ask the child how many are left standing. Then proceed to help the child understand that four bottles down and two bottles up make a total of six bottles. Subtraction at this time is observed but addition concepts must be mastered first. Mastery is gradual and developmental. Therefore, avoid introducing subtraction concepts at this time.

This activity develops

- eye-hand coordination
- gross motor coordination
- skill in aiming
- more of an awareness of "up" and "down"
- more of an awareness of number concepts
- confidence

Age 2 – Week 40

Paper Plate Pull

Punch a hole in the side of a paper or Styrofoam plate. Push a piece of yarn through the hole and tie it securely. Cut the yarn to a length that is suitable for the child to hold the yarn and drag the plate around on the floor.

Place a toy or any small object on the plate and tell the child to pull the loose end of the yarn. The child may be instructed to pull the plate with the object to a specified place. Instruct the child to be very careful to keep the object on the plate. Should the object fall off, tell the child to pick it up and put it back on the plate and continue walking to the designated point.

If the child is successful in pulling the one object, a second object may be added to the plate. Make the child aware that there are now two objects on the plate. He should understand that one and one more are the same as two.

Another object may be added to the plate for the child to carry. Again the child should be made aware of how many objects he can drag by pulling the string before some of them fall off the plate. Each time an additional object is added, emphasize to the child that it is one more than the number of objects that are currently on the plate. The size, shape and weight of the chosen objects should be considered before choosing them for the child to drag, because the child may lose interest if the task is too awkward or difficult. This would be a good time to reinforce the concepts of "light" and "heavy."

As an extension of this activity, the child can use the plate for holding litter that he finds on the carpet or floor. He can drag this to the waste can and place the load of litter in it. This will boost his confidence and motivate him to want to help you more.

This activity develops

- gross motor coordination
- awareness of pulling weight through feeling sensation
- awareness that more objects make the pulling load heavier
- awareness of one more and several
- confidence and independence
- language enrichment

Age 2 – Week 41

Little Boy Blue

Read the rhyme, Little Boy Blue, to the child.

> "Little Boy Blue
> Come blow your horn.
> The sheep are in the meadow.
> The cows are in the corn.
> Where is the little boy who looks after the sheep?
> He is under the haystack fast asleep."

Read the rhyme several times to the child and encourage the child to listen for two animals whose names are mentioned in the rhyme. Help the child if he cannot recall the animals, cows and sheep. Ask the child where Little Boy Blue was when someone was looking for him. If the child cannot answer, read the rhyme again. Make the child aware that Little Boy Blue was supposed to be taking care of the sheep, but instead he was asleep.

This is a good time to tell the child that when you have a job to do you must do the job the best that you can. Talk about simple jobs that the child can do to help you, such as helping to set the table, picking up litter in the home, retrieving small things in another place for you and other little tasks that save you steps.

Tell the child that Little Boy Blue could blow his horn and the sheep would gather together and come to him. Remind the child that when you call him, that it is a signal for him to come to you. Children should obey parents; therefore, you expect him to obey you.

At another time, ask the child what color clothes Little Boy Blue wore. Then read the rhyme again and encourage the child to help you name rhyming words such as: horn, corn, born, torn, and morn. Also introduce rhyming words such as: sheep, sleep, peep, keep, deep, reap, seep and heap.

As an extension of this activity, help the child make a horn. You can make a horn with a paper towel roll or fold cardboard around and staple the edges together to resemble a megaphone. You may also use a large spool such as thread cone from a serger sewing machine for a horn. The child will enjoy blowing either type of horn and will be entertained by the different sounds that he can produce with the pretend horn.

This activity develops

- listening for a specific purpose
- reasoning and memory recall skills
- further awareness of words that rhyme (sound alike)
- free expression (role playing) when blowing the horn
- an understanding of obedience and responsibility

Age 2 -- Week 42

Leaf Matching

Take the child on a nature walk in the Spring. (If you live in an area where there is no change in season, you can still use these ideas to enrich your child's awareness of nature.) Make the child aware that Spring is a waking up time for plants that have been asleep all winter. As you walk along, make the child aware of the different kinds of trees. Find at least five different kinds of deciduous trees, if possible, such as an oak, elm, tulip poplar, maple and mulberry. Pluck two leaves from each of the five trees.

Show the leaves to the child. The names of the trees are not important at this age. Make the child aware that each kind of tree has a different shaped leaf.

If for some reason you cannot go on a nature walk, make green leaves from construction paper that resemble certain kinds of trees. Refer to an encyclopedia for pictures to copy or use another kind of book with pictures of trees.

Begin the activity by placing all of the ten leaves on a flat surface in random order. Encourage the child to find any two leaves that are alike. If the child needs help, pick up a leaf and ask the child to find one like it. When two leaves have been matched, point out to the child that both of the leaves are "green" and that they are alike in every way, i.e., they look the same.

Real leaves can be preserved by sealing them between two pieces of clear contact paper or two pieces of wax paper. If you use wax paper, use a pressing cloth to protect the iron. The heat from the iron will melt the wax of the two pieces of paper and fuse them together when the wax cools.

As an extension of this activity, play the game "I Spy" to look for things that are green. The cardboard magic mirror (that was made earlier in the age 0, week 38 activity) can also be used for additional interest.

This activity develops

- an appreciation of trees
- skill in matching leaves
- more of an awareness of similarity and differences
- more of an awareness of the color "green"
- listening and following directions
- eye-hand coordination
- confidence

Age 2 – Week 43

Place It On or Under

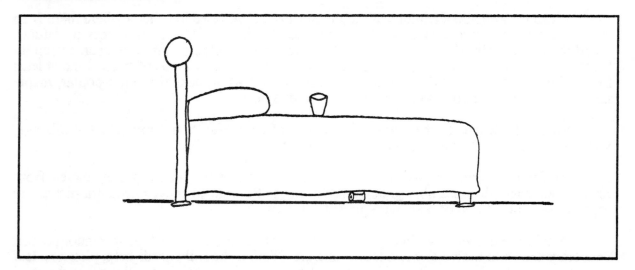

      This activity can be done with any piece of furniture that objects can be placed "on" or "under" it. Select two objects that are familiar to the child. Name them and allow the child to see you place one of the objects "on" a piece of furniture (such as the bed) and the other object "under" it. Ask the child what is "under" the bed. If the child cannot remember, name the object again and place the same object "under" the piece of furniture. Once again, ask the child what is "under" the piece of selected furniture.

      If the child understands, switch the positions of the same two objects. Keep switching them back and forth until the child is secure with the concepts, "on" and "under," and can recall the object readily that is out of sight (under).

      Advance this activity by choosing four different but familiar objects. Place two of the objects "on" the furniture and two "under" the same piece of furniture. Can the child remember the two objects that were placed under the selected piece of furniture?

      This activity should be repeated at various times and often to strengthen the child's understanding, not only of the concepts "on" and "under," but also the child's skill in memory recall. It is advisable not to use more then three objects "on" and three objects "under" a selected piece of furniture for a child this age. However, four or five objects may be introduced when the child is older. This will be a real challenge for a child of age five or six.

This activity develops

- observational skills (number and kind of objects)
- memory recall
- listening
- gross and fine motor coordination in moving and holding the selected objects
- further awareness of the concepts, "on" and "under"

Age 2 – Week 44

How Far Can You Throw?

A wad of cotton or paper wrapped and secured with a rubber band can be used for this activity. A sock ball, nerf ball or bean bag may also be used, but different types of material offer more interest for the child.

Allow the child to throw the wad as far as possible in a designated open area. Mark or place an object to show the distance the child threw the first wad. Tell the child to pick up the wad and throw it again and see if he can throw the wad a greater distance.

Repeat this activity several times and talk about how "far" the child can throw the wad. Emphasize to the child that with practice he can throw the wad even farther. Say, "now see how 'far' you can throw it." Praise the child for any positive response and say, "Look how 'far' you threw the wad."

The child may wish to use other objects for throwing outside. However, remind the child that whatever he chooses to throw outside, he should never throw rocks. Warn him about the danger of throwing rocks so that the child will understand why he should not choose rocks for throwing when he is playing outside.

At another time, if you are near a body of water such as a river, lake or pond, you may allow the child to throw a rock in the water and observe the circular ripples that are produced when the rock breaks the surface tension of the water. Remind the child again of the danger of throwing rocks at someone.

This activity develops

- eye-hand coordination
- gross motor coordination
- awareness of distance
- awareness of the concept "far"
- confidence in developing skill in throwing an object

Age 2 – Week 45

My Color Booklet

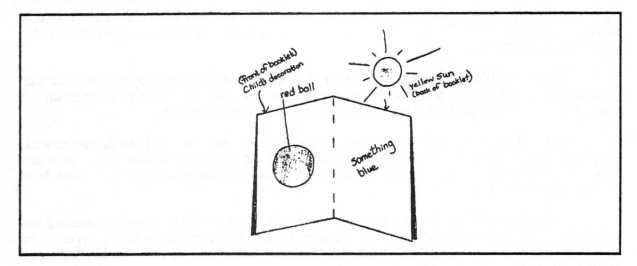

Fold a piece of 8 1/2 x 11 inch paper in half and then in half again, so that the piece forms a four page booklet. Encourage the child to decorate the front cover of the booklet using the eight basic colors at least once. The basic colors are red, orange, yellow, green, blue, purple, brown and black. Name the colors with the child and ask him to pick a special color when you call it by name. Do this several times and take note of the colors that the child is not sure of at this time. At another time, play a game of "Pick Up The Color" with the child using only the colors that he does not know. Continue to play this game with the child at various times until he can identify the colors.

After the front of the booklet is decorated, open the booklet and tell the child to draw a ball and color it "red." Be sure to use the left hand side of the paper because the child should be aware of left and right progression for future reading skills. When the child is finished say, "Red ball."

Move to the page on the right and instruct the child to draw something "blue." When he is finished ask the child to tell you what is blue. Say, "Blue _____" Praise the child for whatever he drew.

Turn the booklet to the back and tell the child to draw a "yellow" sun. When he is finished say, "Yellow sun." Then encourage the child to recall the colors and pictures in his booklet. Look at the front and name all of the basic colors with the child. Open the booklet and allow the child to say, "Red ball." Look at the page on the right and note whether the child remembers what he drew. If not, help him recall. Then turn the booklet over and allow the child to say, "Yellow sun."

Similar booklets may be made at other times. The child can draw an orange pumpkin, some green grass, a purple flower, a brown table and a black boot. The intended concept is to use the colors and be able to recognize them in the booklet. The drawn objects' names can be used for memory recall, but bear in mind that this activity is not intended for reading words.

Also, the picture drawings are not expected to resemble suggested objects. Accept the drawings, ignoring the apparent scribbling, and praise the child even though you cannot recognize any feature of a specific drawing. Allow freedom of expression.

This activity may be done over a period of several days or if the child is especially interested, it can be completed in one sitting. It depends on the child and his attention span and interest. It is advisable to complete a suggested activity even though it requires several sittings to finish.

Read the color booklet(s) often with the child. It will be meaningful to him because he made it (them), and should be able to recall the colors and objects from memory when he looks at it. Other booklets can be made for the child to enjoy. It can be a shape booklet, a special color booklet, a furniture booklet, a toy booklet or a leaf booklet. Pictures for these suggested booklets can be drawn by the child or pictures can be cut from old magazines and glued to the pages of a booklet.

This activity develops

- skill in listening and following directions
- more of an awareness of the basic colors
- skill in identifying objects by color clues (what he drew)
- confidence
- a feeling of ownership (his booklet)
- eye-hand coordination

Age 2 – Week 46

Belongings

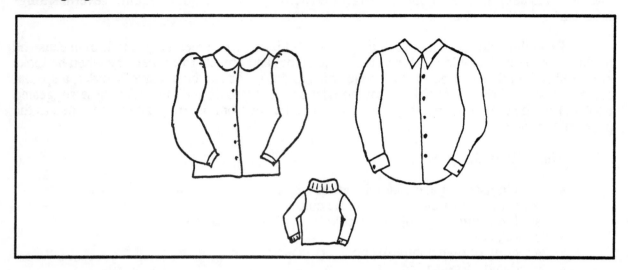

Assemble a shirt or a blouse from each member of the family. If the child has no brothers, sisters or other relatives living within the household, choose additional clothing for those who do. Try to choose ones with color or designs for added interest. Show the child each shirt or blouse and tell the child to whom they belong. For example: "This is Daddy's blue shirt. This is Mother's green blouse."

Once the items have been identified, hold one up and ask the child whose shirt or blouse it is. If the child has difficulty matching the article of clothing with the person, use a picture of that person to help the child. When all of the clothing have been identified correctly, repeat the activity so that the child will feel confident and secure.

At another time, get a shoe belonging to each family member and see if the child can match the person's name with the correct shoe.

As a further extension of this activity, ask the child where a particular family member sits at the table at meal time. Ask the child where each member sleeps. Ask the child to name a favorite food of each person. The child may interject something special that he has observed about a family member. Encourage and honor any contribution the child may wish to make. This helps to establish a good self-image and a feeling of security which is very important to a child.

This activity develops

- further awareness of traits of family members
- skill in matching by association
- language enrichment
- listening skills
- confidence

Age 2 – Week 47

What is its Use?

Assemble various household items. Some examples of suggested items to use are: a spoon, a book, a shoe, a cup, a toothbrush, a towel, money, a key and crayon. Talk about each item as much as you feel is necessary before introducing each item one at a time to the child. Select one of the items and ask the child to tell you its name. Then ask the child to tell you its use. Continue in this manner until the child can name each object and tell you its use. Assist the child whenever you feel it is necessary.

This activity can be repeated at different times over an extended period of time. Choose different items each time if you feel the child was secure with the items that were used previously. If you feel the child needs additional clarification about any item, discuss it further to enrich the child's knowledge and language development.

This activity develops

- language enrichment
- reasoning and association skills
- further awareness that objects have a purpose
- observational skills
- confidence

Age 2 – Week 48

Food, Ordinals and Eating

Use the following suggested foods to help you decide which foods that you wish to use for this activity. Your selection should include a meat, a fruit and a vegetable. The food materials should be prepared in the following manner. Cut a piece of meat, such as a hot dog, into bite size pieces. Count out three pieces of the hot dog. Count out three pieces of a vegetable, such as green beans. Cut a piece of fruit or use raisins. Count out three pieces of that food. Children enjoy feeling and counting jello cubes which is an easy way for a young child to eat jello. This may be used in place of the fruit. Arrange the three foods that you have chosen in three rows from top to bottom. There should be three rows across and three down with a meat row, a vegetable row and a fruit row. Count the pieces in each food row, so that the child will understand that there are three pieces of each kind of food and three rows.

Encourage the child to eat a piece of meat "first," a piece of vegetable "second" and a piece of fruit "third." While the child is eating the foods, continue to offer the meat "first," the vegetable "second" and the fruit "third" until all three pieces of the foods have been eaten. Use the words, "first," "second" and "third" so that the child understands the order of these three concepts.

This activity can be done to make eating more interesting at meal time. Foods should be varied, as well as new ones introduced. Identify the foods for the child so that he can recall their names. At meal time, instead of lining the food in rows, suggest that the child eat a spoonful of meat "first," vegetable "second" and the fruit "third." He can continue in this manner until all of his food is eaten.

As an extension of this activity, the child should be made aware of his "first" and "second" birthdays that have already been experienced. The "third" birthday is coming next. He will then be three years old. Explain this to the child by holding one finger up and saying, "First." Do likewise with the next two fingers by saying, "Second" and "Third" to denote the respective birthdays.

This activity develops

- an awareness of "first," "second" and "third"
- more of an awareness of his age and birthday
- listening and following directions
- vocabulary enrichment (names of foods)

Age 2 – Week 49

Foot Pushing

Establish an area inside that will be safe for the child to move a sock ball or nerf ball. If this is not possible, go outside for this activity. Establish some boundaries for the child to use when he pushes the ball. If the activity is inside, the child can push the ball to a specified piece of furniture. If the activity is outside, it can be pushed to a specified tree or pole.

Tell the child to use only one foot to push the ball to the designated area. He should be instructed not to kick the ball too hard but to control the ball by pushing it gently with his foot so that the ball can be pushed to the given area.

The child should be cautioned that the ball should not be kicked at random. It should be pushed with the foot with controlled short pushes. If the child kicks the ball, stop and repeat the directions.

When the child has developed some coordination, count how many foot pushes he makes to get the ball to the designated area. Repeat this activity at various times and change the designated boundary to add interest to the activity.

This activity develops

- eye-foot coordination (difference in a kick and a push)
- further awareness of a boundary in reaching a goal
- listening (for the count of foot pushes made)

Age 2 – Week 50

Sequence Fun

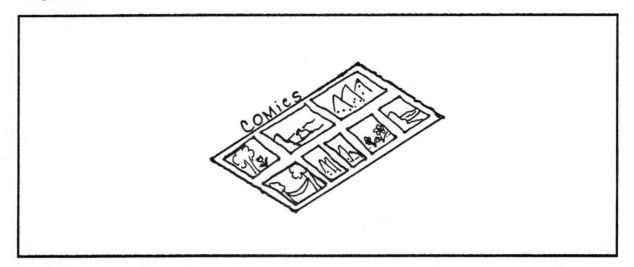

Choose a colored comic strip that you think the child will enjoy such as "Nancy" or "Peanuts." Read the comic strip to your child and explain the humor and sequence of events of the chosen comic. Review the sequence with the child to determine if the child understands what happened "first," "second" and "third."

Cut the comic strip sections apart. Mix the pieces and tell the child to place the comic pictures in the proper sequence. The child may enjoy this activity enough to want to repeat the activity several times.

Encourage the child to retell the story to you and assist him whenever necessary allowing him to verbalize and embellish the story if he wishes.

Allow the child to choose other comic strips. Be sure to review the story and sequence several times. This will enrich the child's experiences with the sequence in a story and will motivate him to feel confident in retelling the comic strip story to other family members.

This activity develops

- memory recall of a brief story in sequence
- language enrichment
- eye-hand coordination
- confidence
- an interest in comics

Age 2 – Week 51

Tiptoe

Show the child how to tiptoe and sing or chant the following:

"Tippy tippy tiptoe here we go
Tippy tippy tiptoe to and fro
Tippy tippy tiptoe through the house
Tippy tippy tiptoe like a mouse"

Use a drum or an empty coffee can with a plastic lid and tap the rhythm of the chant. Encourage the child to tiptoe through the house quietly. Watch and make sure that the child walks on his tiptoes, not on the sides of his feet. When you say the word, "mouse" tell the child to go and hide like a mouse would hide from a cat. Suggest that the child hide behind a piece of furniture or something similar.

To find the child call, "Mouse, where are you?" The child should answer by saying, "Shh, I am here." For interest, pretend to look for the quiet "mouse." As you hunt for the hidden "mouse," talk about how quiet a mouse must be so that a cat will not catch him. When you find the "mouse," tell the child how very quiet he was, because you had difficulty finding him.

Encourage the child to tiptoe again. Check to see if the child is tiptoeing correctly. Assist the child if necessary, because some children have difficulty balancing on their toes. The child may need to practice tiptoeing to develop good balance skills. Repeating this activity will motivate the child to practice his balancing.

This activity develops

- listening and following directions
- awareness of the rhythm of the drum beat
- confidence
- skill in balancing and tiptoeing

Age 2 – Week 52

Color Pieces

Use a piece of red, blue and yellow construction paper and cut five fish shapes from each piece of paper making a total of 15 fish. Paste one fish of each color on a separate paper plate.

Mix the other colored fish and place them individually on a flat surface, preferably the floor. Instruct the child to put all of the red fish in the red plate, all of the blue fish in the blue plate and all of the yellow fish in the yellow plate.

Repeat this activity several times and praise the child for catching so many fish. Count the four fish in the red plate, count the four fish in the blue plate and then count the four fish in the yellow plate. Do not count the fish that are glued on the plates unless the child mentions it. If he does, tell him that one more than four is the same as five. Now would be a good time to make sure that the child knows the three primary colors, red, blue and yellow.

This activity develops

- more of an awareness of red, blue and yellow
- skill in recognizing and matching the colored fish
- skill in following directions
- eye-hand coordination
- more of an awareness of four and one more to make five

Part IV

(Three - Four Years)

Introduction

At the age of three, the child is more self-centered. She aims to please adults and shows signs of more independence. Her vocabulary has increased, and she is very interested in words. She understands simple explanations and is able to reason thoughts accurately.

She may show more of an interest in fine motor activities since she has better small muscle coordination. However, large muscle activities will deplete most of her energy as she engages in more active running, jumping, pedaling, hopping, sliding, throwing and catching a ball and galloping.

Stories, rhymes, rhythms, songs, dramatizations and music are very much a part of her world. She still enjoys fantasizing and may even develop a friendship with an imaginary playmate, even though she is capable of playing for short periods of time with another child.

Simple matching and guessing games are challenging for her. She understands number concepts of two and three even though she may be able to count higher. This is a very inquisitive age in which the child asks many questions as she explores and relates to her environment.

Note: The author and publisher are not liable for any injury or death incurred due to the misuse of the suggested materials and directions. As with all child-related activities, materials should be selected with careful attention to child safety; adult supervision is essential.

Age 3 – Week 1

Ball Bounce

Choose a ball that bounces well and can be easily grasped by the child's hands. However, if the ball is too small it will be more difficult for the child to hold. A ball, approximately eight to ten inches in diameter, is recommended.

Show the child how to drop the ball from the hands and catch it when it bounces up. Emphasis should be placed on watching the ball as it goes down and comes back up so that the child can anticipate the ball's position in order that she can grasp (catch) it at the precise time. Explain to the child that when you drop the ball and it comes back up, that is what is meant as a bounce. Do this several times for the child as you say, "Down and up."

Allow the child to hold the ball, drop it, watch it bounce and attempt to catch it. Stand behind the child if necessary and help her drop the ball. Assist her in determining when to catch the ball. Coordinating the eyes and hands at the correct moment is difficult for some children. Repeat this activity so that the child will develop skill in bouncing and catching a ball.

Encourage the child to catch the ball with the hands without touching the body. If the child uses her body to help catch the ball, avoid negative correction. Simply show the child that she should try to catch the ball without touching her body. If she continues to use her body to help catch the ball, ignore this incorrect style until the child develops more skill in anticipating the timing of the bouncing ball.

At another time, count how many times the child can bounce and catch the ball without missing. This will help the child become aware of her progress, and at the same time enrich her understanding of sequential counting.

To make the bouncing of a ball even more fun, the child may enjoy throwing the ball against a designated inside wall, the side of a building outside or a net pitch back to watch the ball bounce on the floor or ground before catching it. This will serve to help the child improve her skill in catching. She may also develop number skills by counting each time she throws the ball against a wall and catches it.

This activity develops

- eye-hand coordination
- skill in throwing and catching a ball
- further awareness of "up" and "down"
- tactile enhancement (the feeling when catching a ball)
- more of an awareness of counting in sequence
- confidence

Age 3 – Week 2

Early Skipping Fun

Skip around a room or outside as slowly as you possibly can to show the child how to skip. Tell the child that you are skipping and would like for her to learn how. Skip very slowly and say, "Step, hop." Change to the other foot and say, "Step, hop" again. Encourage the child to watch and try to skip as you continue to skip very slowly. Then show the child how much fun it is to skip fast.

Hold the child's hand and encourage her to start with the same foot as you. Continue to say, "Step, hop. Step, hop" as you attempt to skip with the child. The child may "catch on" right away or she may be very awkward and be hesitant to try. If the child seems to have too much difficulty, stop and try again at another time. Tell the child that you will practice "step, hop" later.

Try to interest the child by clapping as you say, "Step, hop"; actually it can be a quick "1-2" count. The child may respond or lose interest. Whichever it is, try to practice often, but do it only when the child is willing to respond. Saying, "step, hop" at different times throughout the days and weeks will help to establish a rhythmic pattern with the child and eventually that rhythm will be transferred to the feet. Keep trying!

If you have had little success with the skipping activity, encourage the child to trot like a pony. This activity is accomplished with short quick steps. The feet will gain very little distance forward with the short quick steps when the child trots. However, the child can be motivated to trot to a designated boundary as you chant the following chant. "Trot, trot, trot. Little pony trot." Keep repeating this and soon the child will repeat the chant too.

This activity develops

- gross motor coordination (leg and foot)
- a sense of rhythm in skipping and trotting
- listening and observational skills
- rhythmic clapping coordination
- confidence

Age 3 — Week 3

Pound, Pound, Pound

A small hammer will be ideal for the child to use with this activity. However, if you do not have a small hammer, Daddy's hammer will suffice. Extreme caution should be emphasized in using the big hammer. You will probably need to help the child hold it or suggest that she use both hands to hold it.

Assemble some nails with large heads and a scrap of soft wood that is suitable for the child to use for driving nails. Tap five nails slightly into the wood leaving several inches between each nail.

Count the nails with the child so that she understands that there are five nails present. Show the child how to hold and use a hammer. Tell the child to hammer one of the nails all the way into the wood. Help the child if necessary. The child will probably insist that she do this independently. In that case, allow her to drive the remaining nails into the wood. It will require much supervision, but the child will thoroughly enjoy the experience.

When the five nails have been hammered into the wood, tap five more nails slightly into the wood for the child. If you feel that the child is adept enough, allow her to attempt to start tapping the nails into the wood. You will undoubtedly need to help her. Count the five nails again with the child so that she understands the concept of five.

After much practice with the hammer, the child can be taught how to join two pieces of wood with a nail. This hammering activity can be repeated many times. The child may just enjoy hammering nails into wood or the child may be motivated enough to want to make a simple toy such as a boat.

As an extension of this activity, the child may enjoy this action finger play:

> "Johnny works with one hammer, one hammer, one hammer
>   (pound left fist gently on the left thigh)
> Johnny works with one hammer and then he works with two
>   (pound left and right fists on left and right thighs)
> Johnny works with two hammers, two hammers, two hammers
> Johnny works with two hammers and then he works with three.
>   (continue pounding fists and begin to tap the left foot)
> Johnny works with three hammers, three hammers, three hammers
>   (continue to move the fists and left foot and begin to move
>   the right foot when the word four is said)
> Johnny works with three hammers and then he works with four.
> Johnny works with four hammers, four hammers, four hammers
> Johnny works with four hammers and then he works with five.
>   (at this point, pound fists, tap feet, and nod the head)
> Johnny works with five hammers, five hammers, five hammers.
> Johnny works with five hammers and then he takes a rest."

This activity develops

- eye-hand coordination and skill in hammering
- confidence and independence
- more awareness of counting and the concept of five

Age 3 – Week 4

Animal Moves

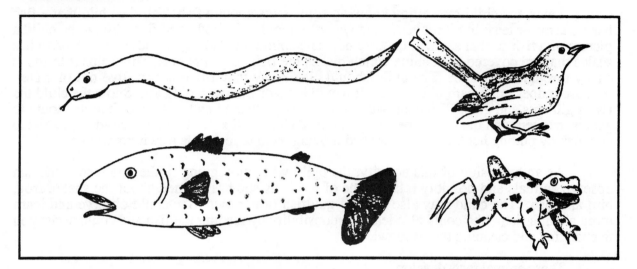

Show the child a picture of a snake and make her aware that a snake has no arms or legs. Tell the child that a snake must wiggle its body to crawl forward. She should also know that a snake has dry scales on its skin and sheds it as it grows. The snake has two eyes but no outside ears. It hears or feels the vibrations of sound through its body. This helps it sense when other animals are near. Tell the child that snakes do not need to eat very often. If you wish, you may tell the child what a snake eats. Encourage the child to wiggle (crawl) like a snake by laying on her stomach and wiggling her body muscles to move forward. Establish a boundary for the child to wiggle (crawl) toward. (If you wish, you may inform the child about poisonous and non-poisonous snakes.)

At another time, talk to the child about a frog. Show the child a picture of a frog and point out the following characteristics of a frog. The frog has four legs, two eyes, smooth skin, a tongue that is attached in the front so that it can throw its tongue out to catch the insects that it eats. The child will probably be interested in knowing that the frog does not have external ears (ears that stick out). The frog moves forward by hopping and jumping. Invite the child to pretend to be a frog and hop around. Place a small pillow on the floor and tell the child to again pretend to be a frog and jump over the pillow. The child may also enjoy hopping and jumping to a specified place.

Later, show the child a picture of a bird and ask the child how a bird is different from a snake. Then ask the child how a bird is different from a frog. Inform the child about the following characteristics of a bird. A bird has two legs, two wings, two eyes, two ears and its body is covered with feathers except its feet. The feet are covered with skin that resembles dry scales. Birds eat mostly insects, worms and small plant seeds. Their mouths (beaks) are specially made to help them get their food. They fly or hop to move forward. The child may note that the frog and the bird have claws which help them to grasp (hold) on to something small. This helps to prevent them from falling. The child can observe this by watching a bird in a tree. Invite the child to pretend to fly like a bird.

The child may enjoy the following rhyme:

"Once I saw a little bird come hop, hop, hop.
So I said, "Little bird, will you stop, stop, stop?"
And was going to the window to say, "How do you do?"
When he flipped his little tail and far away he flew."

Later, the child may enjoy knowing some facts about a fish. Tell the child that a fish has no arms or legs, but it moves in the water by moving its body and fins. Show the child a picture of a fish so that she will understand. The child will also enjoy knowing that a fish has scales that are covered with slime which makes the fish very slippery. This helps it to move easily through the water. The child should also know that a fish cannot live out of water, because it does not breath like we do. It would have difficulty getting air. Show the child the fish's gill slits and gills. The child will enjoy knowing that a fish takes water into its mouth to get air (oxygen) and the water goes back out through the gill slits. Invite the child to pretend to be a fish by putting her hands together and moving them to resemble a swimming fish.

As an extension of this activity, the child will enjoy going to the zoo where she can observe animals and possibly relate some of the facts she has learned about the snake, frog, bird and fish. The child may also enjoy a goldfish of her own. She could observe and learn more about a fish. She could also learn responsibility by feeding the fish and could assist you in changing and cleaning the fishbowl.

These animal facts develop

- awareness of different kinds of animals
- awareness of how different animals move
- language enrichment through listening
- a keener sense of observation
- an appreciation for animals
- dramatization

Age 3 – Week 5

Match Pictures

Obtain two identical magazines or catalogs that have pictures that will be of interest to your child. Select five large colorful pictures from each of the two magazines or catalogs. Glue each of the ten pictures to a piece of construction paper or cardboard. The size of the backing does not have to be uniform. Various sizes will add interest to this activity.

Show the child the matching sets of pictures. Make the child aware that there are two pictures of each that are the same. Discuss each set of pictures so that the child will be able to use picture clues or listening clues to assist her with this activity.

Lay the pictures face up on the floor or table and ask the child to find any two pictures that are the same. If the child has difficulty, pick up a picture and ask the child to find one that is just like the one you are holding. You may assist the child by giving clues such as, "It is in this area," as you point to the area where the matching picture is. Help the child in any way so that she will succeed in matching the pictures. Emphasize the word "same" so that the child understands the concept that same means alike. If you feel the word alike is more meaningful to the child then use it.

To play the game another way, lay five different pictures on the floor or table face up and put the five matching pictures in a pile. Encourage the child to pick up a card from the pile and find the picture that is the "same." Show the child how to organize the pictures that have been matched. Tell the child to put them in a pile, a bag or box so that they are separated from the unmatched pictures. Allow the child to match the pictures independently until all of them are matched. Suggest that the child match them again in the same way. It will probably be necessary for you to sort the pictures and place them properly for the next game.

The game of "concentration" can be used to further challenge the child. To play this game, all of the pictures are placed face down. Each player turns two pictures over in search of two that are the same. If the two pictures that were turned over do not match say, "They are not the same." The pictures should then be turned back over. The child should be told to try to remember what pictures they were and their location on the floor or table. Continue playing this game until all of the pictures have been matched. If the child shows signs of losing interest, turn all of the cards over face up and suggest that she help you match the pictures so that you can put them away. Avoid showing any signs of disappointment.

Duplicate photographs, postcards, art prints, a set of "Old Maid" cards and regular playing cards may be used for this activity to develop the concept of "same" when the child has developed skill in matching simple pictures. If you decide to use regular playing cards, use only a set of five at first. The child will gain confidence and will then ask you to add more to her set of cards. The child may even suggest that she be allowed to play this game independently.

This activity develops

- skill in observing and matching pictures
- eye-hand coordination
- memory recall
- further awareness of pictures that are the "same"
- confidence and independence

Age 3 – Week 6

Colorful Fish

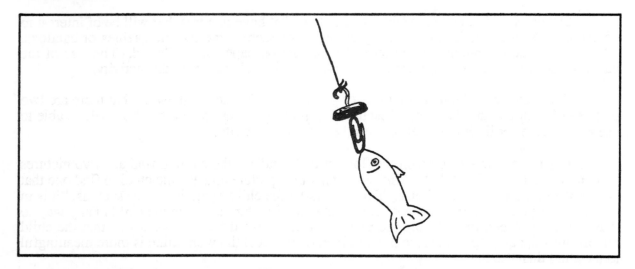

Cut out two construction paper fish from each of the following colors; red, orange, yellow, blue, green, purple, brown and black. The fish may also be made from 3 x 5 inch index cards that have been colored with the suggested colors.

Show the child one fish of each color. Name each color as you place the fish at random on a table or on the floor in front of the child. Tell the child to pretend that the fish are in water.

Encourage the child to pick up a red fish. Praise the child if she is successful. If the child still does not know the color red, show her the correct red fish. Continue this activity until all of the colors have been named and the correct color fish has been found. Make a note of any colors that the child does not know so that you can reinforce these colors at another time with the child. This activity is designed to reinforce the skill of visual recognition and memory recall of the names of the eight colors.

When the child is confident with the colors, place the two fish of each color on the table or floor. Name a color and ask the child to find two fish that are the same color. Praise the child and encourage her to put the fish in a container to represent a pretend fishing pail. Continue the game until all of the fish have been "caught."

This activity may seem simple for the child if she already knows her colors. However, the matching and listening skills that accompany this activity will increase your child's confidence and make her secure in performing not only this activity but others that may be more challenging.

For more interest, put a small paper clip on the nostrils of each fish. Tie a magnet (refrigerator or cup hook kind) to a string and show the child how to actually catch the fish with the magnet. This takes more skill (eye-hand coordination) and may overwhelm the child if this activity is introduced before the child is secure with color recognition and matching. Caution the child to only "fish" with the magnet and string. Swinging the magnet on the string could result in an accident.

As the child becomes more competent in matching colors, allow her to play the game independently. At another time, work with a small number of fish and instruct the child to catch a certain number of fish. Count the number of fish that were caught and then ask the child how many are left.

Identical or matching stickers, numbers, letters and words may be used on the fish at different times. Only use a few fish at first and then gradually add more as the child becomes more confident.

This activity develops

- further skill in color recognition
- skill in matching colors
- listening for the color named in order to find it
- eye-hand coordination
- independence and confidence

Age 3 – Week 7

Climb Up and Down

If you have a short ladder, lay it against something that is stable and a little higher than the floor or ground. Allow the child to climb up and down on the rungs of the ladder. Be sure to hold or brace the ladder to make sure that it is steady and safe.

If you do not have a ladder, allow the child to walk up and down several steps. If you do not have either of these, lean a smooth board or a large piece of heavy cardboard about 18 inches wide against an object to form an incline plane. Hold the board or cardboard steady and encourage the child to hold on to each side as she climbs up. Then tell the child to come down by moving her feet and hands backwards.

Whichever one of these you choose to use with the child, it is suggested that you emphasize the words "up" and "down" in relation to climbing. A child of this age will enjoy experiences on a regular sliding board. If you live near a park or a place where a small sliding board is present, take your child there and encourage her to climb up the ladder and slide down the slide. If you do not have access to a small slide, heavy cardboard can be leaned against a stationary object to form an incline plane. A small set of stairs can be used for the stationary object to support the cardboard. The child will enjoy this homemade sliding board.

A child of this age is agile and likes to climb, slide, run, hop, skip, jump and experiment with different ways to move. She is developing gross motor skills for better coordination of her body muscles. You may think of other ways to satisfy her interests in these activities.

This activity develops

- more awareness of the concepts, "up" and "down"
- eye-hand-foot coordination
- gross motor skill in climbing and sliding
- confidence and independence

Age 3 – Week 8

Obstacle Line

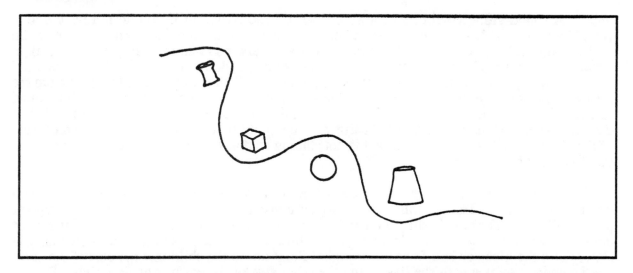

Lay a long piece of wide colored yarn on the floor. The yarn can extend into another room if there is enough open space. Position the yarn so that at intervals the yarn curves left and right in a snake fashion. Place a small object at each curved indentation. These objects will serve to establish boundaries for the child to go around. (This is a follow-up activity of age 1, week 6).

Show the child how to walk with one foot exactly in front of the other. Then tell the child to start at one end of the yarn and walk on the yarn with one foot in front of the other until she gets to the other end of the yarn. Tell her the objects have been placed to remind her to be careful as she walks along on the curved yarn strip.

For additional interest, a toy or stuffed animal can be placed at the end of the yarn. The child should be instructed to pick it up when she gets to the end of the yarn and bring it back to you.

At another time, pieces of different colored paper can be placed at the end of the yarn. The child should be told to pick up a specified colored piece and bring it back. This activity involves listening and associating which color to pick up. If the child is still having difficulty with colors, be sure and identify the color by picking it up and matching it with something else that is that color. If the child knows only a few colors, then play this game using only three colors. If the child knows all of the colors, pastel colors, such as pink, lavender, lime, tan and gray, may be introduced to add more interest for the child.

This activity develops

- eye-foot coordination
- skill in balance
- skill in following directions
- more awareness of colors
- observational skill
- confidence

Age 3 – Week 9

Day and Night

A round globe would be ideal to use for this activity, but if you do not have one, a round ball will do. Lower the shades and close the curtains to darken a room. Take the child to that room and tell her that you have made the room darker so that you can pretend it is night time. Turn on a flashlight so that the light shines on the globe or the ball. Make the child aware of the light that is reflected from the globe or ball. Tell the child that the light from the flashlight is like the light that comes from the sun. Also, tell her that the globe or ball is round just like the earth that we live on. When the sun shines on the earth we have day time. When the sun does not shine on parts of the earth we have night time. Show the child the dark side of the globe or ball where the flashlight is not shining so that she will understand some of what you have told her.

Take a piece of masking tape or cut a piece of paper in the shape of a house and tape it on the globe or ball. Tell the child to pretend her house is there on the earth where the tape or paper is located. Turn the flashlight on and tell the child to pretend that it is day on this side of the earth where her house is. Encourage the child to hold the flashlight and watch as you slowly turn the globe or ball from left to right. Point out to the child that the part of the earth that is having day is where she lives, and the other side of the earth is having night. Repeat this activity so that the child is aware that day time is caused when the sun shines on one part of the earth and night is caused where the sun cannot shine until the earth turns to face it. The child should then realize that her "house" changes position in relation to the sun.

When it is night time, talk to the child again about why it is dark outside. Ask the child where the sun is. If she does not know, simply tell her the sun is shining on the other side of the earth.

At various times, continue to talk about day and night and allow the child to pretend to be the earth. Hold the flashlight and tell the child to turn around slowly while you hold the light in one position. Through this experience, the child should realize that the light from the flashlight can only shine on one side of her at a time. Therefore, the concept of the cause of day and night should be fairly well understood by the child.

This activity develops

- awareness of day and night
- awareness that the earth is round and turns
- awareness that the sun gives us light and heat
- role playing
- awareness of reflected light
- language enrichment

Age 3 – Week 10

Scissors

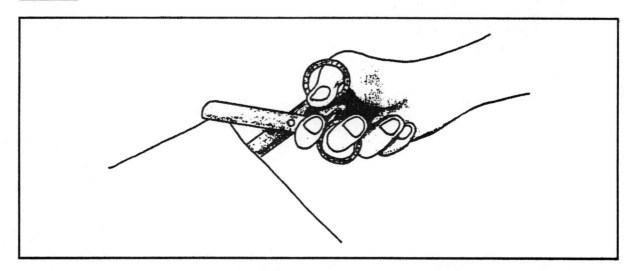

Scissors can be fun but they need to be used with care. Buy a pair of scissors that have been recommended for children and make sure that they have blunt ends.

Show the child how to hold scissors. The thumb should be placed in the top hole and the middle finger should be placed in the lower hole. The pointer (index) finger should rest just below the rim of the lower hole and provide support to the scissors. The ring and little fingers have no real function in cutting.

Remind the child that the thumb should always be "up," i.e., it should always be in the top hole of the scissors. Many children try to cut upside down or sideways. Some children put the pointer finger in the lower hole with the middle finger. If possible, try to avoid this. However, if the child cuts satisfactorily with both fingers in the lower hole avoid correcting her until she is more secure in cutting.

Use a wide felt marker and draw a line from the top to the bottom of a half sheet of typing or similar paper. Instruct the child to cut closely beside the line. If the child is right handed, the wide line should be on the child's left. If the child is left handed, the wide line should be on the child's right. Scissors for left handed people are available, and there are also special scissors with blunt ends that can be used for both left and right hand cutting.

As the child cuts the paper, make certain the scissors are perpendicular to the paper. Each "bite" into the paper should be made in the middle of the scissors' blades, not at the blunt ends. The child will need much guidance and patience in learning to coordinate the scissors. It is not advisable to leave a child this age alone with scissors. This will avoid damage to curtains, furniture, clothing and hair. Children enjoy "cutting" and may cut anything in sight.

Continue to draw lines for the child to practice her cutting. Soon the child will develop enough skill to cut a picture from an old magazine. With more practice, the child will be able to cut around curves and in corners. It will be easier for the child to manipulate the paper and the scissors if you will remove the page from the magazine before the child begins to cut. Remind the child to cut closely beside the line, not on the line.

If the child has difficulty cutting, allow her to cut cooked spaghetti into pieces. This will give her better control of the scissors and help her develop more confidence in cutting.

This activity develops

- skill in cutting
- eye-hand coordination
- visual skill in watching the cutting line
- skill in following directions
- confidence

Age 3 – Week 11

Me

A child of this age is very egocentric. She is anxious to please but still thinks primarily of herself. She wants to know as much about herself as possible. Read the following poem to your child and explain the meaning of "name," "age" and "birthday."

> "My name is (full name)
> And I am three years old
> My next birthday is _____.
> Then I'll be four years old."

Tell the child that a name is what we are called. She should be aware of her first, second and last name. The last name is the family's name. The child should understand that four is one more than three, and that every time someone has a birthday that means that they are one year older.

Read the rhyme several times to the child and pause before the last word of each line and give the child an opportunity to fill in the last word. If she is still interested, continue repeating the rhyme until the child can tell her full name, age and birthday. If the child loses interest or cannot recall it all, try again at another time.

As an extension of this activity, draw a simple cake and add three candles while the child watches. Count the candles, 1-2-3 as you point to each one. Say to the child, "On your next birthday I will add one more candle. Then you will be four years old." Add the fourth candle and count 1-2-3 and one more is four.

As a further extension, choose a cardboard box (round or square) and punch four holes in it. The holes should be large enough to support four old table candles that you may have on hand. If you do not have candles, use pencils with no points. Allow the child to add the "candles" to the pretend birthday cake. The child can be encouraged to count as she places the candles 1-2-3-4.

This activity develops

- awareness of full name
- awareness of age
- awareness of birthday
- awareness of the family last name
- more awareness of the number concepts (1-2-3-4)
- memory recall
- language enrichment

Age 3 – Week 12

Circle and Square

Children love to draw. Allow your child to help you trace around a saucer or plate with a pencil. This should be drawn on a piece of poster board or cardboard so that it can be made into a stencil. To make the stencil, carefully cut out the circle that was drawn leaving a hole in the cardboard. Use a ruler and draw a six inch square on another piece of cardboard. Carefully cut out the square to make a square stencil.

Place the circle and square stencil each on a separate piece of paper and tape them to a flat surface. Ask the child to name the two shapes. Assist the child if necessary.

Instruct the child to select a crayon and color inside the circle stencil using back and forth strokes until the circle is completely colored. Allow the child to choose a different color and color the space inside the square stencil.

Remove the tape and stencils and the child will discover a neatly colored circle and square. The boundaries of the stencils help to control the child's coloring yet allows the child some free movement of the crayons. Invite the child to cut out the circle and the square. Assist her if necessary.

Hang the colored circle and square up for others to admire. The child should know the names and colors that were used in this activity.

If the child does not know the colors and shapes, reinforce her memory recall by playing the game, "I Spy." For example, say, "I spy something red." Make sure the child points or finds something red. Continue to play the game until the child knows the two colors that were used in this activity and also the two shapes.

This activity develops

- more awareness of the shapes, "circle" and "square"
- more awareness of colors
- freedom of choice in selecting colors
- eye-hand coordination
- language enrichment
- confidence

Age 3 – Week 13

Hit or Miss

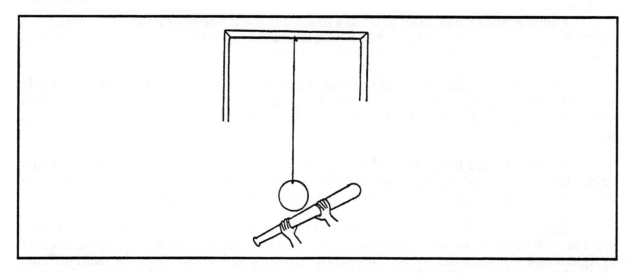

Suspend a nerf ball, sock ball, yarn ball or a stuffed paper bag from an open doorway by attaching a piece of yarn or string at the top of the door frame and tying it to one of the balls or the bag. The yarn or string should be long enough so that the ball hangs at the child's eye level.

Place a yardstick or plastic bat in the child's hands. Show her how to grasp it comfortably with the hands near the middle, yet leaving enough space in between to be used for hitting the ball. Instruct the child to keep her eyes on the ball as she moves the yardstick or bat forward to hit the ball. The hit ball will move away and return for the child to hit it again, because it is suspended from the yarn or string to which it is attached. Therefore, the child should be instructed to continue to watch the ball. Also, the child should be reminded to tap the ball gently. If it is hit hard, the attached ball will strike the wall or the ceiling and will not return to a position for the child to hit it again.

The child should continue to hit the ball each time it returns. It is important for the child to remain in one position so that the ball will swing in clear view in order for her to tap the ball each time it returns.

As an extension of this activity, the child will enjoy counting the number of times she can hit the ball. Allow the counting to continue as long as the child is interested. This activity can be done independently with little supervision from you.

This activity develops

- skill in aiming at a target
- eye-arm coordination
- skill in timing or anticipating the return of the ball
- skill in counting
- more awareness of a boundary

Age 3 — Week 14

The Hole Punch Row

Punch at least ten or more holes in a row along the top edge of a piece of cardboard or poster board that is approximately 2 x 8 inches. Place the cardboard on top of a piece of paper and tape this to a flat surface to prevent it from slipping.

Give the child a fine tipped felt marker or pencil and show her how to color in the holes that have been punched. Encourage the child to move from left to right. However, if the child skips some holes and moves at random allow her to fill in the rest of the holes without interruption.

When the child has finished the first row, remove the tape and show her the colored circles that she made on the paper underneath. Move the cardboard down to make a new row and encourage the child to make another row of circles using the hole punched cardboard.

Observe the child. Does she take time to fill in the entire hole or does she just make a mark in each hole? Emphasize the word "row." Again encourage the child to move from left to right as she colors in the holes. Throughout the days and weeks show the child different kinds of rows, such as rows of words in a book, rows of designs in cloth, rows of chairs in a building, etc. This will enrich her knowledge of the concept and enable her to become more perceptive.

As an extension of this activity, the child can use a metal hole puncher and punch holes at random. This can be done on the newspaper, a magazine page or a scrap piece of paper. If your hole puncher is too difficult for the child to grip and punch a hole, assist her until she develops the necessary strength and coordination to successfully punch holes for herself. The child may also enjoy having you draw a line on paper and allowing her to punch holes along the line.

This activity develops

- eye-hand coordination
- skill in focusing on detail
- more awareness of left and right
- more awareness of a "row"
- awareness of movement along a line
- independence and confidence

Age 3 – Week 15

Name the Sound

Assemble three things that the child can name but are small enough to hide in a paper bag. Some suggested items are a bell, a bunch of keys hooked together, two wooden blocks or any similar items that can be used to make a sound. Place each kind of item in a small paper bag.

Name and show the child what is in each bag. Shake each bag so that the child can listen to the sound that the objects make inside the bags. Close the bags and change their positions.

Shake one of the bags and encourage the child to listen, think and name what is inside the bag. If she has difficulty, show her what is inside and repeat the activity using the same bag. Continue until the child has succeeded with the three bags several times.

At another time, repeat this activity but substitute different objects to be placed in the three bags. The objects that you choose should make a distinct sound so that the child can distinguish the sounds easily. To vary the game, you can name the object for the child to choose. The child should then shake each closed bag and by listening select the correct bag.

This is a good listening activity and should be repeated often.

As an extension of this activity, a tape recording can be made of some familiar home sounds such as the sound of a vacuum cleaner, radio, clock, dishes rattling, pouring water, hammering, etc. The recording can be played for the child and as she listens, she should be encouraged to identify the respective sound. If she has difficulty, produce the real sound for her and try the tape recording again. This will serve to improve the child's listening skills immensely.

This activity develops

- skill in identifying objects
- listening for a sound to help in making a selection
- skill in distinguishing different sounds
- confidence
- language enrichment

Age 3 – Week 16

Listen and Draw Book

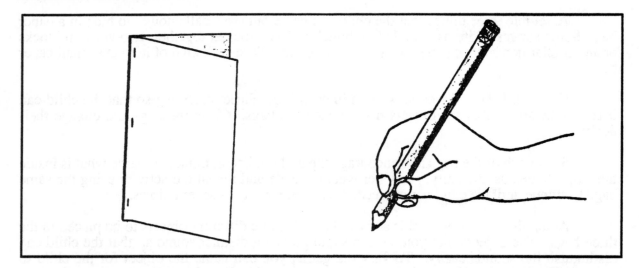

Obtain two pieces of typing paper to form a booklet. Staple the left hand side to secure the pages. Tell the child that she is going to make another booklet and that you will tell her what to draw. Show the child the front, inside and back of the book. Count the front page as 1, the left inside as 2, the right inside as 3 and the back as 4. The child should then be aware that there are four pages to her booklet. Remind the child that earlier in the age 2, week 45 activity she made a color booklet. This time you will make another kind of booklet.

Hand the child the booklet and a pencil or fine tipped marker and tell her to draw a picture of herself on the front. Check to see if the child is holding the pencil or pen correctly. If not, show her the proper way by instructing her to hold the pencil or pen with the thumb and index finger placing the middle finger behind to help support the pencil or pen. The ring and little fingers have no real purpose in drawing or writing.

The child may begin immediately to draw or she may ask you to help her. If she needs help, say, "You have a head." Make a circle with your hands to show the child that the head resembles that shape. Then say, "You have a body." Use your hand to move from your head down to your legs. Then say, "You have two arms." Move your arms and make the child aware of their position on the body. Then say, "You have two legs." This should be enough of a stimulus to motivate her. Accept whatever the child draws and praise her for her efforts.

When the front picture of the child is complete, open the booklet and tell the child to draw a house. Be sure the child begins drawing on the left inside page. To motivate the child, you can show her a simple picture of a house from a magazine. Refrain from drawing a house for the child to copy. However, you can suggest that the child draw a square. You can draw the outline of a square in the air to show the child what you mean. Remind the child that a house needs a door, windows and a roof and talk about why a house needs these. The word, "chimney," may be mentioned. If it is, suggest that the child draw a chimney for the house. If the child wants to draw smoke coming from the chimney, allow her to do so. Accept whatever you see and praise the child for following your directions.

When the house is finished, instruct the child to draw a ball on the right inside page. The child should be able to do this independently. However, if the child asks you for help, draw a circle in the air with your hands and tell the child to try to draw a ball.

When the ball is finished, turn the booklet to the back page and tell the child to draw anything she would like to draw. This gives the child time to think. If the child says that she does not know what to draw, make a few suggestions such as a favorite toy, a tree, a bird, etc. Again, accept what you see and praise the child for her efforts.

These four drawings need not be done all at one sitting. Look at the booklet with the child when it is finished. Ask the child what is on each page? If the child cannot recall, tell her what she drew on each page. At another time, invite the child to tell you about her booklet. Hopefully she will be able to recall what she drew in the booklet. If not, rename the pictures and try again later.

Other booklets may be made for the development of fine motor control as well as memory recall of what was drawn. The booklets should contain pictures of different things. With practice, the child's artistic skill will improve and the drawings will be more meaningful to her. If the child is interested in coloring what she draws, allow her to do so.

This activity develops

- skill in listening and following directions
- eye-hand coordination
- more awareness of left and right
- memory recall
- skill in turning a page
- confidence

Age 3 – Week 17

Guess What?

Children enjoy riddles and they stimulate thinking and reasoning. Simple riddles can be developed quickly and are a good traveling activity which can be used as a peaceful game when a child has been very active. Here are some suggestions for you to try:

Guess what is green and brown and grows very tall?	(tree)
Guess what has four wheels and Daddy drives it?	(car)
Guess what has a front and a back and has pages?	(book)
Guess what has a head, foot and four legs?	(bed)
Guess what has four legs, a back and you sit on it?	(chair)
Guess what has panes that you can see through?	(window)
Guess what lets you in and out?	(door)
Guess what has two wheels, pedals and handlebars?	(bike)
Guess what is round, square, or other shapes and holds clothes together?	(buttons)
Guess what shows a picture and makes a sound?	(TV or movie)
Guess what twinkles at night?	(star)
Guess what is yellow and gives us heat and light?	(sun)
Guess what opens and closes and keeps things neat?	(drawer)
Guess what is soft and helps rest your head?	(pillow)
Guess what is hot and makes wood burn?	(fire)
Guess what is long, thin and you can write with it?	(pencil)
Guess what has one eye and uses thread?	(needle)
Guess what has four legs and a top?	(table)
Guess what is black and white and is read all over?	(newspaper)
Guess what is clear and you drink it?	(water)
Guess what is (describe the child)?	(child's name)

These riddles develop

* active thinking and reasoning
* skill in listening for clues
* awareness of characteristics of different things
* an interest in creating other riddles
* language enrichment

Age 3 – Week 18

Create With Tape

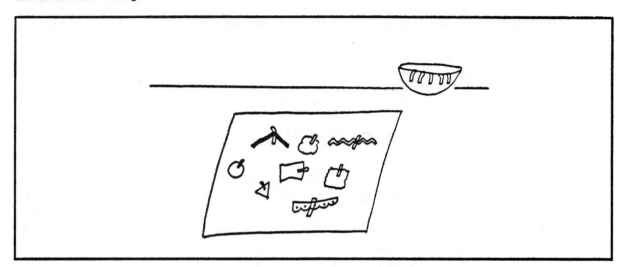

Gather an assortment of materials for the child to see and feel. These items could include small pieces of colored paper, baggie ties, lace scraps. rick rack scraps, bits of cloth, several buttons, cotton balls, felt pieces, string or yarn or anything similar that you happen to have on hand.

Allow the child to feel and explore the materials. Talk about the materials and their uses. You can also tell the child where you found these materials in the house.

Encourage the child to tape some of the materials on a piece of cardboard or heavy paper to make a picture. It will be easier for the child if you will cut the tape in 2 inch lengths and line them up on the rim of a non-breakable large mixing bowl or something similar. In this way, the child can choose a material and tape it down independently. However, it will be necessary for you to show the child how to lift up a tape length and use it to attach a material on the cardboard.

This activity can be repeated at another time using materials from outside such as leaves, sticks, small flowers, feathers or whatever the child might choose from outside that is not dirty or litter.

This activity develops

- freedom of choice
- creativity
- more awareness of the textures of a variety of materials
- eye-hand coordination
- confidence and independence
- language enrichment

Age 3 – Week 19

Jumping Fun

This activity will probably function better outside; however, it can be done inside with closer supervision. Some suggested items that can be used for inside jumping are a steady chair, stairs, sofa, low table, trunk, sturdy suitcase or stool.

A child of this age enjoys jumping from a higher to a lower level. The suggested items are of different levels and any chosen item may be used exclusively. You may vary the items to be used for jumping at other times. To avoid over stimulation, one jumping item at a given time is recommended. Jumping activities should be repeated often to help the child gain better coordination.

To begin a jumping activity, the child should be helped if needed to stand on the chosen object. Count 1-2-3. On the count of three, the child should use that as a cue to jump from a higher to the lower level. The child will most likely enjoy doing this jumping activity and may be anxious to continue for awhile. At the conclusion of the jumping activity, a quieter activity should be encouraged to settle the child down.

If this activity is performed outside, the child may help you select places where she can practice jumping from a higher to a lower level. The main thrust of this activity is to develop skill in jumping from a higher to a lower level, not distance. The child needs to feel (experience) the sensation of moving through space in this manner when she jumps.

This activity develops

- gross motor coordination
- awareness of high and low
- awareness of the different heights of the objects
- listening for a cue to jump
- more of an awareness of the order of counting 1-2-3
- skill in body balance as the child moves through space

Age 3 – Week 20

Where Does It Belong?

Collect a key, a small juice can, a spoon, a large button and a small envelope. Trace the outline of each object on a piece of paper.

Place the objects in a box and encourage the child to choose an object and place it on the correct shape. This activity will be simple for the child.

To further challenge the child, choose ten buttons of various sizes and trace their outlines on paper. Place the buttons in a container and encourage the child to place the buttons on the correct shape. An assortment of spools, pencils or spoons can also be used.

This activity can be even more challenging for the child if a collection of different keys are used. Keys are similar but the teeth positions vary on each side. In this activity, the child will have to find the correct side of the key before placing it on the matching shape. At first the child may need help, but with practice the child will soon learn to do this activity independently.

As an extension of this activity, clay may be used to make impressions of various materials such as a spool, button, key, popsicle stick, pencil, scissors, etc. The child will enjoy matching the objects on the impressions or indentations made in the clay.

This activity develops

- further awareness of the different shapes of objects
- eye-hand coordination
- observational skills
- matching skills
- awareness of sizes
- problem solving
- confidence

Age 3 – Week 21

Print Painting

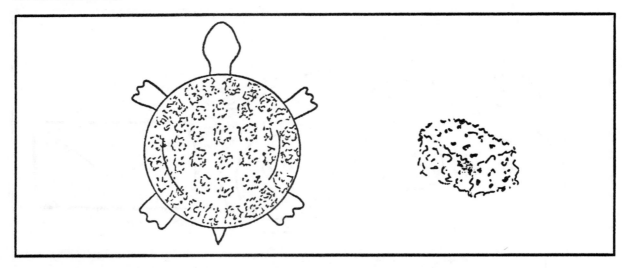

This activity can be done with diluted water base paint that was left over from a home project or tempera paint. Draw an outline of a turtle on construction paper or use a paper plate. Glue or staple a paper head, four legs and a tail. Tear or cut a sponge piece so that it is about 2 to 3 inches long and 1/2 inch wide. A sponge with big holes will work better for this activity.

Show the child the turtle. Count the legs and make the child aware that a turtle has four legs, a tail, a head and a hard shell with a design on it. Tell the child that she will be able to print a design on the paper turtle's shell. Show the child a picture of a turtle and tell the child any other facts about a turtle that you feel will be of interest to her.

Pour a little paint in a shallow tray or dish and show the child how to dip the sponge in the paint with the narrow part in the paint. Carefully press the wet part of the sponge on the paper turtle's shell and print several dabs on the shell. Dip the sponge in the paint and repeat the printing until the shell has enough paint dabs to make a nice design on the paper turtle. Allow the paint to dry while you talk to the child about wet and dry paint. The child should understand that the liquid part of the paint evaporates just like water evaporates from wet clothes. When all of the liquid has evaporated from something, it is then dry.

At another time, other objects may be used for printing a picture. Some suggested items for you to use are an old toothbrush, bottle cap, old comb, a spool, golf tee, pencil eraser, and a clothespin.

This activity develops

- awareness of another way to paint
- awareness of wet and dry
- language enrichment
- awareness of a turtle's characteristics
- tactile sensitivity when painting
- confidence

Age 3 – Week 22

Nuts and Bolts

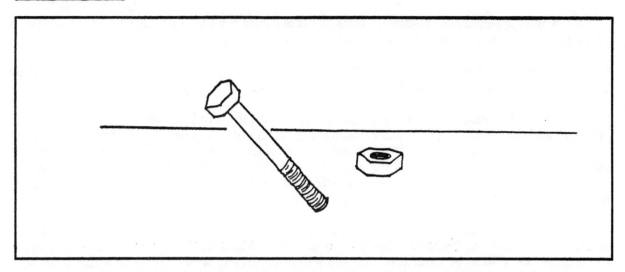

Assemble ten different sizes of metal nuts and bolts if possible. The different sizes will make this activity more interesting. If you do not have various sizes, make certain that the bolts you choose to use have nuts that fit the threads of the bolts properly.

Mix the assortment of nuts and bolts in a flat tray. Show the child how to screw (turn) a nut on a bolt. Allow the child to explore and attempt to fit the proper nuts on the bolts. Help the child if necessary.

Once all of the nuts and bolts are threaded properly, tell the child to unscrew the nuts, mix the nuts and bolts and start again.

If the child has problems with the nuts and bolts suggest that the child sort the nuts and bolts according to size and try to thread them later. It may be necessary for you to help the child sort them. If you are using nuts and bolts of various sizes, you and the child can put them in order from the smallest to the largest. This should give the child some sense of organization and help her to match the nuts and bolts correctly.

This activity develops

- matching skills
- eye-hand coordination
- problem solving skills

Age 3 – Week 23

Pouring

A plastic pitcher with various sizes of glasses and cups will be suitable for the child to practice the pouring of a liquid. Go outside or use the kitchen sink for this activity.

Put some water in the pitcher and line up the empty glasses and cups so that it will be convenient for the child to pour the water from the pitcher into the glasses.

Allow the child to hold the pitcher of water. Tell the child that the cups and glasses are "empty" and that she is to pour water into each of them until they are "full" of water. As each container is filled make the child aware that the container is not "empty" any more. Allow the child to pour the water until all of the water has been emptied from the pitcher. Tell the child that the pitcher is "empty" and that you will need to get more water before she can fill the remainder of the glasses and cups.

When the child has filled all of the glasses and cups, empty the water back into the pitcher and allow the child to continue to pour the water to "fill" the glasses and cups. Encourage the child to be careful so that she will not spill any water. If some water spills say, "Oops, a spill" and allow the child to continue. With much practice the child will become more skillful in pouring a liquid. However, at this age I would only recommend allowing the child to practice her pouring skill independently at the kitchen or bathroom sink.

Throughout this activity much conversation should take place. For example you could say, "Water is wet, you can pour it and it is clear. Containers can be filled with water and we need to drink water for good health." The child should also be made more aware of the concepts "empty" and "full," as well as "heavy" and "light" in relation to the full and empty pitcher.

This activity develops

- skill in pouring a liquid
- more awareness of "empty" and "full"
- observational skills
- language enrichment
- awareness of the feel of something "heavy" and "light"
- confidence

Age 3 – Week 24

Money Talk

Assemble five pennies, five nickels and two cups. Allow the child to hold a penny and encourage her to look at the man's face on the front of the penny. Tell the child it is the face of Abraham Lincoln. Also tell the child that he was a famous man and was once the president of the United States. Turn the penny over and tell the child that the building on the back side of the penny is a picture of the Lincoln Memorial. At this time, tell the child anything else that you can recall about Abraham Lincoln that you feel will be of interest to her. The child will probably notice the small letters and numbers on the coin, but it is not necessary for you to say anything about them. Tell the child the coin is called a penny and it is worth one cent.

Allow the child to hold a nickel. Identify the likeness of Thomas Jefferson on the front of the nickel. Tell the child that Thomas Jefferson was a famous man too, and also was once president of the United States. Turn the coin over and tell the child that the picture on this side is a likeness of Thomas Jefferson's home. The home is called Monticello. Add any more information about Thomas Jefferson that you wish to tell the child. Tell the child that the coin is called a nickel and is worth five cents. It is worth (will buy) as much as five pennies.

Mix the pennies and nickels and place them on a smooth work area. Tell the child to pick up all of the pennies and place them in one of the cups. Tell the child to dump the pennies out and mix them with the nickels. Then instruct the child to put all of the nickels in the cup. Tell the child to dump the nickels out of the cup and this time instruct the child to put all of the pennies in one cup and all of the nickels in the other cup. At the conclusion of this activity, pick up a penny and ask the child to identify it. Likewise, pick up a nickel and ask the child to identify it. Correct the child if she confuses them.

Instruct the child to count out five pennies. Help the child to count in sequence "1-2-3-4-5." Hold the five pennies in one hand and tell the child to hand you one nickel. Place that nickel in the other hand and open the palms of your hands to show the child the coins. Again tell the child that the five pennies will buy the same thing as one nickel. This concept may be a little difficult for the child. However, if you allow her to pretend to buy something that is worth five cents, using either five pennies or a nickel, she will better understand. If you can "find" something in a store that costs only five cents, this experience will be even more realistic for the child.

Place the nickels in a row from left to right and tell the child to put a penny on each nickel. Then ask the child how many nickels she has. The child should realize that she has just as many nickels as she does pennies. She may also enjoy counting all of the coins so that she realizes that she has ten coins in all and that number means more than five. The child may also note the nickel is bigger than the penny. Again, make the child aware that it takes five pennies to buy the same thing for one nickel.

Dimes and quarters may be introduced in the same way, but make certain the child understands the money value of a penny and a nickel before attempting to work with coins of higher value. It will be difficult for the child to realize that a dime is worth more than a penny and a nickel even though it is smaller. Therefore, go slowly in teaching money value and your child will gain confidence and learn the concepts rapidly.

"Money talk" should be an on-going activity until the child can accurately identify all of the coins including a half dollar and a silver dollar.

This activity develops

- awareness of the different money coins and their value
- sorting skills
- looking for detail
- awareness of "same" and "different"
- language enrichment
- confidence

Age 3 – Week 25

Which Egg is It?

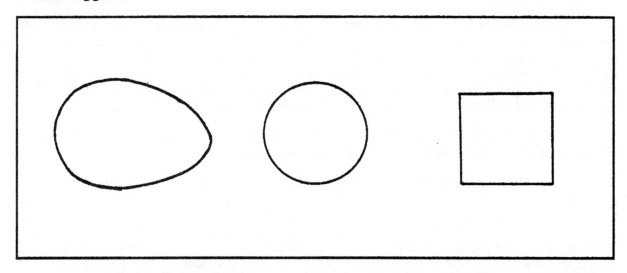

Cut out five different colored eggs about the size of your fist. They should be red, blue, yellow, orange and green. Plastic eggs may also be used for this activity.

Show the child the eggs and place them on the floor. Play the game "Pick Up" with the child. To play this game, name a color and instruct the child to pick up the egg with that color. Do this with each of the colored eggs to make certain that the child can find a specified color when it is named.

Count the five eggs with the child as you instruct her to place them in a basket or other container. Place the basket or the container in a position so that the child cannot see inside the container of eggs. Place four of the five eggs on the floor. Ask the child which color egg is missing. Name the colors of the eggs that are on the floor with the child. If the child has difficulty recalling the missing color, show the child the colored egg that was left in the basket. Change the color and continue playing this game until the child gains confidence and can readily identify the missing colored egg.

Make the child aware that the egg is a different shape from a circle and square. Review the shapes of the circle and square if the child does not seem to understand. To do this, simply draw a circle, square and an oval on a piece of paper. Tell the child that the egg shape is called an oval.

This activity develops

- memory recall of the colors and shapes
- skill in recalling something that is out of sight
- further understanding of the number concepts 1-5
- confidence
- listening skills

Age 3 – Week 26

Two Parts Make a Whole

Cut out five large colorful pictures from a magazine. Show the pictures to the child and talk about each picture. Glue each picture to cardboard or heavy paper. When the glue is dry cut each picture in two pieces with one or two curves or points in the cutting. The cut should be from the top to the bottom. Each picture will then have a left and a right side. Show the whole picture again to the child and make her aware that the two pieces make a "whole." This type of puzzle was first introduced in the age 1, week 24 and the age 2, week 1 activities.

Mix the puzzle pieces and tell the child to put the pictures back together. Praise the child and encourage her to repeat this activity as long as she appears to be interested.

At another time, pick up the left side of one of the pictures and ask the child to tell you something about it. Accept whatever the child says. Do the same with the right side of the same picture. Put the two pieces together and ask the child to tell you something about the whole picture. Accept what the child says and add whatever else you wish to convey to the child regarding the picture. Follow the same procedure with the other pictures. During your conversation with the child be sure to refer to the left and right sides of each picture and make the child fully aware that the picture has two parts. You may mention that each part is called a "half" and it takes two "halves" to make a "whole" thing. The words "left" and "right" can be mentioned, but it is not necessary to emphasize "left" and "right" at this time. You can refer to them as "this side" and "that side." The child may also have difficulty understanding the concept, "half."

Remember to repeat some of the previous activities, especially those that seem to challenge the child. What may seem simple to you, may not be that simple for the child. She may appear to understand a concept, but at another time show little or no recall. That is why it is very important to play the same games and repeat activities to firmly instill these concepts in your child.

This activity develops

- further awareness of "left" and "right"
- awareness that the left and right sides of a picture are not necessarily the same
- eye-hand coordination
- further awareness that two parts make a "whole"
- language enrichment
- confidence

Age 3 – Week 27

In and Out of the Box

Obtain a corrugated cardboard box that is large enough for the child to crawl in and sit down in easily when the box is placed on its side.

Select two sets of eight colored strips of paper or crayons. Place a set of each in a small paper bag or similar container. The colors should be red, orange, yellow, green, blue, purple, brown and black. Place one of the bags in a corner of the inside of the box. The other bag should be placed in front of the child who should be close to the corrugated box.

Tell the child to choose any color from the bag that is outside the box. The child should then examine the color, name it and put it beside the bag that is outside of the box. The child should then crawl into the box, sit down, find the matching color in the bag that is inside the box and crawl back out of the box. The matched colors should be placed beside each other outside the box. The child should choose another color and repeat the activity until all of the colors have been matched and are outside of the box.

Repeat this activity often. If the child knows her colors then other objects may be used for the child to name, retrieve and match. However, if the child still does not know her colors, continue to use only the basic colors. As the child learns the colors, use only the ones in which the child has difficulty recalling. To reinforce the child's confidence, once again use all eight colors so that the child will realize that she can recognize all of the colors. You may also use identical or matching shapes, numbers, letters and words with this activity

This activity develops

- memory recall
- skill in color naming and matching
- gross motor coordination
- eye-hand coordination
- confidence

Age 3 – Week 28

On and Off

This activity can be done during one sitting as a game or it can be done at any convenient time throughout the day while you are working in one particular place.

The child should be allowed to cut appliances "on" and "off" with adult supervision. This type of an experience will enable the child to develop self-confidence and independence. A lesson in safety should be emphasized as each appliance is turned "on" and "off." Children delight in pushing buttons, flipping switches and turning knobs.

A good place to begin is at a light switch. Allow the child to turn the light "on" and then turn it "off." Perhaps you and the child can walk through the house and count the total number of light switches.

At another time, the child should be allowed to cut on a lamp. Some lamps have a knob to turn, while others have a slender knob switch to push back and forth to obtain light. Several older lamps may have a short chain to pull for the light to come "on" and go "off." More modern lamps are simply touched for the light to come "on" and "off." The child should be encouraged to observe the different methods of activating lamps and perhaps try them all with supervision.

Other appliances that the child will delight in operating are vacuum cleaner, food processor, mixer, toaster, dishwasher, garbage disposal, radio and television. The child can be invited to turn on these appliances when the appropriate time arises. The washing machine and dryer may be difficult for the child to reach, but activating them can be a thrilling experience for her. Caution and safety should be emphasized.

This activity develops

- a sense of responsibility and helping
- eye-hand coordination
- awareness of the different kinds of switches
- a different tactile sensation when an appliance is activated
- confidence
- language enrichment

Age 3 – Week 29

Tearing Strips

Assemble five meat trays, plastic lids or something similar. Use a wide felt marker and number the trays 1-2-3-4-5. Arrange them in numerical order from 1-5. Give the child several strips of paper that have been cut from a magazine. The strips should be about an inch wide. The length depends on the size of the magazine.

Show the child the plastic tray with the "1" written on it. Point to the "1" and say, "This is the picture of the number one." Tell the child to tear off one piece of paper from a strip and place it in the tray. Repeat this procedure for "2," "3," "4" and "5." For example, the child should tear off two pieces of paper to place in the "2" tray, three pieces for the "3" tray and continue in the same manner for "4" and "5."

When the child is finished, count the pieces in each tray with the child. Emphasize the recognition of "1," "2," "3," "4," and "5." Encourage the child to do the tearing, counting and placing of the counted pieces, again tearing pieces from the remaining strips that were previously cut. The child may need you to begin, but encourage her to work independently if possible. Help the child only if it is absolutely necessary. Discard the torn pieces and start with new strips to tear each time that the child does the activity.

At another time, mix the five numbered trays. Instruct the child to find tray "1," "2," "3," "4" and "5." Then tell the child to put them in order from "1" - "5" from left to right. Sweep your hand in the direction of left to right so that the child understands what you mean. Mix the trays again and observe the child. Can she put the trays in numerical order without your help? The child will not be ready for number concepts of "6" - "10" until she thoroughly understands and recognizes the numbers "1" - "5."

Continue to work with number concepts from "1" - "5" and introduce other small materials for the child to count and place in the trays. The objects that you use for a specific tray do not have to be exactly alike (same). The child should become competent with these concepts if this activity is repeated often. Remember, "practice makes perfect."

This activity develops

- eye-hand coordination
- further awareness of parts of a whole by tearing from a whole strip to make smaller pieces
- skill in counting and recognizing "1," "2," "3," "4," "5"
- matching skill (pieces with numbers)
- confidence

Age 3 – Week 30

Three Triangles

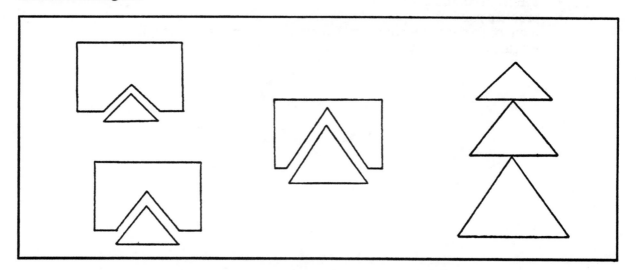

Assemble three pieces of cardboard about the size of a sheet of typing paper. Cut out one triangular piece from a long side of each piece so that there is a small, middle size and large triangle. The remaining cardboard of each piece will be used as the frame for each of the three triangles.

Show the child the three triangles. Fit the smallest triangle in the frame from which it was cut. Say, "This is a small triangle." Fit the middle size triangle in place in the frame and say, "This triangle is larger than the small triangle." Fit the largest triangle in place in the frame and say, "This is the largest triangle."

Take the three triangles out of the frames and place them on top of each other with the largest one on the bottom. Make certain that the child sees you do this.

Encourage the child to put the triangles in the correct frames. Allow her to do it independently but give help if she does not seem to understand. Take the frames out of order and allow the child to place them again in the correct frames. Help the child if necessary.

Tell the child to stack the triangles with the largest one on the bottom. Then arrange the three triangles to form an evergreen tree. Ask the child if that shape looks like anything she has seen before. If the child does not know, tell her and talk briefly about evergreen trees.

Talk about a triangle. It has three sides and three points. Draw a square on paper and ask the child if she remembers its name. Help if necessary and count the sides and corners of a square. Tell the child she should try to remember them because a triangle has three sides and corners and a square has four.

As an extension of this activity, allow the child to draw triangles and squares. It will be helpful, if you will make dots and let the child connect them to form the shapes of the triangle and the square.

Allow the child to work independently with the triangle cardboard shapes and frames at various times so that she will understand the shapes and various sizes.

This activity develops

- more of an awareness of size
- eye-hand coordination
- problem solving
- more of an awareness of the difference in a square and a triangle
- language enrichment

Age 3 – Week 31

Hoops

Assemble three different sizes of embroidery hoops. There should be a large, middle size and small one. Lay them down so that the child can see them in order from the smallest to the largest. Ask the child to identify the shape of the hoops. Make certain that she understands that they are in the shape of a circle.

Lay the hoops inside each other for the child to see. Instruct the child to pick up the smallest and the middle size hoops. Ask the child which hoop is left on the floor. Help the child if she does not understand that it was the largest one. Talk about the word "large" and tell the child it means big. Then show the child the two hoops that were removed and say, "Of these two which one is larger?" The child should begin to understand that comparisons are relative. It depends on what you are comparing.

Allow the child to roll the smallest hoop. When it stops, allow the child to roll the middle size hoop. When that one stops, allow her to roll the largest hoop. Ask the child which one went the farthest? Allow the child to play with the hoops and perhaps discover some things on her own about hoops.

If you have a hoola hoop, show it to the child and ask her which hoop (circle) is the largest now. Allow the child to roll the hoola hoop. She may prefer to lay it down and compare it with the three embroidery hoops. In either case, allow her to explore and manipulate the hoops as she wishes.

As an extension of this activity, the child may enjoy collecting objects and forming sets of one, two, three, four and five. You can suggest that one of the sets be placed inside a hoop. Identify which one by calling each one by name such as the smallest, next to the smallest, next to the largest and the largest (if you are using the hoola hoop too). The child may also enjoy using the hoops to play toss rings. A wooden chair can be turned upside down for the child to toss a hoop and try to ring one of the chair legs. With practice, the child can develop skill with this activity. She can also identify which hoop (small, middle size or large) was rung. The hoola hoop should not be used for this tossing activity.

This activity develops

- further awareness of comparative sizes
- more awareness of the shape of a circle
- eye-hand coordination
- further awareness of different objects moving through space
- free exploration
- confidence

Age 3 – Week 32

Foot Shapes

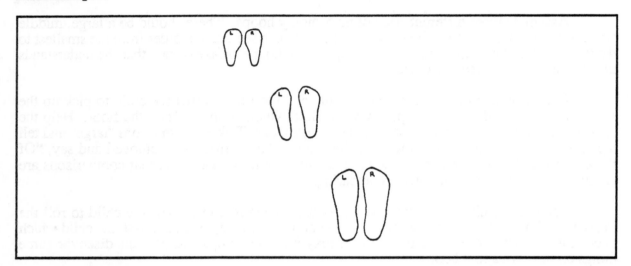

Assemble a pair of shoes that belong to Daddy, Mother and the child. Use a piece of heavy paper or cardboard and a felt marker or crayon to trace an outline of each pair of shoes on the paper. Cut the shoe shapes out. Mark all the left shoe shapes with a green felt marker by writing the letter (L) at the toe of each one. Similarly, mark all of the right shoe shapes with a red felt marker by writing an (R) on the toe of each.

Allow the child to examine all of the shoes. Count the shoes. Tell the child that there are six shoes, but two shoes belong to each person. The two shoes belonging to each person are called a pair. Instruct the child to match the pairs of shoes. Then tell the child to place the sorted pairs in order from the largest to the smallest. Point out to the child that other things come in pairs too. For example; hands, ears, eyes, cheeks, arms, legs, etc., come in sets of two or pairs. The child should also realize that gloves, mittens and socks come in pairs.

Show the child the shoe shapes with the correct sides up so that the child can see the green (L's) and the red (R's). If the child asks what the (L) and (R) mean, tell her the (L) is a letter at the beginning of the word "left"; (R) is a letter at the beginning of the word "right." Tell the child that people have a left and right foot.

Encourage the child to match the shoe shapes. Then mix up the shoe shapes with the correct sides facing up. Ask the child to find the largest shoe shapes, the middle size shoe shapes and the smallest shoe shapes and place them in a row from the largest to the smallest. Help the child if necessary. The child may enjoy doing this several times. If not, try this activity again at another time.

This activity may be further extended by turning the marked sides of the shoe shapes down at random. The child should then be instructed to turn them over and match each pair, or some shoe shapes can be facing down and some up. Challenge the child to turn them all face up. The child may enjoy putting all of the left shapes together and all of the right shapes together. The words "left" and "right" may be mentioned, but it takes time for the child to completely master the skill of distinguishing left and right without becoming confused.

At another time, the child may enjoy arranging the shoe shapes in left and right positions so that she can walk on them and pretend that they are stepping stones.

For safety reasons use masking tape to secure the shapes.

This activity develops

- eye-hand coordination when matching
- more awareness of left, right and six
- more awareness of shoes, shoe shapes, sizes and pairs

Age 3 – Week 33

How Does It Taste?

Assemble some sugar, salt, cocoa and vinegar. Identify each of these items for the child. Place a little sugar on a paper towel and allow the child to taste it. Tell the child that sugar tastes "sweet." Allow the child to smell it.

Place a little salt on a different paper towel and allow the child to taste it. Tell the child that the salt tastes "salty." Allow the child to smell it.

On another paper towel place some cocoa and allow the child to taste it. Tell the child that cocoa tastes "bitter," but when sugar is mixed with it the taste will change. Allow the child to smell the cocoa.

Allow the child to smell a little vinegar that has been placed in a small glass. Then let the child taste a little bit of the vinegar. Tell the child that vinegar is "sour."

Emphasize the four words, "sweet," "salty," "bitter," and "sour." Ask the child what part of her body helped her to taste. Use a mirror and allow the child to see her own taste buds which are on the tip, sides and back of the tongue.

Ask the child what helps her to smell. This is a good time to talk to the child about the danger of smelling and tasting unknown things. Talk about poison. Emphasize that too much of anything is a poison and sometimes just a little bit can be too much.

At snack or meal times, encourage the child to tell how different foods taste. If she forgets the four kinds of tastes, repeat the sugar, salt, cocoa and vinegar test. Some foods are bland and the child may have difficulty. Explain that some foods have stronger tastes than others. Therefore, it is best to talk about foods with a distinct taste such as cake, crackers, pickles, etc. The "bitter" taste is apparent in many herbs. Children will not readily identify with the "bitter" taste since most bitter herbs are blended to alter and enhance the taste of other foods.

As an extension of this activity, pictures of foods can be identified and discussed. The child will be interested in knowing new food names and how they taste. However, if a food is familiar to the child, she may readily be able to identify its tastes by a picture without tasting it.

This activity develops

- awareness of a purpose of the tongue
- awareness of different taste groups
- language enrichment
- awareness of poison
- skill in identifying foods by taste
- more awareness of the sense of smell and taste

Age 3 – Week 34

Sort the Tableware

Collect an assortment of plastic or metal tableware such as forks, knives and spoons. Mix them up in a dishpan or similar container and tell the child to sort the tableware by putting the forks in one pile, the knives in another and the spoons in a third pile.

You may also use a tableware compartment tray for the sorting of the tableware. The child may need a little help to get started. To help the child, place one of each kind of tableware piece in place and encourage the child to begin to sort the tableware.

Once the child becomes proficient in sorting the tableware allow her to unload the dishwasher's tableware section. Be sure to remove any sharp knives or other dangerous objects from the tableware basket.

The child may also be encouraged to set the table at meal time. She should be instructed as to the correct placement of one place setting and then be allowed to place the other tableware at the correct places at the table. You may need to make a few adjustments, but be sure to praise the child for her efforts. With encouragement she may soon learn to do this independently.

Encourage the child to tell you which piece of tableware is the longest, which is the next to the longest and which is the shortest. To assist her, the tableware should be lined up side by side with the lower ends even. In this way, the sizes will be obvious to the child. The child may also enjoy counting the tableware pieces. It will be necessary for you to assist her with this.

This activity develops

- more skill in sorting
- more skill in counting
- an interest in helping
- confidence
- more of an awareness of lengths or sizes
- eye-hand coordination

Age 3 – Week 35

Sink or Float

Place five things that float and five things that sink in a bowl or pan. Some suggestions for items to use are: a cork, spool, plastic block, candle, jar lid, nail, bolt, metal nut, shell and a large button. Allow the child to work at a sink where a dishpan has been half filled with water.

Show the child that a metal spoon will sink when it is placed in water and that a wooden spoon will float. Push the wooden spoon down to try to make it remain submerged. Allow the child to observe the wooden spoon rise and float again.

Place the metal spoon on the left side of the sink and tell the child to test the items in the bowl to see whether they sink or float. If they sink they should be placed with the metal spoon. If they float they should be placed on the other side. Point to the right side as you lay the wooden spoon there.

Observe the child as she works independently. Help her only if necessary. When the child is finished, test the objects again in the water to determine if they sink or float just as you did for the metal and wooden spoons.

This is a good time to talk to the child about swimming. Tell the child that she can float if she balances her weight correctly on the surface of the water. If she does not do this, then she will sink. Discuss water safety and the uses of water such as drinking, cooking, washing clothes, cleaning, watering plants, swimming, boating, solvent (dissolving sugar, salt, etc).

At another time, different items may be selected to test for floating and sinking. The child may be interested in selecting these items independently and may want to count how many objects sink and how many float. Allow the child to explore the uses of water with moderate supervision.

This activity develops

- more of an awareness of the uses of water
- problem solving (sinking and floating)
- confidence and independence
- more awareness of the properties of water
- language enrichment

The Alphabet Song

Sing or chant "The Alphabet Song" with the child even if she already has heard it. The following words will help you if you do not recall the song.

"ABCDEFG, HIJKLMNOP, QRS, TUV, W, X, Y, and Z.
Now I know my ABC's, tell me what you think of me?"

Print the upper and lower case letters on a piece of paper for the child to see and sing the song again.

Repeat the song several more times and tell the child the ABC's are pictures or symbols. When they are put together in a special order they form a word. Make the child aware that the names of people are words too. Write the child's name and say, "See, your name is a word."

Obtain an alphabet book from the library or buy one. The book should have colorful pages with large letters and a picture of something that begins with each letter. This type of book will be especially appropriate at this time. It can be looked at, read and the pictures and letters discussed. The child should also be encouraged to look at the book many times independently.

Repeating "The Alphabet Song" with the child will help her to memorize the alphabet. Singing or chanting the letters very slowly will help to ensure that the child hears the letter names clearly. Rapid repetition tends to slur or blend the letters and the child confuses the letter names.

When reading stories to the child, point out a certain letter. Looking for just one letter throughout the book can be fun for the child. If the child is still interested, name another letter and look through the book for that particular letter. If the child does not appear to be interested in learning the alphabet, continue to sing or chant "The Alphabet Song." The child will eventually learn the alphabet without realizing it.

It is necessary for a child to know the alphabet for many reasons such as reading, writing, alphabetizing, using the dictionary, a typewriter, a computer, etc. It will also be helpful for you to play games with the child concerning the order in which a letter comes before or after another. For example, what letter comes before "k," what letter comes after "d" or what letter is between "d" and "f"? A homemade alphabet chart can be used for this game. Use one concept at a time when playing the game. Avoid interchanging "before," "after" and "between" during one game activity. This type of game can be played up to kindergarten and first grade or longer if the child still needs reinforcement. Use the upper case letters first, then progress to the lower case letters when playing this game.

If the child questions you about the lower case letters, explain that you can pretend that each letter has a "mother" and "child" letter. The big (upper case) letter is the "mother," the little (lower case) letter is the "child." Avoid introducing formal writing of the letters to this age child. However, the child may enjoy forming the letters with clay, cooked spaghetti, paper strips or yarn pieces.

This activity develops

- awareness of the alphabet
- awareness of the upper and lower case letters
- awareness of the letter sequence
- awareness of the concepts, "before," "after" and "between"
- listening for a specific letter
- confidence

Age 3 – Week 37

Fabric Match

Assemble some fabric scraps and cut out two 3 x 3 inch squares of eight different kinds of colored material. The squares will be similar to those used in the age 0, week 37 activity. Some suggested fabrics are plaids, polka dots, tweeds, stripes, flowers, abstract designs, etc. These fabric squares should be glued to cardboard squares that have been cut to the same size. This will make the squares more durable and easier to manipulate.

Mix the fabric squares and ask the child to match the like squares. The game can be extended by placing the squares with the fabric side down. Two cards may then be turned up (over) to determine if they match. If they match, the squares should be removed from the pile. If they do not match, turn them face down again and tell the child to try to remember what they are. Continue turning two fabric squares over until all of the fabric squares have been matched.

Encourage the child to find a certain color in the fabric squares. Change the color when the child is confident with the previously specified color. Identify as many colors as possible in the fabric squares.

As an extension of this activity, encourage the child to make a square shape with the fabric squares. It can be an outline of a square or a square made with all of the squares with four squares in each row.

Count all of the fabric squares. Then match all of the eight sets again and count the sets of two. If the child seems to enjoy this type of counting, suggest that the child select a given number of squares. Help the child count these. At another time, you can instruct the child to find a certain number of the squares that have red or some other color in them. Be certain to check the squares for colors before telling the child to count out a specific number of squares with a particular color. Allow the child to suggest other ways to count the squares.

This activity develops

- a further awareness of a square
- a further awareness of colors
- matching skills
- skill in looking for a specific color
- counting skills
- memory recall
- confidence

Age 3 – Week 38

Shadow Fun

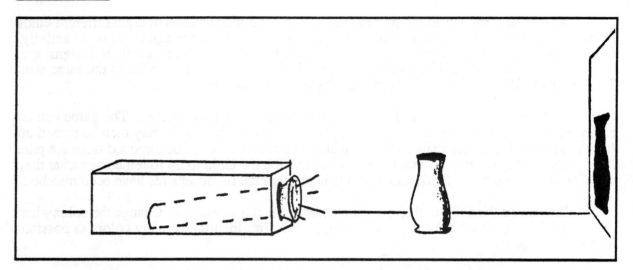

Use a spotlight type flashlight or some other kind of bright flashlight. Collect various items throughout the house that can be used to project an interesting shadow on the wall. Some suggestions are a candlestick holder, a figurine, a stuffed animal, a book end, a bowl, a vase, a box, a basket, etc.

Punch a hole in a shoe box to hold the barrel of the flashlight if you are using a cylindrical shaped flashlight. This will serve to stabilize the light. Place one of the objects on the floor near a light colored plain wall in a darkened or semi-darkened room. Move the light back until a shadow of the object is projected clearly on the wall. Repeat this activity until all of the objects' shadows have been projected on the wall. Discuss each one as you project its image on the wall. The child will enjoy seeing the shapes of the various objects and will probably comment on how different they look.

Name the objects for the child. Then place the objects out of the child's view and project an image of the object on the screen. Ask the child to identify the object. If the child cannot remember the name of the object, allow her to select it from the group of objects that you are using. Continue to do this until all of the objects have been used or the child loses interest. At another time, the child may enjoy challenging you to name the object as she selects an image to project for you.

Discuss with the child what causes a shadow. Since light cannot go through these objects, it goes straight past them, thus forming an image or shadow on the wall. Explain to the child, that light will go through a clear window pane and this is why we can see through it.

Use a piece of paper approximately 5 x 5 inches and cut a shape from the center of the paper smaller than the face of the flashlight. Secure the cut paper to the face of the flashlight with a rubber band. Shine the flashlight on the screen. The child will delight in observing the image of the shape that was cut. Repeat this activity with other shapes.

At another time when it is sunny, take the child outside in the early morning. Stand at a given point and note where the child's shadow falls. At noon, repeat the activity with the child standing in the same place. Observe the child's shadow. In the late afternoon, go outside again and note where the child's shadow is this time.

Tell the child the sun is like a big flashlight, but in the morning it is on one side (east), at noon it is directly overhead and in the afternoon the sun is on the other side (west) of us. That is why shadows are formed on the west in the morning, under us at noon and on the east in the afternoon.

As the child plays with outside shadows, she will notice that they are the longest in the early morning and late afternoon. This will make the child aware of the change in time.

As a further extension of this activity, hang a black piece of construction paper on the wall with tape (the kind that will not mar the wall). Seat the child on a stool with her body sideways to the wall so that when a light shines on the child, a silhouette is formed of her on the black paper that is taped on the wall. The light should be placed on a low table. A slide projector light works better, but a stable flashlight will do. Some adjustment may be necessary for you to obtain a sharp image of the child's head on the wall. Once the child's head silhouette is clear, stand to the side of the projected silhouette and carefully and quickly trace the child's head silhouette with white chalk. Turn the light off, remove the paper and cut out the silhouette with scissors. Turn the silhouette over and mount it with rubber cement on white construction paper. This silhouette can be framed or filed for a keepsake.

This activity develops

- an interest in shadows
- more awareness of light and shadows
- awareness that outside shadows vary in size during the day
- awareness that light will not go through some objects
- more awareness of different shapes
- memory recall of the different shadows of the objects
- language enrichment
- confidence

224

Gallop Fun

Obtain an old large colored plain sock. Allow the child to help you stuff the old sock with crushed newspaper, old stockings or fiberfill. Use selected felt pieces and cut two large green oval eyes, a red triangular nose, two brown triangular ears and a red smiling U shaped mouth. Arrange the pieces on the stuffed sock to resemble a horse's head. Assist the child in using fabric glue to attach the pieces. Place a line of glue behind the ears to the neck (cuff of the sock) and attach pieces of yarn for the mane. Insert a yardstick or old broom handle in the cuff of the sock. Push the stick or handle as far up in the stuffed sock (horse's head) as possible. Secure the cuff to the yardstick or old broom handle with a strong rubber band or tie it together tightly with yarn or string. You now have made a hobby horse with the child.

Show the child how to gallop. A gallop is accomplished by stepping forward with one foot and hopping as the back foot is brought forward. Step forward with the same front foot and repeat. Practice these steps with the child and then allow the child to straddle the stick hobby horse and gallop like a cowgirl or cowboy.

Galloping and skipping differ. When galloping, do not alternate feet forward as you do in skipping. Chanting "gall-op" or clapping the galloping rhythm will assist the child as she gallops in an open, safe designated area.

Once the child is coordinated with galloping, encourage the child to dismount the horse and practice skipping which was first introduced in the age 3, week 2 activity.

This activity develops

- leg-foot coordination
- awareness of the parts of a horse's head
- role playing
- confidence
- independence

Age 3 – Week 40

Trace the Shapes

Assemble a plastic or non-breakable mixing bowl, a book, a coaster, a teddy bear, a magazine, a jar lid, a shoe box or similar items.

Show the child how to hold a pencil. The thumb and forefinger should be used to grasp the pencil while the middle finger supports the pencil behind. The ring and little fingers serve no purpose in holding a pencil.

Allow the child to place the mixing bowl face down on a sheet of plain paper. Hold the bowl steady while the child traces around the outside edge of the bowl. Remove the bowl and ask the child to identify the shape. If she cannot recall the name of the shape, identify it for her.

Give the child a wide felt marker and instruct her to trace over the pencil line very carefully. Emphasize that speed is not important, but doing her best is important.

Once the felt marker tracing is completed, instruct the child to choose a green crayon and color the circle. Scribbling up and down, back and forth and round and round is to be expected. Tell the child again, that speed is not important, however, coloring neatly and carefully is important. Allow the child to cut out the circle with a pair of scissors. Tactfully, instruct the child in handling the scissors correctly with regard to the placement of the fingers in the holes, as well as the position of the scissor blades to the paper. Remind the child to cut closely beside the line, not on it.

At another time, follow the same procedure with the book. Trace around the shape first with a pencil, then use a felt marker to trace over the pencil line. Color the book yellow and cut it out. Continue with the other objects that you have selected at various times. Allow the child to choose a different color each time she makes a new shape. A brief activity at one time is more meaningful than a long tiring activity, just to get the job done.

This activity develops

- more awareness of different shapes
- skill in selecting a specified color
- eye-hand coordination
- more skill in cutting
- confidence

Age 3 – Week 41

I Can Do It

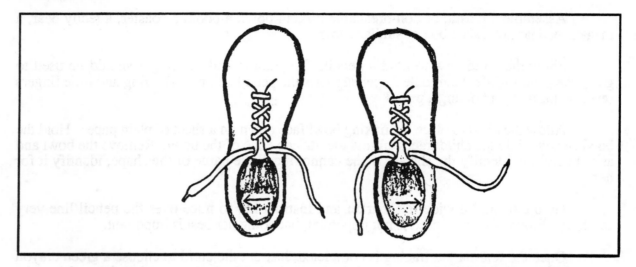

This activity was introduced at age 1, week 49. It is important that a child of this age learn to dress and undress herself. However, many children have difficulty connecting the two sides of a jacket in order to zip it and often rely on adults to do this for them.

If your child has difficulty with this skill, now is a good time to practice with her. Use a large zipper that functions well. Use an old candle or a bar of soap to lubricate the teeth of the zipper. Go through each step carefully with the child and allow her to do as much as possible on her own. Assist her only when necessary. Encourage her to practice this over and over until she is skillful in joining the two sides of the jacket and then zipping it. It is easier for the child to do this when the jacket is not being worn. However, once she has mastered the zipping skill with a jacket "off," encourage her to put the jacket "on" and practice. The skill should be practiced at various times until the child is confident and can accomplish this skill independently.

Many children have difficulty manipulating buttons and buttonholes. This skill can also be mastered in a leisurely manner if the child is encouraged to do a little buttoning at a time and using a garment that is not being worn. Select a blouse or a shirt for the child on which to practice. The smaller the button, the more difficult it seems to be for the child. If your child experiences difficulty with these, select a garment with large buttons and buttonholes. Be available to help the child when necessary, but try to allow her to do this activity as independently as possible. Once the large button skill is mastered, reintroduce the blouse or the shirt. With practice, the child will soon learn to button and unbutton her own clothes.

Many children have difficulty with slipping on boots. To make the task easier, slip a plastic bag over the child's shoes and encourage her to put on the boots. Allow her to take them off and put them back on. Try to buy boots that are a little larger than the child's shoes. If boots fit too tightly, they are almost impossible to put on and take off.

Left and right shoes often confuse children. If you will draw an arrow with a felt marker inside the heel of each shoe, the child can look at the arrow and determine on which foot to put the shoe. For example, the left heel should have the arrow pointing to the outside of the shoe. Similarly, the right heel should have the arrow pointing to the outside of that shoe.

The child will learn another beneficial manipulative skill if she is allowed to lace her shoes. Start with a shoe that is easy to lace and is not on her foot. Instruct the child how to lace and then allow the child to do as much independently as possible. If the child shows signs of frustration, stop and try again later. Once the skill of lacing is mastered, the child can be taught to tie her own shoes. This takes much practice. If your child seems to be disinterested, try to introduce this skill later.

Continue to practice zipping, buttoning, slipping on boots and shoes and lacing. These skills are necessary for a child to learn to become independent and should be mastered by the time the child goes to kindergarten. Much practice is recommended.

This activity develops

- eye-hand coordination
- small muscle refinement
- skill in fastening clothes
- confidence
- persistence in staying on a task and completing it
- independence

Age 3 – Week 42

Fold It and Discover

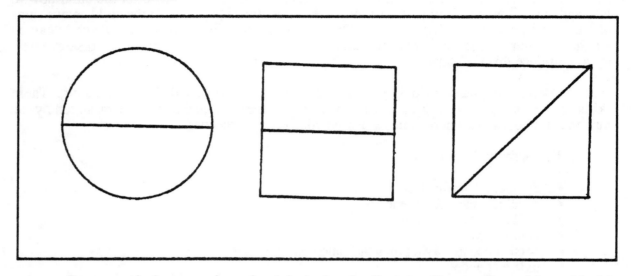

Cut out a circle approximately eight inches in diameter. Draw a line with a wide felt marker across the middle. Cut out two squares approximately eight inches wide. Draw a line with a wide felt marker parallel across the middle of one square and diagonally across the middle of the other square.

Show the three shapes to the child. Make certain that the child can identify the circle and the two squares with confidence before proceeding.

Point to the line across the middle of the circle. Tell the child to fold the circle in half on that line. Make certain that the child understands that the fold will produce a crease on the line. Assist the child if necessary. Tell the child the circle is now folded in half. Open the folded area to show the child the whole circle, then refold it to emphasize the half circle.

Point to the parallel line in the middle of the square. Instruct the child to fold the square on the marked line. Tell the child that the new shape that is formed is no longer a square. This new shape from the folded square is called a rectangle. Open the paper to reveal the square, then fold it again to show the child the rectangle. Point out the two long sides and the two short sides of the rectangle. Count the corners. Tell the child that both the square and the rectangle have four corners, but they are different shapes. Open the square and show the child that the square's sides are the same size. Fold it again and emphasize the rectangular shape that was formed when the square was folded in half.

Take the square with the diagonal line and tell the child to fold the square on that line. Ask the child if she remembers the name of that shape. If not, refer to the activity in age 3, week 30 and identify the triangle, the shape with the three sides and three corners.

Draw a circle and ask the child to name it. Draw a square and ask the child to name it. Draw a rectangle and ask the child to name it. Then draw a triangle and ask the child to name it. Review the names of the shapes with the child and note the names of any shapes that seem to confuse the child. Isolate these shapes and reinforce the names of those shapes that the child has difficulty recalling. You can play the game of "Pick Up" with the child. Draw and cut the shapes out, and then instruct the child to pick up the one that you name. At another time, select a shape and ask the child to identify that shape. In this way you will know which shapes to continue to emphasize.

Allow the child to fold the shapes again, one at a time, and emphasize how a fold makes a difference in a shape. On a separate sheet of paper make some dots in the shape of a circle, a square, a rectangle and a triangle and allow the child to connect the dots with a pencil or felt marker.

As an extension of this activity, identify the shapes again and tell the child to look for something in the house that may have one of these shapes. Some expected answers may be: a cake is in the shape of a circle, a box is the shape of a square or a rectangle, a book is in the shape of a square or a rectangle, a slice of pie is in the shape of a triangle. You may also include the oval shape which was mentioned in the age 3, week 25 activity.

This activity develops

- more awareness of the basic shapes
- skill in identifying the shapes (circle, square, rectangle and triangle) by observing the number of corners and sides
- eye-hand coordination in folding and connecting dots
- confidence
- language enrichment

Age 3 – Week 43

Magnet Fun

Obtain two small strong refrigerator magnets for holding notes on the doors or buy two U-shaped magnets for this activity. Assemble a collection of objects such as a button, a paper clip, a pencil with a metal end, a hole puncher, a nail clipper, a rubber eraser, a piece of chalk, a clothespin, a spool or any other safe object that you may choose to use. Place the objects in a box so that they can be removed one at a time.

Hold a magnet close to a steel nail and allow the child to observe that the nail is attracted to the magnet. Remove the nail and hand the child the magnet. Instruct her to remove an object from the box and hold it close to the magnet. If the object is attracted to the magnet, instruct the child to put it on the left side of the box. If the object is not attracted by the magnet, tell the child to place it on the right side of the box. Allow the child to continue with this activity until all of the objects have been sorted.

Count how many objects were attracted by the magnet. Count how many objects were not attracted by the magnet. Ask the child which side has more objects. Match the objects one to one to prove which side has more. The child will discover from this experience which number is greater.

Use a paper, Styrofoam or plastic plate and place one magnet on the top and one on the bottom of the plate in line with the one on the top. Move the bottom magnet slowly across the bottom of the plate. Tell the child to watch the movement of the magnet on top. Allow the child to explore with this until her interest wanes.

At another time, allow the child to use a magnet and discover other things in the home that are attracted by a magnet by walking around and testing the furniture, lamps, hinges, doorknobs, toilet handle, refrigerator door, etc.

This activity develops

- awareness of magnetism
- awareness that only some objects are affected by magnetism
- skill in sorting
- enhancement of the sense of touch in feeling the pull of magnetism
- problem solving
- free exploration
- confidence and independence

Age 3 — Week 44

Yes or No

This activity can be played at anytime and is also a good traveling activity. Below are some suggestions. Other statements can be added as the child becomes more confident. These statements should serve to stimulate the child's thinking and encourage her to reason and ask more questions. Tell the child to answer the following statements by saying either "yes" or "no."

The grass is red.
Stars appear to twinkle at night.
Birds fly in the water.
Rocks are good to eat.
Pages are in a book.
Plants grow in washing machines.
Clouds are white.
Easter comes at Christmas time.
A camera takes medicine.
A chair is for sitting.
Mother cooks in the bathroom.
Fire can be dangerous.
I can swim in the bathtub.
I can pour juice in a fork.
I can wear mittens on my hands.
Snow is hot.
Sugar is sour.
Daddy can buy bananas at the grocery store.
Elephants are little animals.
Fish live in the water.
I wear shoes on my ears.
Cars have doors.
Lamps give us light.
Mother washes clothes in the dishwasher.

This activity develops

* listening skills
* thinking skills
* skill in making a decision
* language enrichment
* association skills
* confidence

Age 3 – Week 45

Clothespin Toss

Assemble ten clothespins (colored ones will add more interest). Count the clothespins with the child. Place the clothespins in a paper bag. Make a line with yarn or place a marker to use as a boundary. Place an empty dishpan or trash can a short distance from the boundary line.

Choose one clothespin from the bag. Stand behind the boundary line and show the child how to aim and toss the clothespin so that it will land in the empty container. If you miss the container when tossing the clothespin, try again. Tell the child that with practice anyone can improve.

Allow the child to aim and toss a clothespin towards the container. Praise the child to motivate her to try to do her best. If the child misses the container say, "One out, try to get one in." Continue until all of the clothespins have been tossed. Count the clothespins that went into the container first. Invite the child to help you count. Praise the child even if there are none in the container. Invite the child to help you count the ones that landed outside the container. Ask the child which number is more: the number of clothespins that went into the container or those that landed outside. Emphasize the concepts "in" and "out."

Repeat the game often and emphasize the word "more." When you feel that the child understands the concept of "more," talk about the word "less." Avoid using these words interchangeably with the child until you are certain that the child understands the difference. It would be easier to play the game by asking the child to note whether there are "more" clothespins in the container than outside. Then at another time, play the game and ask the child to tell you which is "less," the number (set) of clothespins in the container or the number (set) of clothespins that is out of the container. When the child develops more skill, the container should be moved farther away to challenge the child more.

This activity develops

- eye-hand coordination
- skill in aiming at a target
- awareness of a set of ten objects
- more awareness of the concepts "more" and "less"
- an understanding of "in" and "out" of a container
- skill in making a decision
- confidence

Age 3 – Week 46

Listen and Move

Choose a low table that is suitable for a child to sit on and go under momentarily. Obtain a strong box that is large enough for the child to crawl inside. Place the table and the box close to a window and a door that can be opened and closed with ease. Allow the child to choose a small toy or stuffed animal to use with this activity.

Tell the child to listen and follow your directions. Address the child by name and tell her to lay the toy or stuffed animal down. Then begin by giving the commands listed below to the child. If the child does not seem to understand, calmly repeat the command again and show the child what the command means.

> Step over the toy or stuffed animal.
> Crawl under the table.
> Get in the box.
> Get out of the box.
> Open the door.
> Walk around the toy or stuffed animal.
> Stand between the box and the table.
> Stand behind the table.
> Look outside the window.
> Look inside the box.
> Close the door.
> Walk toward the window.
> Walk backwards five steps.
> Stand beside the table.
> Stand beneath (whatever is convenient for the child).

These activities should be repeated often. Variations of these commands will stimulate more interest for the child and she will be further motivated to follow different commands. The materials (props) should also be changed. For example, you can use the bed, dresser and toy chest in the child's room and give her commands using different selected toys for placement during the activity.

This activity develops

- listening skills
- following directions
- more awareness of spatial concepts
- gross motor coordination
- tactile enhancement of the various materials used
- confidence

Age 3 – Week 47

What is Missing?

Assemble any four small objects and place them in a row. Some suggested objects are: a spool, a key, a cup and a toy. Name the objects from left to right and encourage the child to name them independently for you. Tell the child to turn around with her back to you. Remove one of the objects and place it behind you or somewhere else where the child cannot see it. Ask the child to turn toward you and tell you what object is missing. Praise the child if she is correct. If she is not correct, show her the missing object and repeat the process.

As the child becomes more adept in identifying the missing object, change the positions of the objects for more interest and challenge.

This activity may be varied to use four shapes, four colors, four numbers or four letters, etc. However, I recommend using the shapes and colors first and then introducing the numbers and letters when the child readily recognizes them.

This activity develops

- memory recall
- skill in identifying an unseen object
- skill in using visual clues for association and identification
- confidence

Age 3 – Week 48

Tell Me How

Discuss with the child something simple that can be made in the kitchen. It will be more interesting if it is something the child likes to eat. Some suggestions are;

> Make a peanut butter and jelly sandwich.
> Fix a bowl of cereal with fruit.
> Prepare an orange for eating.
> Make chocolate pudding from a prepared mix.
> Prepare some jello.
> Make a grilled cheese sandwich.

Allow the child to decide what she would like to help you make. Ask the child how to make it. Tell the child to instruct you what should come first, second, third, etc. Listen to the child and attempt to prepare it just as the child tells you to do it. The sequence may not be in order or a step may be left out, but listen. The child will be watching and helping and may realize her mistake(s). However, once the task is completed, review with the child the logical sequence of events and why one step should precede another.

Children enjoy helping in the kitchen. Repeat this activity at other times and you will be amazed at the logical sequence that will develop as you prepare different things with the child.

As an extension of this activity, ask the child to tell you how to do things in the proper sequence. Some suggestions are:

> Get ready for breakfast.
> Plant a seed.
> Put on a jacket.
> Wash clothes.
> Put on play clothes.
> Get ready to go on a picnic.
> Set the table for a meal.

This activity develops

- skill in recalling things done in sequence
- problem solving
- language enrichment
- a sense of helping
- confidence

Age 3 – Week 49

<u>Families</u>

Tell the child that all members of the family belong together because they are related to each other. They are different in many ways but all families have one thing in common. It is the family's last name. Say the child's last name and recall the names of all of the family members. Tell the child her full name. Ask the child to repeat it. If the child does not know it, practice it before continuing with this activity. At this age, a child should know her full name, sex and age. Birthdate, telephone number and address can gradually be taught later, but the child should know these before entering kindergarten.

Once the child understands the family name concept, tell her to listen for the words that you say. Tell the child that the things that you name will be different; nevertheless, these names should remind her of a special group to which they belong. Because they are grouped together for a special reason, we say that they belong to the same "family." Say the words, "dog," "cat" and "house." Ask the child which two things belong in the same family. The child should say, "dog and cat" because they are animals and belong to the animal family. A house is not an animal and does not belong to this group.

Review the following words with the child and add others as you think of them. Allow the child to reason as to which two things belong in the special family. You may enrich the activity by discussing each special family group with the child after the child has had a chance to identify which two things belong to the special family.

coat - jacket - rug	(clothing family)
book - table - chair	(furniture family)
book - mitten - glove	(clothing family)
orange - apple - turkey	(fruit family)
lamp - one - two	(number family)
bus - car - house	(transportation or things that go family)
TV - hamburger - fries	(food family)
bed - dresser - towel	(furniture family)
bug - flower - tree	(plant family)
bib - crib - daddy	(baby family)
stool - socks - shoes	(clothing family)
paper - mixer - toaster	(appliances or kitchen family)
washer - dryer - porch	(appliances or laundry room family)
green - red - paint	(colors family)
pillow - bear - bunny	(animal family)
biscuit - rolls - knife	(bread or food family)
juice - milk - box	(liquid or drink family)
suitcase - trunk - grass	(travel or stores clothes family)
spoon - helicopter - airplane	(flying family)
breakfast - lunch - eraser	(meal time family)

These suggestions offer opportunities for you to talk with the child about many different things. Through this experience, you will enrich the child's knowledge and vocabulary, as well as provide her with more skill in thinking and reasoning. Repeat this activity at various times. Use it as a quiet game and also as a traveling game. It will serve to keep the child occupied and challenged.

This activity develops

- more of an awareness of a family and the family name
- memory recall of her full name, age and sex
- skill in associating and reasoning
- language enrichment
- confidence

Age 3 – Week 50

Hopscotch Fun

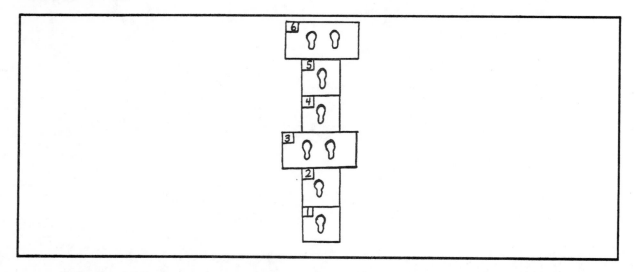

Place a piece of yarn on a carpet to make an outline of a hopscotch area. Chalk can be used outside on the sidewalk or a stick can be used to draw the hopscotch lines in sand or dirt. If you use the yarn indoors, write a separate number "1, 2, 3, 4, 5 and 6" on index cards and place them consecutively in the top left corner of each box of the hopscotch boundary lines. If this activity is done outside, the numbers can be drawn consecutively in each box of the boundary lines. Identify each number with the child.

Instruct the child to hop on one foot into the first box. Then she should hop to the second box and proceed to the third box and land on both feet in that box. Then she should hop into box four on one foot, then to five on one foot and land with both feet in box six. Instruct the child to come back and start again at the number 1 box. Allow the child to do this several times or until her interest wanes.

At another time, use a bean bag or any safe object that will not roll. Tell the child to gently throw the object into the first box. If the object lands in that box, she should then hop into the second box, the third and land on both feet, then proceed to the fourth, the fifth and land on both feet in the sixth box. At that point, she should hop back in the same manner and pick up the object that was tossed into the first box before hopping out of the hopscotch boundary. The child should then be instructed to toss the object into the second box, continue forward and turn around at box six and return to pick up the object in the second box. The child should continue with this activity until the object has been tossed to each box.

If the child seems to have any difficulty, practice tossing the object into each box and then proceed with the hopping and retrieving of the object from each box. With practice, the child will enjoy this activity and at the same time learn to readily recognize the numbers 1 - 6. She should also become aware of what number precedes or follows the other.

This activity develops

- gross motor coordination
- skill in aiming
- more awareness of number sequence
- skill in balancing
- skill in identifying the numbers 1 - 6
- confidence and independence

Age 3 – Week 51

Finish It

This is an activity that allows the child to think and verbalize. Tell the child that you will say a part of a sentence and she should complete it. Tell the child that a sentence is a group of words that makes sense. This is an activity that should be repeated many times. It is also a good traveling game. Many different suggestions can be added to the list below.

Some suggestions are:

I went to the _____.

I am going on a vacation to see _____.

Yesterday I _____.

Mother and I took a walk and _____.

Daddy gave me _____.

A tree is _____.

My car will _____.

My name is _____.

I am _____.

I like to _____.

This activity develops

- listening skills
- skill in thinking and associating ideas
- memory recall
- freedom of expression and language development

Age 3 – Week 52

Actions

Invite the child to listen and do the correct action. If the child has difficulty with any one of these suggestions, take time to practice that action before proceeding with this activity.

Some suggestions are:

> Jump on two feet five times.
>
> Hop on one foot three times.
>
> Tiptoe until I tell you to stop.
>
> Stamp your feet gently six times.
>
> Clap your hands four times.
>
> Walk in place alternating (changing) feet.
>
> Count 1, 2, and tell the child to walk until you say, "Stop."
>
> Tap your foot gently ten times.
>
> Hop on three feet (two feet and one hand) three times.
>
> Hop on four feet (two feet and two hands) five times.
>
> Crawl like a snake until I tell you to stop.

As an extension of this activity, sing the following chant as the child pretends to be a teddy bear.

> "Teddy Bear, Teddy Bear hops on one foot, one foot, one foot.
> Teddy Bear, Teddy Bear hops on two feet, two feet, two feet.
> Teddy Bear, Teddy Bear hops on three feet, three feet, three feet.
> Teddy Bear, Teddy Bear hops on four feet, four feet, four feet.
> Teddy Bear, Teddy Bear, that will do."

The child should then stop and rest. This activity can be repeated not only for fun, but it is a good motor skill activity and teaches the child the number sequence of one through four.

This activity develops

- listening skills
- following directions
- gross motor coordination
- skill in performing a task a certain number of times
- confidence

Part V

(Four - Five Years)

Introduction

A child of four can do more. He is more developed socially, mentally and physically. Interaction with other children of the same age is conducive to proper development. The child learns not only fair play, but he is exposed to others that are different from himself. This aids in broadening his outlook on life and assists him in adjusting outside his home environment. Play is a child's way of learning. Children learn from each other. Therefore, play should be guided and nurtured to ensure that the child develops good play habits.

Children of this age are very curious. They have more confidence and begin to show more of an interest in numbers and letters. Most four year-olds enjoy being read to and looking at pictures. Some children can recognize letters in words or may even be able to read some words as they look for more detail.

A four year old may delight in distinguishing similarities and differences in pictures, shapes, colors, sizes, letters and numbers.

Coordination of hand skills is much improved by this age and the child is more interested in various activities of this nature which promote further refinement of the small muscle control and coordination. This is necessary for writing and other fine motor skills that the child will encounter upon entering school.

Large muscle coordination vastly improves at this age, although some children have difficulty in catching and throwing a ball, jumping rope, balancing and skipping. Practice will serve to refine the necessary coordination that a child needs in order to master any deficit that he may have with any of these skills.

Note: The author and publisher are not liable for any injury or death incurred due to the misuse of the suggested materials and directions. As with all child-related activities, materials should be selected with careful attention to child safety; adult supervision is essential.

Age 4 – Week 1

Playing With Shapes

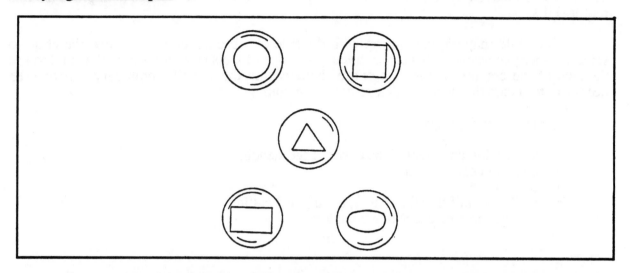

Cut out each of the following shapes from the center of a separate paper plate: a circle, a square, a triangle, a rectangle and an oval. The size should be approximately five inches at the widest point. It will be easier for the child to use if you cut the shapes so that the frame of the paper plate remains intact.

Ask the child to name each shape and assist him if necessary. Encourage the child to feel the open cut out shape (stencil) that remains in the middle of each paper plate. Guide the child's index finger around the edge of each shape so that the child can feel and be able to identify the shape by feeling.

Tell the child to close his eyes and feel the edge of the open cut shape (stencil) and try to identify the shape. Give the child clues to help him identify the shape if necessary. Continue with this feeling activity until the child can readily name each shape by feeling the edge of each open cut shape (stencil).

Give the child a crayon, a felt marker or a pencil and a sheet of plain white or colored construction paper. Instruct the child to trace carefully around the edge of the circle stencil to make a circle the same size as the hole in the stencil. Allow the child to use blunt scissors to cut out the drawn circle. Remind the child to hold the scissors properly and make sure that he cuts beside the line, not on the line. Follow the same procedure for the other four shapes and ask the child to name each shape. Help the child if necessary. If he knows all of the shapes be sure to praise him. In addition, evaluate the child's technique of cutting, and if you feel that he can do a better job of cutting, encourage him to repeat the activity and practice his cutting. Children this age usually need much practice in cutting and are often willing to continue to practice.

As an extension of this activity, encourage the child to help you place the five cut out shapes in a row from left to right. Ask the child to "read" the shapes. Make sure that he starts on the left. Tell the child to turn his back while you remove one of the shapes. The child should then be told to turn around and tell you which shape is missing. This is a game he can play independently with a friend.

If the child enjoys tracing and cutting out the shapes, allow him to use old newspapers or magazine pages to save paper. You may allow him to use scissors independently if you feel that the child is sufficiently responsible. If you are uncertain about his behavior, observe and monitor the child carefully while he uses the scissors.

Retain the paper plate shape stencils and reintroduce them at another time. This is an activity that a child enjoys repeating even though he is unaware that it helps to improve his fine motor skills.

The child may enjoy coloring with the side of a broken crayon. Allow the child to select a paper plate stencil. Instead of tracing the edge of the shape, encourage the child to use the side of the crayon to color the entire shape within the stencil's boundary. It may be necessary to secure the stencil with tape before beginning.

This activity develops

- sensitivity to the feel of the edges of the stencils
- eye-hand coordination
- confidence
- skill in identifying the shapes, tracing and cutting
- more of an awareness of a boundary

Age 4 – Week 2

Junk Box

Allow the child to help you collect many simple items in the house. The child may want to carry a plastic grocery bag with handles as the two of you search and collect discarded items (junk). Some items that may be of interest to the child are: a bolt, a pencil, a paper clip, a feather, a piece of cotton, a bottle cap, a button, a badge, a key, a spool, a little magnet, an eraser, dice, a Cracker Jack prize, a small comb, a plastic flower, a small car, etc. The items may then be placed in a special box (e.g., shoe box) and labeled "Junk Box." More items may be added as the child finds other special items.

Keep the box of junk indefinitely because children enjoy examining and experimenting with little items in many ways. He can feel them, look at them with a magnifying glass, sort them, count them, trace around the outside edges of them and discover other ways to use them such as: Selecting things with a certain color, choosing animals, identifying things that travel or discussing selected objects individually.

Make red X's at random on a large piece of newspaper. Instruct the child to choose any item from the junk box and place one of the items on each of the red X's. Ascertain if the child missed any when he says that he is finished. Show the child which X's were missed, if any.

At another time, line different color X's in rows on the newspaper. Space them close together but far enough apart to prevent overlapping. Instruct the child to begin on the left and place the objects one by one toward the right side. Show the child where to begin in the next row on the left. Tell him to pretend that each time he places an object on an X, he is "reading," because people read words from left to right in this order.

This activity can be repeated at various times and the child will enjoy using the "Junk Box" independently. Make certain that the items in the "Junk Box" are safe for the child to use independently or with another friend.

This activity develops

- freedom of choice
- more awareness of one to one matching
- enhancement of the sense of touch with the "junk."
- skill in following directions
- more awareness of left to right progression
- confidence and independence

Age 4 – Week 3

A Dozen

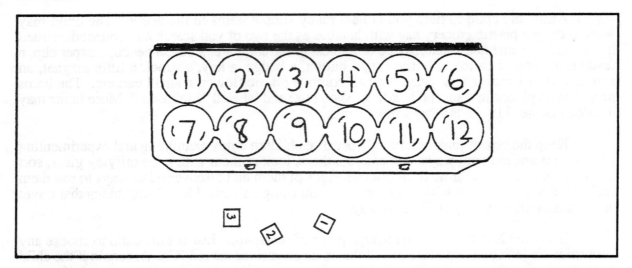

Show the child an empty egg carton. Ask him what it is. Tell him if he does not know. Move from left to right and count the spaces in the top row. Move to the left in the bottom row and continue to count to twelve. Tell the child that twelve of anything is called a dozen.

Use a fine felt tip marker and number the egg cup spaces from one to twelve beginning at the top left. Cut twelve small squares or circles from index cards or cardboard and number them one to twelve with the fine felt tip marker.

Count the spaces in the egg carton again and point to the numbers as you count. Hand the child a small circle or square with the number (1) on it. Instruct the child to put it in the number (1) compartment. Tell the child to continue to do this, as you hand each consecutive number to him, until all twelve pieces have been placed correctly. You may need to do this several times to make certain that the child knows where to look for the correct number on the egg carton.

When the child is confident with this activity, mix the numbered pieces and allow the child to hunt for the number (1) piece, then the number (2) piece and continue until the child has placed all twelve pieces in a row from left to right correctly. Then encourage him to match these numbers with the ones in the egg carton independently. This activity should be repeated many times to allow the child to develop confidence and accuracy. Retain the numbered egg carton to be used with other number activities.

This activity develops

- awareness of a dozen
- skill in matching numbers 1 - 12
- more skill in left to right progression
- sequence counting and recognizing numbers 1 - 12
- confidence and independence
- eye-hand coordination

Age 4 – Week 4

Mail

Use a large index card or a large envelope and print the child's name carefully on it. Write the child's address below the name so that it resembles a piece of mail (letter). Use upper case (capital) letters only at the beginning of each word and lower case letters for the remainder of each word. Glue a used stamp in the top right hand corner and write the return address of a special relative at the top left. Write a message on the back of the index card or use a sheet of paper for the message if you are using an envelope. The message should be brief and signed "With love."

To make this activity more realistic, a relative may have already sent a postcard or a letter, or you may suggest that a relative do this especially for the child.

Whichever method you choose, present the piece of mail to the child. Tell the child that this is a piece of mail with his very own name on it. Point to the child's name as you move your hand from left to right. Then say, "Your house number and street name are right below your name." Point to this as you move your hand again from left to right. Tell the child this is called the family's address; that is where we live. The mail person (man or woman) knows just where to bring our mail, because he or she can read our address and knows where we live. Read the message on the postcard or the letter to the child. Discuss what it says.

Read the address several times and ask the child to repeat it after you. Remember to move your hand from left to right as you read it to the child.

To further extend this activity, write the child's name and address on five envelopes or cards and five other names and addresses on five different envelopes to represent letters. Use two paper bags to represent mailboxes. Attach the big original letter to one of the bags and leave the other bag unlabeled. Mix the letters and tell the child to put all of his mail in the correct bag and the other mail in the unmarked bag. Show the child how to match the names if he does not quite understand. Then allow him to work independently.

At other times, review the child's address with him to make certain that he can recall it from memory. Encourage the child to repeat the address-matching activity. He may also suggest that he dictate a letter to a special friend or a relative. This would be an opportune time for the child to begin to express his thoughts while you write them on paper. He will delight in watching you write what he says.

This activity develops

- skill in recognizing a name in print
- an interest in learning to recall the correct address
- skill in matching the correct address
- more awareness of mail and delivery of mail
- language enrichment

Age 4 – Week 5

<u>Letters and Lines</u>

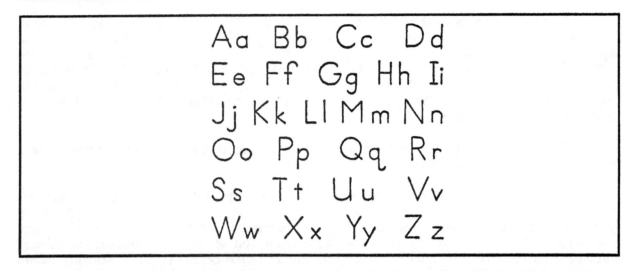

Review The Alphabet Song that was introduced in the age 3, week 36 activity. Tell the child that letters are fun and we can play many games with them. Show the child a picture of all the letters including both the big and little letters (upper and lower case).

Use the printed letters on a tablet or make your own. However, be aware that there is a special way to form each letter. Therefore, an accurate model for the child to see at this time is recommended to avoid correcting mistakes at another time.

Assuming that you are using an accurate model, point out to the child that the letters are made of straight lines, curved lines or part straight and part curved lines. Ask the child if he can find the letters in his name. Help the child to find them. To make it easier for the child, print his name for him to use to match each letter in his name. First, use all big letters (upper case), then use all little letters (lower case) to print the child's name for him to use as a guide. At this time, point out to the child that in kindergarten the teacher will write his name so that the beginning letter is capitalized (big letter) and the rest of the letters are written with little letters (lower case). This is important for you and the child to know, because the teacher very often must "unteach" the child if he learns to write his name with a mixture of upper and lower case letters. Some pre-schools teach children to write their names in all capital letters because it appears easier for the child. Most children at this age are not ready for formal writing of the letters. The child may be shown the correct way to form letters, but his hand coordination may not be refined enough to hold a pencil for making the configurations of the letters.

Cook a little spaghetti, wash, drain and blot it with a paper towel. Allow the child to cut the spaghetti with a pair of blunt scissors. Encourage the child to look at the picture of the letters and use the cut spaghetti pieces to form some of the letters. Make a few letters for the child to motivate him to copy your letters. Start at the top whenever possible and form letters. It may be easier for the child, if you write the upper case letters on individual cards for the child to use as a model for forming letters. Later, the lower case letters can be introduced if the child shows an interest in this activity. Allow the child to form only a few letters during an activity because forming too many letters at one time could be overwhelming for him. This may cause frustration and the child will not be interested in pursuing this activity.

The spaghetti pieces may be stored in the refrigerator in a plastic bag for several days. The spaghetti may also be used to form numbers. However, do not work with letters and numbers at the same time. Children have difficulty distinguishing the meaning of the words, "letter and number." Slow and steady is the way to ensure that the child will be ready (sufficiently skilled) to succeed easily in school.

This activity develops

- more awareness of the names of the letters
- skill in matching letters in a name
- more awareness of the shapes of the letters
- eye-hand coordination
- confidence and independence

Age 4 – Week 6

Sewing is Fun

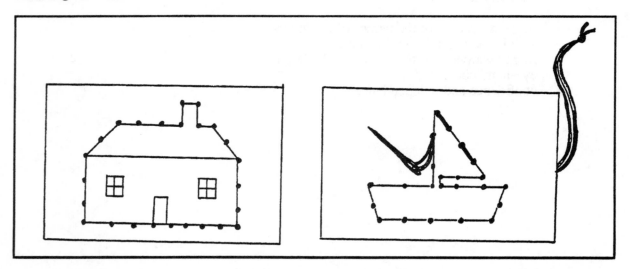

Assemble five blank pieces of corrugated cardboard or poster board about the size of typing paper. Choose five large pictures from a coloring book or magazine. Try to choose pictures with little detail. Cut the pictures out and glue them on the heavy board. Allow the glue to dry. Use an awl, ice pick, sharp pencil or large nail to punch holes about two inches apart around the shapes of the pictures.

Give the child a threaded blunt large tapestry needle. Use yarn approximately one yard long, make a double length and tie a knot to join both ends. Make certain the knot is big so that the yarn will not slip through the hole around the pictures.

Show the child how to move the needle in and out of the holes to lace around the pictures. The child will need you to help in cutting the yarn and tying the knots so that he can continue to lace around the other pictures. This activity may require a little coordination but the child can develop a skill and can become quite adept in sewing a running stitch.

Lacing pictures can also be made by tracing around a stuffed animal to produce a shape or by using carbon paper to trace around a picture to make an outline on the cardboard.

This activity develops

- eye-hand coordination
- skill in the fundamentals of sewing
- more awareness of the different shapes of objects
- confidence and independence

Age 4 – Week 7

The Telephone

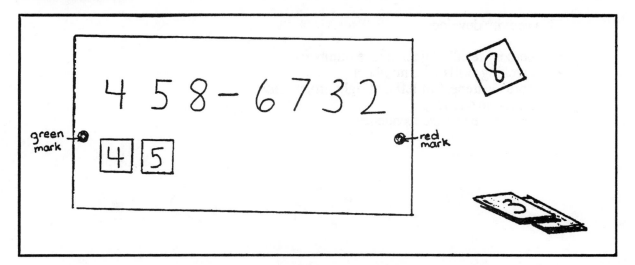

The child should be taught the proper use of a telephone. He should also know the emergency number 911 or whatever the emergency number is where you live. To do this activity, it would be ideal to use real telephones that can easily be disconnected. If this is not possible, try to obtain two toy telephones with the numbers on them. You can also make two telephones from cardboard by using your telephone as a pattern to trace and mark. They can then be cut out and yarn or string can be used to attach the receiver to the side of the telephone base.

Give one of the two telephones to the child. Name a number and tell the child to find it on his telephone. Do this with all of the numbers. The child may ask questions about other buttons or markings on the telephone. Answer the questions as briefly as possible and tell the child that you will tell him more about the buttons or markings later. The child will undoubtedly notice the letters of the alphabet on the same buttons as the numbers. Tell the child that you can also use certain letters instead of the numbers to make telephone calls, but at the present time numbers will be easier to use.

Tell the child his telephone number and encourage him to repeat it after you several times. Then tell the child to find the same numbers on one of the two telephones that you are using for this activity. Call each number one at a time so that the child will be able to listen, think and find each number. Do this several times and then ask the child to recall his telephone number from memory. Assist him if necessary. Praise him for any positive response to help him establish confidence.

If you know the telephone number of your child's friend, allow the child to press or dial the correct number on the real telephone. However, before doing this instruct the child to identify himself by name and then ask to speak to his friend by name. For example, the child could say, "This is (child's name) calling. May I speak to (friend's name)?" The child should also be aware that he must have a reason to call a person. Discuss and practice proper telephone etiquette. Perhaps you can suggest a reason for his calling the friend.

Write your telephone number on a large piece of paper. Read each number and point to it as you say the number. Tell the child that this will be his telephone chart. Then write each number separately on a small index card or something similar. Mix the number cards and tell the child to put them in the correct order by using the telephone number chart that you made. Put a green mark on the left of the number chart and a red mark on the right. Remind the child that he should start on the green side and stop on the red side. Encourage the child to repeat this often so that he will know his telephone number from memory.

This activity develops

- memory recall of a telephone number(s)
- matching skills with numbers
- more awareness of left and right progression
- telephone courtesy
- confidence and independence

Age 4 – Week 8

More About Me

Find a colorful full view picture of a boy or girl from a magazine or some other source. Cut the picture out and ask the child if the picture is of a boy or girl. The child should be able to answer this question correctly. This should serve to make the child confident before he begins the following activity.

Give a blunt pencil or retracted ball point pen to the child. Instruct him to touch the body parts on the picture as you call them by name without talking. Help the child if necessary and praise him for any positive response that he makes.

The body parts to touch are:

- head/hair
- eye
- nose
- ear
- cheek
- lips
- neck
- arm
- elbow
- wrist
- waist
- stomach (tummy)
- knee
- ankle
- heel
- foot/toes
- hips
- hand/fingers

Give the child a yarn ball, bean bag or a balled up piece of paper and instruct him to use this to touch the different parts of his body as you call the same body parts that were previously named. Remind him that he must not talk while you call the words. He should listen very closely so that he does not make any mistakes. Help him if necessary but try to allow him time to listen, think and touch each body part with the yarn ball, bean bag or paper ball.

Make a mental note of those body parts that the child missed or confused and repeat the activity with the picture and then ask the child to find them again on himself.

Give the child a blank piece of paper and a crayon or pencil. Tell the child to draw a picture of himself. Remind him to try to include all of the body parts. Accept the results and praise the child for his efforts regardless of what the picture looks like. Keep the picture in a safe place and at various times throughout the weeks and months encourage the child to draw other pictures of himself. Date each picture and compare them each time the child draws. You should see gradual progress with each picture.

This activity develops

- reinforcement of the body parts
- skill in listening and locating body parts
- skill in drawing a self "portrait"
- language enrichment
- confidence

Age 4 – Week 9

Fun With Letter Aa

The alphabet was first introduced in the age 3, week 36 activity. At that time an explanation of distinguishing the upper and lower case letters was suggested in which the upper case letter was referred to as the "mother" because it is often called the "big" letter. Consequently, the lower case letter is small and is referred to as the "child."

I have chosen to introduce a letter each week in alphabetical order. You will note that the upper and lower case letters are introduced together. The reason for this is that children are often taught to print words using all upper case letters. In school, children are taught that only proper names, important places and things should begin with an upper case letter. The additional letters of each word are written with lower case letters. All other words are written with lower case letters.

Teachers often need to "unteach" improper methods of printing. Therefore, I feel the child should be introduced to both the upper and lower case of each letter together. Simply referring to the "mother" and "child" technique should clarify any confusion.

In this activity, in which the first letter of the alphabet is introduced, print a large upper and a lower case (Aa) on the left hand side of a half sheet of typing paper. Draw a line at the middle of the paper from the top to bottom of the longer sides. Draw a large apple on the right hand side of the line that was drawn on the paper, Tell the child to color the apple red. Print the word "apple" in lower case letters below the picture of the apple.

Show the child the paper with the upper and lower case Aa and the colored apple. Fold the paper on the middle line so that the blank sides are facing inside. Apply glue to the folded blank (back) side of the paper. Cut a piece of heavy paper or cardboard half the size of the paper. Insert it in between the folded paper to give it support. Before sealing the two sides slip a cardboard strip in between. Extend the strip several inches longer than the paper so that the child can use this as a handle for a stick puppet.

Tell the child the word "apple" begins with the letter Aa as you point to the word. Also tell the child that there are many words that begin with the letter Aa. Give the child an apple to eat, if possible, for interest and better association of the relationship between the letter Aa and the word apple.

Making letter puppets may seem redundant to you, but young children are more secure with repetition and make better associations when they are secure. Varying the introduction to each letter may confuse the child. Therefore, I have chosen to be consistent with the puppets and to vary the activities related to the letters. Your consistency and enthusiasm in stimulating the child is the key to success.

At another time, give the child a red fine tip felt marker and an old magazine. Tell the child to put a red circle around every word that begins with the letter Aa in the magazine. If the child marks the Aa's in the middle of the word accept it. However, try to emphasize the words, "beginning" and "starts with" or "first letter" to impress upon the child what you mean. Help the child, if necessary, and then allow him to work independently. Praise him and encourage him to find Aa's on several pages.

The child will delight in playing with the puppet and can chant "Aa is for apple and it is red." When he is finished show him how to store the puppet in a shoe box for later use. As other letters are introduced they too should be kept in the shoe box for use with additional games.

At various times throughout each day, allow the child to find (Aa's) in words on cans, in books, in magazines, on mail, on license plates, signs, etc. If the child points to Aa's in the middle of a word, simply tell him that an Aa can be anywhere in a word.

This activity develops

- awareness of the letter Aa and its short vowel sound as in apple
- visual skills in identifying Aa
- eye-hand coordination
- memory recall

Age 4 – Week 10

Bouncing Bb

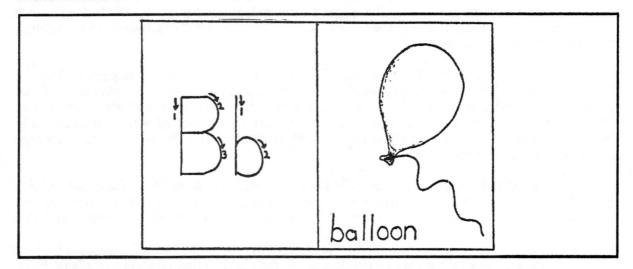

Show the child a ball and bounce the ball. Blow up a balloon. Tie the end of the balloon and allow the child to try to keep it up in the air.

At another time, print a large upper and lower case Bb on the left hand side of a half sheet of typing paper just as you did for the letter Aa in age 4, week 9 activity. Draw a line to separate the left from the right. Draw either a ball or a balloon on the right hand side of the paper. Tell the child to color the ball or balloon blue. Print the appropriate word in lower case letters below the picture you have drawn. Make this into a Bb puppet just as you did for the letter Aa. When it is finished, allow the child to play with the puppet if he wishes. The child can chant "Bb, Bb, look and see. The ball/balloon is blue and was made by me."

If the child is interested in looking for Bb's in magazines, allow him to do so. For more interest, allow him to use a magnifying glass to look for the letters. A blue fine tip felt marker can be used to mark the Bb's if you have one.

At another time, show the child a book. Tell him that the word "book" begins with the letter Bb. Read a story in a book and ask the child to listen for the Bb words in the story as you read. Ask the child what he liked best about the story. Reread it if necessary.

Later, read the following paragraph to the child and tell him to listen for all the Bb's in the short story:

"Betty Burch had a big brown button on her blue blouse. Her bike bumped into a big black box. Betty Burch fell with a bash, boom, bang. She nearly broke her back. Betty's brother brought her back home and put her to bed."

Ask the child to tell you as many words as possible in the story that begin with the same sound as ball/balloon. Show the child the Bb puppet to help him remember the beginning sound of ball/balloon. Help the child recall the Bb words in the brief story and encourage the child to try to think of his own Bb story. You will need to guide and help the child to motivate him.

Show the child the Aa puppet in the shoe box and ask him to recall the letter and the picture. Then review the letter Bb and the word, ball/balloon, on the other puppet. When the child is finished with the two puppets encourage him to put them in the shoe box. Tell him that other puppets will be made and put in there too so that you will be able to play some letter games together.

This activity develops

- awareness of the letter Bb
- visual skills in identifying Bb
- listening skills
- eye-hand coordination

Age 4 – Week 11

Cc, Cc, Cc

cake

Print a large upper and lower case Cc on the left side of a piece of paper just as you did for the letters Aa and Bb. Draw an outline of a cake on the right side. Print the word "cake" in lower case letters below the picture of the cake. Ask the child how old he is. If he does not know, tell him. Show the child four fingers and say, "This is how old you are." Count the fingers to show the child what four means. Tell the child to color the cake any color he wishes. When he finishes, encourage him to draw four candles on top to show that he is four years old. If the child does not know his birthday, now is a good time to explain his birth date to him. Ask the child to repeat it several times so that he will remember it.

Make the Cc and cake paper into a puppet as suggested for the previous letters Aa and Bb. Allow the child to play with the puppet and chant, "Cc is for candles on my cake." Emphasize that "candles" and "cake" both begin with the letter Cc.

The child may suggest looking for Cc's in a magazine or you may suggest that he do it at another time. The child may also enjoy playing with all three puppets independently.

A game can be played with the child to reinforce the letters or sounds of Aa, Bb and Cc. The puppets can be used with the pictures of the apple, ball/balloon and cake facing down. All three letters on the puppets should be facing up. Ask the child to pick up the letter that "apple" begins with. Check for accuracy and put the puppet back in place. Follow the same procedure for the "ball/balloon" and "cake." Change the positions and repeat the activity. Later, the letters can be placed face down and the child can be asked to identify the letters for the beginning sound of "apple," "ball/balloon" and "cake." The cards do not have to be in alphabetical order. However, you can mention that the letter Bb is between the letters Aa and Cc in The Alphabet Song.

The child may also enjoy turning his back while you remove one of the three puppets. He must then try to identify the missing one by letter and picture name. The child may even suggest that the two of you make up a Cc story. Some words that can be used in the story are crate, cape, carry, cash, count, cover, coconut, complete, cook, can. Avoid words such as check, chicken and circus. (At another time the child will learn that Cc has no sound of its own. It borrows its sound from the letters, Kk or Ss.)

When the child is finished with the puppets for the day suggest that he put the puppets in the shoe box so that when he needs them he will know where they are.

This activity develops

- awareness of the letter Cc
- listening skills
- skill in associating the letters Aa, Bb and Cc
- more awareness of age, four and birthday
- memory recall

Age 4 – Week 12

Dig Deep

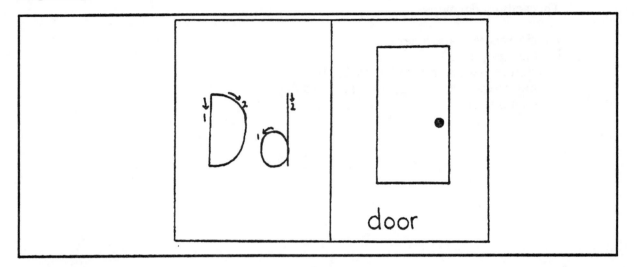

Make a Dd puppet as was suggested for the previous letters. Print a large upper and lower case Dd on the left and draw a door for the picture on the right. Print the word "door" in lower case letters under the picture. Allow the child to choose a crayon and color the door. Make certain the child can identify the color, the letter and the picture before proceeding with this activity.

A chant for the letter Dd can be introduced when the child is playing with the Dd puppet. The chant is "Dd is for door and I am four." The child should enjoy saying this and will probably be able to recall it at a later date.

The child may suggest looking for the Dd's in a magazine. This activity is beneficial for several reasons. It reinforces the visual skills in recognizing the letter many times in words. It also is good for fine motor coordination when the child uses the felt tip pen to circle the respective letters. It also serves to increase the child's attention span and motivates him to work independently. If the child shows no interest in looking for the letters in magazines, suggest that he look for Dd's when you read him a story or when you go to the grocery store. He will undoubtedly recognize the letters on signs and buildings.

If the child has a sandbox, he may enjoy playing the Digging Deep game. If you do not have a sandbox, rice in a container can be used indoors. Use an old shower curtain or large garbage bags underneath to catch the rice spills. If you feel that rice will be too messy, use shredded newspaper, clean kitty litter or plastic packing pellets for this activity. Any of these materials can enhance tactile sensory development.

To begin the game, print the letter Dd on ten pieces of cardboard about an inch square. Hide these ten cardboard pieces in the sand, rice, shredded paper, kitty litter or plastic pellets. Instruct the child to dig deep and find the ten cards with the Dd on them. For variation, Aa's, Bb's and Cc's can be hidden with the Dd's. No more than three cards of each letter should be used. Too many will be confusing. After the child finds the cards in the sand, rice, shredded paper, kitty litter or plastic pellets, suggest that he put all of the Aa's, Bb's, Cc's and Dd's together in separate piles.

You can also use the four puppets and place them in alphabetical order. Ask the child what letter is between Aa and Cc, and what letter is between Bb and Dd. You can also use the puppets and call a letter for the child to pick up and identify the picture on the puppet. The puppets can then be turned over and the pictures can be used to identify the beginning letter of each puppet. When you are finished, remember to put the puppets in the shoe box for later use.

This activity develops

- awareness of the letter Dd
- skill in listening for letter sounds
- skill in matching letters
- tactile sensory enhancement
- confidence

Eggs in the Basket

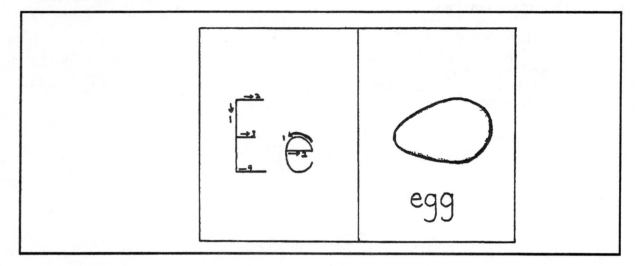

Make an Ee puppet as suggested for the preceding letters. Print a large upper and lower case Ee on the left hand side of the paper and draw a large egg for the picture on the right side. Print the word "egg" in lower case letters under it. Tell the child that an egg is an oval shaped object and the word "egg" begins with Ee.

A chant for Ee that the child can say while he is playing with the egg puppet is, "Eggs in the basket, Ee, Ee, Ee. One fell out and hit my knee."

Some suggested activities for using the letter Ee are:

The child can look for Ee's in a magazine.

The game, "Which Letter is Missing" can be played. The letter puppets should be placed in a row and one of the puppets is removed when the child turns his back. The child then must guess which letter puppet is missing.

The letter side of the puppets can be placed face down. The child should "read" the picture and tell what letter the word begins with.

The game can be reversed with the pictures down and the letters up. The child must name the letter and tell the picture whose name begins with that letter before turning it back over to check.

A new game that the child can play is to draw ten eggs on white paper, each approximately three inches long. Allow the child to color and cut them out. Use a felt marker and write the letters Aa, Bb, Cc, Dd and Ee on the ten eggs so that you have two eggs with each letter. Put these paper eggs in a small basket. Allow the child to choose an egg and name the letter. Do this until all the eggs have been called by the correct name.

As an extension of the egg game, the eggs can be hidden in different obvious places in a room. The child should then be encouraged to go and find them. As he finds each egg, he must identify the letter that is written on it and place it in the small basket.

The child should be encouraged to keep all of the letter puppets in the shoe box. He should also be reminded to practice the chants that correspond to each letter. The chant will help to reinforce the name and the sound of each letter in a fun way.

This activity develops

- awareness of the letter Ee
- skill in distinguishing letters
- memory recall and association skills
- eye-hand coordination
- confidence

Age 4 – Week 14

Let's Go Fishing

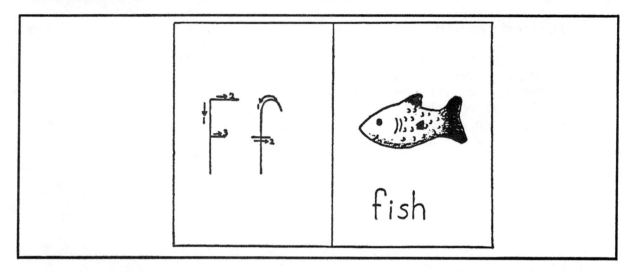

Make an Ff puppet using a half sheet of typing paper as previously suggested for the other puppets. Print the Ff on the left side of the paper and draw a fish on the right hand side. Print the word "fish" in lower case letters under the picture. Tell the child to color the fish orange. Check to see that he chooses the correct color.

A chant for the child to use with the Ff puppet is: "Fish, Fish, Fish in the water. Ff is for fish and also Father." When the child finishes with the puppet, remind him to put it in the shoe box with the other puppets. Tell him that he can play with them at another time.

The child may suggest that he play one of the letter games that he has especially enjoyed, or you may suggest one for him to play. Remember that young children learn best through repetition.

The child may also enjoy repeating the magnetic fish activity in which he made paper fish and matched the colors. This time he will be using letters instead of colors. Draw twelve fish that are each approximately five inches long on colored construction paper. Allow the child to cut them out. Letter the fish with the letters Aa through Ff twice. Place a paper clip on the nostril of each fish or staple two staples on the nostril area. Tie one end of a piece of string or yarn to a stick or pencil. Attach a refrigerator magnet (or one with a cup hook) to the other end of the string or yarn.

Lay the twelve colored fish on the floor and tell the child the floor represents the "water" where the fish live. Invite the child to go "fishing." The child should hold the stick or pencil as if it were a fishing rod. The magnetic end should be referred to as the "hook." Tell the child that as he catches the fish he must tell you the name of the letter on the fish. All correctly named fish may be kept out of the "water." If he does not know the name of the letter, tell him the letter name and instruct him to put the fish back into the "water." The game can be varied by calling a letter by name and requesting the child to catch that fish. The child may also enjoy matching the two fish with the same letter.

As an extension of this activity, you and the child can make up a story about a fish. You can write the words as the child makes up the story. Then you can read the child his story.

The child may also enjoy finishing this story: "The funny fish did flip flops in the water. Her four fins were like fans. She found a famous friend named Freddy Fish. He flipped and flopped his four fins and flung water on the funny fish. The funny fish _____."

This activity develops

- awareness of the letter Ff
- memory recall skills (letters Aa - Ff)
- visual discrimination skills
- eye-hand coordination

Age 4 — Week 15

Goo Goo Goggles

Make a Gg puppet using the same procedure as before with the other letters. Print the letter Gg on the left hand side of the paper and draw a pair of glasses that have enlarged frames on the right hand side. Call these big glasses "goo goo goggles" and print the words "goo goo goggles" in lower case letters below the picture you have drawn. Allow the child to draw over the outline of the enlarged glasses that you have drawn with a green crayon or felt marker.

Introduce the following chant to the child. "Gg is for goo goo goggles to wear over your eyes." Allow the child to wear a pair of old sunglasses for a while or make some play sunglasses from pipe cleaners. If your child wears prescription glasses, try using the pipe cleaner glasses. However, if the child is sensitive about wearing glasses, try varying the chant by substituting the word "glasses" instead of "goo goo goggles"

Repeat any of the previous letter games to suit the interest of the child. A new game for the letter Gg can be called "Goo Goo Goggles." Print the letters Aa through Ff twice on separate index cards that have been cut in half. Print the letter Gg on four of the cards. Shuffle the cards and place them face down in a stack on the floor. Two or more persons can play this game. The first player turns over a card and says the letter name on the card and places the card upright beside the deck. The game continues until someone turns over a Gg card. That person must say, "Goo goo goggles" instead of "Gg." If that person says "Gg" instead of "Goo goo goggles" then he must take all of the cards that are face up and the card with the "Gg" on it. The winner is the one with the fewest cards when all of the cards have been played. If none of the players has any cards left, that signifies good memory and concentration for all players. The game may also be played without saying a word except for the letter names and the word, "Goo goo goggles." If a person talks, then he too must take the discarded cards beside the deck. Be certain to tell the child the names of any letters that are missed. Do not penalize the child in the game because he does not know the letters. Practice will help him to learn the letters.

Invite the child to develop a story with words that begin with the letter Gg. A suggestion that may help to stimulate the child would be to ask him to finish this brief story: "Gertie Groundhog lived with her grandfather in a green garage. Gertie giggled at her shadow. Grandfather groaned because _____." Perhaps the child could be encouraged to draw a picture about his story.

This activity develops

- awareness of the letter Gg
- skill in distinguishing the letters Aa - Gg
- memory recall skills
- listening skills
- eye-hand coordination
- confidence

Age 4 – Week 16

The Hat Game

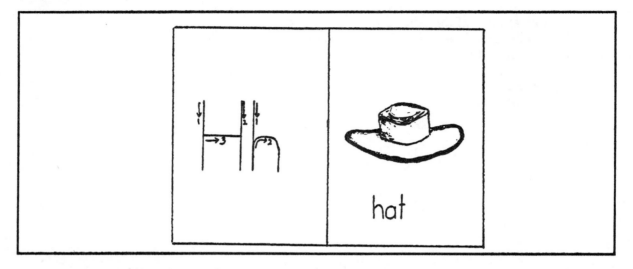

Make a puppet for the letter Hh like the others that were made previously. Print the letter Hh on the left hand side and draw a picture of a hat on the right hand side. Write the word "hat" in lower case letters under the picture of the hat.

When the child is playing with the letter Hh puppet, he can use the following chant: "(child's name) says this and that. Did you know that rhymes with hat?" When the child is finished with the puppet, remind him to put it in the shoe box with the other puppets. These will be used in some of the future activities. The child may also enjoy looking for words that begin with the letter Hh in magazines.

Invite the child to suggest one of the previous letter games to play or introduce a new game called the "Hat Game." Use one color of construction paper to draw and cut out sixteen hats that are approximately four or five inches wide. Allow the child to help you draw and cut out the paper hats if he is interested. Print the letters Aa through Hh so that there are two hats with each letter. Place the hats with the letters face down. Each player turns over one hat and then another in search of the two hats that have the same letter. If the player finds two hats that are the same, he puts the matched hats in a pile beside him and continues to search for two more that are the same. If he turns over two hats that are not the same, then the two hats must be turned back over face down. The next player then has a turn. Remind the child to try to remember where the replaced hats are. When all of the hats have been matched, count the hats with the child. The player with the most hats wins. Emphasize to the child that even though the object of a game is to win, there is only one winner. Games should be played for fun, because everyone cannot win.

If this game seems too difficult for the child, play the matching game with all of the hats facing up. The game can be played alone or with another person. However, if it is played with another person, they can take turns finding a set of matching letter hats. Count all of the hats when the game is over. The child will delight in noting how many hats he matched.

The child may want to tell or have you write a story with him about a "Big Hat." This helps the child to formulate sentences in order for him to speak in complete thoughts. He will also enjoy hearing his story reread to him and to other family members.

This activity develops

- awareness of the letter Hh
- visual discrimination of the letters Aa - Hh
- eye-hand coordination
- association skills (matching letters)
- memory recall of the letter names

Age 4 – Week 17

Indian Boy

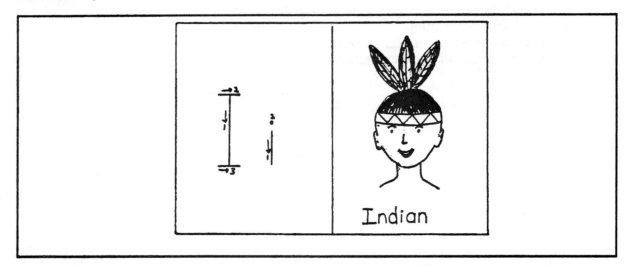

Make the Ii puppet to add to the letter puppet collection. Print the letter Ii on the left hand side of the paper and draw an Indian boy's face on the right hand side of the paper. Add a headband and put three feathers in it. Allow the child to color the feathers different colors. Print the word "Indian" under the picture.

A chant for the child to use as he plays with the Indian puppet is: "I'm an Indian. Look at me. I have three feathers. Don't you see?"

Draw a headband on light cardboard or heavy paper that can be decorated and worn by the child. Measure the child's head to determine the length of the headband. Then encourage the child to decorate the headband. Draw three feathers and allow the child to color and cut these out. Then glue or staple them to the headband. Place the headband around the child's head and secure with a paper clip or staple it together. Invite the child to repeat the Indian chant as he plays with the Ii puppet and wears the Indian headband.

For interest, the child can learn to sing the song "Ten Little Indians." Use your fingers to count while you sing or chant the finger play song. Encourage the child to move his fingers also at the correct number as you sing or chant.

At another time, allow the child to play with all of the letter puppets and suggest that he name all of them for you. Help him if necessary.

The child may also enjoy playing "What's Missing?" with the letter puppets. I suggest that you use only four letter puppets at a time. Ask the child to identify the letters on the puppets that you plan to use. Tell the child to turn around while you remove one of the puppets. When the child turns around, ask him to tell you what puppet is missing. Tell the child the name if he does not recall it. Continue to play the game with any of the four puppets. This is good for the child's memory recall.

This activity develops

- awareness of the letter Ii
- more skill in distinguishing letters Aa - Ii
- role playing
- eye-hand coordination
- memory recall skills
- confidence

Age 4 – Week 18

Jack-in-the-Box

Jack-in-the-box

Make the Jj puppet to add to the puppet collection. Draw a Jack-in-the-box for the picture and print the name below the picture. A suggested chant for the Jj puppet is: "Jj, Jj, Jack-in-the-box, open the lid and out he pops."

Obtain a large box in which the child can stand or squat momentarily inside. The top should be attached on one side with the other three sides free so that the child can push the lid up when he pretends to pop up like a Jack-in-the-box.

Before beginning, allow the child to decorate the outside of the box. Then invite him to get inside. Chant again, "Jj, Jj, Jack-in-the-box, open the lid and out he pops." Tell the child to open the lid when you say, "pops" and jump up like a Jack-in-the-box.

Allow the child to play with the large box independently and encourage him to say the chant. The letter puppets can be placed inside the large box and the child can substitute one of the puppets to pop out when the word "pops" is said.

The child should be encouraged to use the letter puppets (Aa through Jj) with other previously suggested games. However, he should be reminded to put all of the puppets back in the shoe box when he is finished. You can also suggest that he look for the letter (Jj) in magazines using the magnifying glass to help to "spy" the letters. The letters can then be marked with a fine red tip felt marker for additional interest.

This activity develops

- awareness of the letter Jj
- skill in distinguishing letters
- role playing
- listening skills
- eye-hand coordination
- creativity in decorating the box

Age 4 – Week 19

The Kite

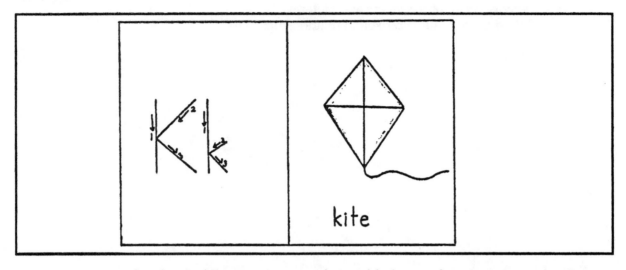

kite

Prepare and make the Kk puppet as was done with the previous letter puppets. Draw a kite on the right hand side, print the word "kite" in lower case letters below the picture of the kite and allow the child to color the four sections of the kite a different color. Ask the child to name the colors that he chose. A suggested chant for the child to say is: "Kk is for kite that flies so high. If I let it go it will touch the sky."

Buy or make a kite for the child. The child will delight in helping you make or assemble the kite. A homemade kite can easily be made by cutting off the corners of a piece of paper about the size of a piece of typing paper. Allow the child to decorate the kite before he cuts off the corners. Staple a piece of yarn to the middle of the top section. Staple another piece of yarn to the bottom tip of the kite to represent a tail. Tie a knot at the end of the two pieces of yarn before stapling them to the kite. This will prevent the yarn from slipping under the staple. Give the kite to the child and allow him to pretend to fly his kite indoors.

To emphasize the letter Kk and its beginning sound, such as in the word kite, print the upper and lower case "Kk" on a Styrofoam meat tray or plate (a paper plate will not suffice). This can be accomplished by drawing a kite at the top of the inverted tray or plate and printing an upper and lower case "Kk" below it with a pencil. Show the child how to use a nail about two inches long to punch holes along the lines of the drawn kite and the letters. Try to encourage the child to start at the top of each letter when he begins to punch (print) the "Kk's" since this is a rule in forming block (printed) letters in school. This same activity can also be used with other letters and pictures that are on the other letter puppets.

Play the game "Find Me" with all of the letter names and pictures. Spend a little time with each letter and emphasize the beginning sound of the word under the picture. For example Aa--"a"pple, Bb--"b"all, Cc--"c"ake, etc. The child may comment that the "Kk" and "Cc" sound alike. Acknowledge the comment by saying, "Cc" has no sound of its own. It borrows from the letters "Kk" (as in kite) or "Ss" (as in circus).

274

This activity develops

- awareness of the letter Kk and its initial sound as in the word kite
- eye-hand coordination
- dramatization as in pretending to fly a kite
- tactile sensory perception (punching holes)
- confidence in beginning to form letters
- memory recall of the letters and pictures
- skill in associating letter/sound relationships

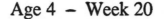

Age 4 – Week 20

Lollipop Fun

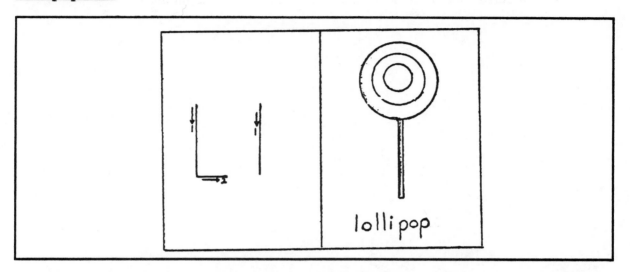

lollipop

Make an Ll puppet using a picture of a colorful lollipop as the picture clue. This can be drawn by using several different colors to make concentric circles with the given circular shape of the drawn lollipop and then adding a line for the lollipop stick or holder. Print the word "lollipop" in lower case letters below the picture. The suggested chant for Ll is: "Ll is for lollipop, yummy to eat. It's tasty and sweet and hard to beat."

The child may enjoy making a colorful lollipop by cutting several sizes of circles and gluing them on top of each other. For example, the first circle can be five inches in diameter, the second colored circle can be four inches, while the third, fourth and fifth circles can be three inches, two inches and one inch, respectively.

Place all of the letter puppets in alphabetical order and encourage the child to recall the letter names. Make a mental note of those with which the child may seem to have difficulty and practice naming them several times. If the child knows all of the puppet letter names, play the game "Listen and Find." Ask the child to listen for the letter name that you say and find that letter in the alphabetical row of puppets. Do this until the child readily listens and finds the correct letter.

At another time, the child may enjoy lining up toothpicks or paper pieces to form "Ll's." Draw a line on a piece of paper and encourage the child to form toothpick or paper strip upper case "L's" on the lines. Draw another line and allow the child to make a row of lower case "l's. The child may comment that the lowercase "l" looks like the number one (1). Acknowledge the comment by saying that they do resemble one another but they mean two different things.

The child may enjoy making other letters that are made primarily of straight lines such as the upper case "A," "E," "F," "H," "I" and "K."

276

This activity develops

- awareness of the letter Ll
- skill in visual recognition of the letters
- listening skills
- memory recall
- awareness of the letters that are made primarily of straight lines

---
Age 4 – Week 21

My Mittens

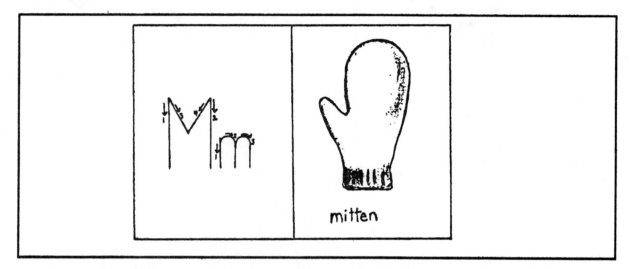

mitten

Make an Mm puppet. Trace around the child's hand for the picture clue for the initial sound of Mm. Print the word "mitten" under the drawing and allow the child to decorate the mitten. The suggested chant for the letter Mm is: "Mm is for mitten, but Kk is for kitten."

Allow the child to play with the puppet if there is interest and encourage him to say the chant. If there is no interest, put the puppet in the shoe box with the other letter puppets and tell the child that you will work with them later.

At an opportune time, read the "Three Little Kittens" rhyme to the child. Talk about the words that rhyme such as kitten and mitten, dear and fear, cry and pie, etc. This is also a good time to talk about obedience and the meaning of the word naughty.

Children enjoy rhyming words. Your child will probably spontaneously begin to rhyme words. Even if the rhymes are not authentic words, your child will be exploring with sounds. This activity will be a good traveling game. For example, you name a word and the child responds with a rhyming word. Likewise, the child can say a word to you and you tell him a word that rhymes with the word he said to you.

If the child enjoyed having you trace around his hand for the letter puppet, he may also enjoy making a pair of mittens in a similar manner. Fold a piece of paper in half and trace around one of the child's hands. Cutting through both thicknesses of the paper will produce two paper mittens. Turn one of the paper mittens over so that the left and right thumbs face inside toward each other. Point out the left and right mitten to the child and tell him that he now has a pair of mittens to decorate. Tell him that the mittens should look alike. Therefore, whatever he colors on one mitten, he must do the same on the other mitten. In that way, they will look the same.

278

This activity develops

- awareness of the letter Mm
- listening skills
- rhyming skills
- more awareness of left and right
- more awareness of a pair
- confidence

Age 4 – Week 22

Night Time

Make an Nn puppet to correspond to the other letter puppets. Allow the child to color the picture section of the paper black to represent night. You may prefer to glue a black piece of construction paper to the paper instead of allowing the child to color it black. Draw a crescent moon and two or three stars on a small piece of paper. Tell the child to color them yellow. Help the child to cut out the moon and stars and glue these in place on the black paper so that it resembles the moon and stars at night. Paste will not adhere to wax crayon. Therefore, be certain to use a type of glue that will adhere to the wax or staple them in place. Write the word "night" on a slip of paper and glue this below the moon and stars. A suggested chant for the child to use is: "Nn is for night when I sleep tight."

Allow the child to play with the puppet and repeat the chant several times. Give the child the shoe box with the other puppets and encourage him to recall the other letter chants. The chanting activity is fun, yet very important because it indirectly emphasizes the initial sound of each letter. This type of skill will be helpful to the child when he begins to read. Over eighty percent of the words in the English language are spelled phonetically (sound reading). This sound awareness skill will also be helpful to the child in spelling.

If the child does not appear to be interested in the letter puppets, try to casually chant the different letter chants when you are doing house work, riding in a car or talking with the child. Children approach learning in many different ways. What appeals to one child may not appeal to another. Therefore, try to use the suggested ideas and explain them in a way that will be most beneficial to the child.

Another way to emphasize the name and sound of the letter Nn is to sing or chant, "Twinkle, twinkle little star. How I wonder what you are. Up above the world so high, like a diamond in the sky. Twinkle, twinkle little star. How I wonder what you are." When the child has listened to the song several times ask him when the stars shine.

This is a good time for you to talk to the child again about day and night. This activity was introduced in the age 3, week 9 activity. Encourage the child to tell you what he likes about night or ask him to relate things that the family does at night. Refer to the Nn puppet and point out the dark night and the bright moon and stars.

The child may also enjoy watching you draw a five-pointed star. If you dot the lines on paper, perhaps the child can learn to draw stars too. Use the words, start, across, down and up as you show the child how to draw a star. The child may also be interested in drawing a six-pointed star by overlapping two triangles to form one.

This activity develops

- awareness of Nn
- more of an understanding of letter/sound relationships
- vocabulary enrichment
- eye-hand coordination
- more awareness of rhyming as in the chant and song
- listening skills

Age 4 — Week 23

Octopus

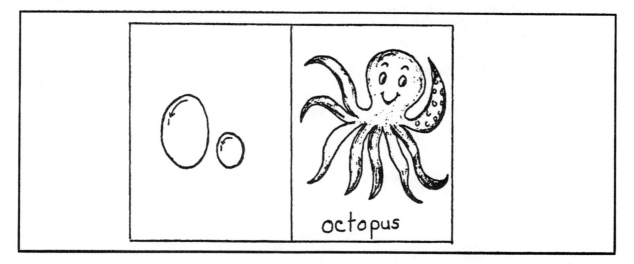

Make an Oo puppet similar to the other letter puppets. When drawing an octopus, remember that he has eight tentacles. The word "octopus" should be printed in lower case letters under the picture. The octopus was chosen for interest, and because it is easy for the child to relate the initial short vowel sound of the word. The other letter puppets whose names begin with vowels that have been introduced also include the short vowel sounds. They are Aa (apple), Ee (egg), Ii (Indian) and Oo (octopus). The child need not be told that these words are vowels, although he may ask you why they appear so many times in words. You can simply tell him that they are necessary for us to pronounce (say) words correctly.

The child may enjoy playing with the octopus puppet as he chants the following chant: "Oo is for octopus that swims along. His body and suckers are very strong." The child may also be interested in knowing some facts about an octopus. An octopus has two large shiny eyes and strong hard jaws that come to a point like a bird's beak. These help him to get his food. The octopus can squirt a liquid in the water to make it cloudy. In this way, other animals that would eat the octopus cannot see him in the water. He has no bones and his body is soft. His eight arms or tentacles have suckers on them that allow the octopus to attach himself to an object or to capture his prey for food. He draws water into his body and squeezes it back out with a strong force. This expulsion forces his body to move through the water.

If your child has a keen interest in an octopus, he may enjoy making a model from a paper or Styrofoam plate. Punch eight holes evenly around the rim of the plate. Strips of cloth or yarn can be plaited to make the tentacles. The eight tentacles can then be attached through the holes in the plate and secured with a knot or they may be stapled to the plate. The strips of cloth or yarn may be knotted to represent the octopus' suckers. The child can then add two eyes on top with a crayon or felt marker. It can be suspended with a string or rubber band for the child to hold. This will give the illusion of a swimming octopus.

The child will enjoy counting the eight tentacles. Show the child the number 8 so that he can associate the symbol with the eight tentacles.

The letter puppets should be placed in order and identified at optimum times. Some of the games should be played and the chants repeated to reinforce the letters and sounds without the child feeling pressured to do so. Workbooks and structured materials are good "time fillers," but there is nothing like personal contact and interaction with the child.

This activity develops

- awareness of the letter Oo
- language enrichment
- dramatization (playing with the swimming octopus)
- eye-hand coordination
- more skill in sound/letter relationships

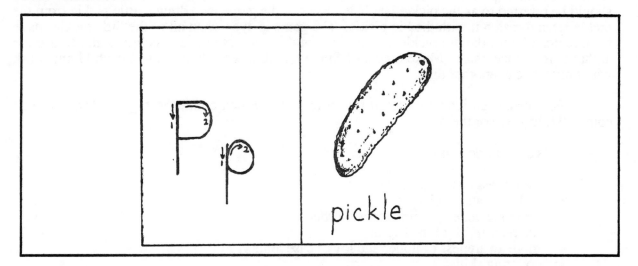

Age 4 – Week 24

The Pickle Jar

Make the Pp puppet and draw a large pickle for the picture clue to emphasize the initial sound of the letter Pp. Print the word "pickle" in lower case letters below the picture. Tell the child to color the pickle green. Check to see if the child chooses green. Tell the child that pickles are made from cucumbers. The child should know that a cucumber is a vegetable, that it grows from a seed and that it is related to the watermelon family. The child may say that it looks like a little watermelon. At this time you can explain to the child how they are different. Size, inside color and taste should be enough to convince the child that they are different.

The child may enjoy the suggested chant for the letter Pp. The chant is: "Pp is for pickle, and it won't tickle." Encourage the child to place all of the letter puppets in a row. As you call a letter beginning with Aa, encourage the child to find the Aa puppet and place it in a new row under the other row. Continue to call the letters in alphabetical order and help the child place them in the new row. When you name the letter Pp, which is the last one that has been introduced, tell the child that he has put the letters in alphabetical order. Say, sing or chant the alphabet song and continue to sing until the end of the song. At this time, tell the child that when you finish making puppets that he will have twenty-six in all. Count the letters from Aa through Pp and tell the child that he now knows sixteen letters and has sixteen puppets. That means that he will make ten more puppets which will give him a total of twenty-six puppets. Encourage the child to try and guess what the other puppets will be to motivate him and keep his interest keen.

The child may suggest an alphabet game from a previous letter activity when he is looking for something to do. If at all possible, try to encourage this. Repetition and reinforcement will provide the child a firm foundation for future reading skills.

Another game the child may enjoy is the "Pickle Jar Game." Invite the child to help you make some big and little pickles. Draw sixteen big pickles and sixteen little pickles on green construction paper. Allow the child to help you cut out all of the paper pickles. Print one upper case letter (from A through P) on each of the big paper pickles. Similarly, print one lower case letter (a through p) on each of the little paper pickles. Use the words "big" and "little" when you make the paper pickles. Make a reference chart by printing the letters (Aa through Pp) on a piece of paper.

To begin the game, place all of the big (pickles) letters face up in a row on a table or the floor. The little (pickles) letters should all be in a large plastic jar or other container which should be referred to as the pickle jar. The object of the game is to draw a little pickle from the pickle jar and match it with the big pickle. The game is over when all of the little pickles have been matched with the big pickles. Help the child if necessary and encourage him to use the alphabet reference chart. Make a note of the letters that seem to confuse the child and work with only those at another time.

For further enrichment, count the little pickles, then count the big pickles, and then count all thirty-two of them.

This activity develops

- awareness of the letter Pp
- skill in matching letters
- more awareness of alphabetical order
- memory recall of the letters
- more awareness of upper and lower case letters
- counting skills
- confidence

Age 4 – Week 25

My Quilt

Make a puppet for the letter Qq and draw a nine-square quilt for the picture clue to reinforce the Qq sound. The letter sound for Qq actually sounds like (kw) blended together. For interest, the drawn quilt can have different colored squares and the child can choose different colors to make a pretty quilt. While the child is coloring the quilt you can explain what a patch quilt is i.e., cloth squares that have been sewed together. Remember to print the word "quilt" in lower case letters under the picture of the nine-square quilt. A suggested chant for Qq is: "Qq is for quilt. It's not made of silt." Count the nine squares with the child and write a "9" on a piece of paper so that he will relate the concept of nine with the symbol "9."

Allow the child to play with the quilt puppet and recall the different colors that were used in the paper quilt. This will be a good time to give the child only the letter puppets that seem difficult for him. Review them briefly and play "Find the Letter." That is, you call a letter by name and the child either points to or hands the correct letter puppet to you.

At another time, the child may enjoy using all of the letter puppets to form a letter quilt or a picture quilt depending on the side of the puppet he wishes to use. The letter puppets can be counted for number concept reinforcement.

This activity develops

- awareness of the letter Qq
- more skill in identifying and associating letters
- language enrichment
- more awareness of the number concept "9"
- eye-hand coordination
- language enrichment
- more confidence

Age 4 – Week 26

The Rocket

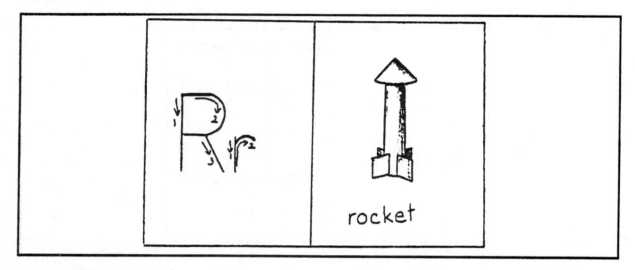

rocket

Make an Rr puppet and draw a rocket to represent the picture clue for the Rr sound. Print the word "rocket" in lower case letters under the picture. Allow the child to color the rocket. The suggested chant for the letter Rr is: "Rr is for rocket that blasts up high. It moves very fast in the big blue sky."

Allow the child to play with the rocket letter puppet and any other puppets that he may choose to enhance his dramatic play activity. A fun action that the child may enjoy is to squat and pretend to be a rocket. Tell the child to listen as you count backwards, 10, 9, 8, 7, 6, 5, 4, 3, 2, 1, 0 and after zero say, "Blast off." At that time, the child should jump up very high as if he were a rocket.

The child may also enjoy making a rocket from a paper towel roll. A circle, a little larger than the circumference of the roll, should be drawn on a piece of paper. A line should also be drawn from the edge of the circle to the center. Allow the child to cut out the circle and the line that was drawn to the center. Overlap the cut edge of the circle and staple or glue this to form a cone. This cone can be attached to the paper towel roll with tape. Four slits can be cut at the opposite end of the roll. Two rectangular cardboard pieces can then be inserted to form the base. The child may suggest that he fly his rocket outside. It will not go far, but the child will enjoy trying and playing with it.

To reinforce the letter Rr and its sound, the child may enjoy drawing a large rainbow with red, orange, yellow, green, blue and purple colors and realize that the word rainbow begins with the same letter and sound as the word rocket. This will be a good time to name other words that begin with the letter Rr. Some suggestions are: rain, ring, ripple, rhyme, rip, roar, rag, rich, ram, rough, rug, riddle, roll, rocker, etc.

This activity develops

- awareness of the letter Rr
- skill in identifying the letters (visual discrimination)
- role playing
- memory recall
- more awareness of words that begin with the letter (Rr)
- confidence
- eye-hand coordination

Age 4 – Week 27

Make a Snake

Make an Ss puppet and draw a snake as a picture clue to reinforce the Ss sound. Print the word "snake" in lower case letters under the picture. Allow the child to color the snake. The suggested chant for the child to use when he is playing with the Ss puppet is: "Ss is for snake that you see. Take a look and he will flee."

Talk to the child about a snake. Ask questions such as, "Where does he live? How does he move? What does he eat? Can he hear?" The child will enjoy seeing pictures of different kinds of snakes and may recall a previous activity in which snakes were discussed. You may also encourage that he try to move like a snake. In fact, you could choose a starting and stopping boundary to stimulate the child to want to try and move like a snake.

At another time, allow the child to make a paper snake. Assemble a piece of construction paper or any kind of heavy weight paper. Cut the corners from the paper to form a circle. Use a pencil and draw a continuous spiral line from the outside of the circle to the center leaving approximately one and one-half inches between the line as you draw the spiral line to the center. Use a wide felt marker and allow the child to trace over the pencil line. Then assist the child in cutting beside the spiral line to the center leaving a small section to represent the head in the middle. Add eyes, mouth and spots to make the spiral snake look more realistic. The child should enjoy playing with the paper snake. He should be encouraged to recall the Ss chant to reinforce the letter name and sound.

The child should also be encouraged to look for words in a magazine that begin with the letter Ss. He should also be motivated to try to name words that begin with the letter Ss. Some suggestions are: seal, sew, some, sick, same, sip, sag, supper, soup, sing, sister, etc. Words that begin with (sh) should be discouraged at this time since the Ss sound is altered when it is followed by an (h). This is a skill that should be taught later.

This activity develops

- awareness of the letter Ss
- more skill in distinguishing letters
- memory recall
- gross motor coordination (moving like a snake)
- language enrichment
- more awareness of words that begin with the same letter
- confidence

Age 4 – Week 28

Tree Tops

Make a Tt puppet and draw a tree to use as a picture clue to reinforce the letter sound. Print the word "tree" in lower case letters under the picture. Ask the child what colors should be used for the tree. Allow him to choose green and brown. If he confuses the colors in making the choice, point to a real tree or use a picture to reinforce the correct color choice. The chant for the tree puppet is: "Tt is for tree. It bows for me." (that is, when the wind blows). Explain that a hard wind can make a tree bend over and bow. Ask the child to bend over and bow. He can also be encouraged to move his arms to represent the tree branches.

Some of the alphabet games using the puppets may be reintroduced and the chants reviewed. You may be tired of reviewing these, but a young child needs much repetition in order to feel secure. The more comfortable a child feels with the letters and sounds, the more freely he will begin to use them.

The child may enjoy playing the game called "Tree Tops." Assemble some green and brown construction paper. Draw twenty green scalloped ovals to represent tree tops. Then draw twenty brown tree trunks. Encourage the child to help you cut them out. Use a felt marker and write the upper case letters (A through T) on the green tree tops and write the lower case letters (a through t) on the brown tree trunks.

Line the tree trunks in a row. Make a printed alphabet guide on a separate sheet of paper and help the child rearrange the tree trunks so that they are in alphabetical order. Place the green tree tops in a separate container and encourage the child to draw one and place it on the correct tree trunk. Allow the child to continue with this activity until all of the trees are complete with top and trunk.

Count the twenty trees with the child several times and invite the child to repeat the game. If there is no interest, suggest that the child place them in a container for later use. The Tt puppet should also be placed with the other puppets in the shoe box.

At another time, the child may be encouraged to pretend to be a tall tree. To do this, the child should try to stand as tall as possible. Then tell the child to pretend to be a short tree. The child should then be encouraged to squat as low as possible to resemble a short tree. The child should enjoy doing this at various times on command.

To reinforce visual recognition of the letters and their positions, introduce the game "Move the Trees." For example, tell the child to line up all of the tree tops and trunks in alphabetical order. Help the child if necessary. Then instruct the child to move the (Bb) and the (Dd) trees. Ask the child how many trees he moved. Increase the number of trees for the child to pick to three. If the child is confident, he can pick up more trees. It may seem awkward for the child to pick up both the top and trunk of each tree, but this activity is a good experience in manipulating materials for fine motor control. Count the trees for accuracy with the child and take note of any letters with which the child may have had difficulty.

This activity develops

- awareness of the letter Tt
- skill in distinguishing letters
- skill in matching upper and lower case letters
- language enrichment
- confidence

Age 4 – Week 29

The Umbrella

umbrella

Make a Uu puppet and draw an umbrella to be used as the picture clue to reinforce the short vowel Uu sound. Print the word "umbrella" in lower case letters under the picture. Tell the child to color it red. The chant for the umbrella puppet is: "Uu is for umbrella you wear over your head. The one that I have is colored red."

Allow the child to play with the Uu puppet and chant the rhyme. Then encourage him to put the Uu puppet in the alphabet letter puppet shoe box.

Show the child a real umbrella. Ask the child what it is used for. Also ask the child why an umbrella has ribs. Allow the child to open and close the umbrella. Emphasize the concepts: open, close, and under.

Open the umbrella and tell the child that you will use the alphabet puppets to play the game, "Under the Umbrella." A puppet is taken from the box. The child must name the letter on the puppet. If the child is correct he can then put the puppet under the umbrella. If the child has difficulty with a letter, he should be told the letter name again and the picture clue on the other side of the puppet should be identified for reinforcement. This puppet must then be put back into the shoe box. The game continues until all of the letter puppets have been named correctly and placed under the umbrella.

To vary the game, use the pictures on the puppets instead of the letters. The child then should be challenged to name both the picture and the letter before placing the puppet under the umbrella.

This activity develops

- awareness of the letter Uu
- more skill with letter recognition
- more skill with picture clues to reinforce the initial sounds
- more awareness of the concepts, open, close and under
- memory recall
- language enrichment

Age 4 – Week 30

The Pretty Vase

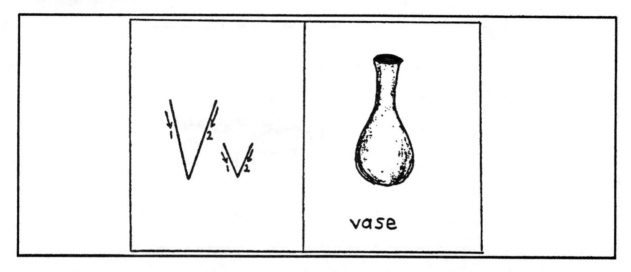

vase

Make a Vv puppet and draw a vase to use as a picture to reinforce the Vv sound. Print the word "vase" in lower case letters under the picture. Allow the child to color the vase. The chant suggested for the Vv puppet is: "Vv, Vv, Vv is for vase. Never carry it in a race."

The child should be encouraged to walk or dance around with the puppet and repeat the chant as he moves around. The puppet should then be placed in the alphabet shoe box with the other puppets.

Show the child a pretty vase. If possible collect some pretty flowers with the child and help him place them in the vase. If you do not have any real or artificial flowers, make some from construction paper. Attach the paper flowers to pipe cleaners or cardboard to represent stems. Count the flowers as you put them in a vase.

As an extension of this activity, draw twenty-two tulips on colored construction paper. Encourage the child to help you cut out the paper tulips. Use a felt marker and write a letter from Aa through Vv on each of the paper tulips. Tell the child to put the tulips in a vase one at a time. Help the child count the tulips as each one is placed in the vase. Then instruct the child to identify the letter on each tulip as he removes them one at a time from the vase. He may enjoy doing this several times. The game can then be reversed. The child can name the letter on the tulip as he places it in the vase. Similarly, he can count the tulips as he removes each one from the vase.

This activity develops

- awareness of the letter Vv
- skill in identifying the letters Aa - Vv
- skill in identifying the initial sound of Vv as in vase
- skill in counting to twenty-two
- confidence

Age 4 — Week 31

My Wagon

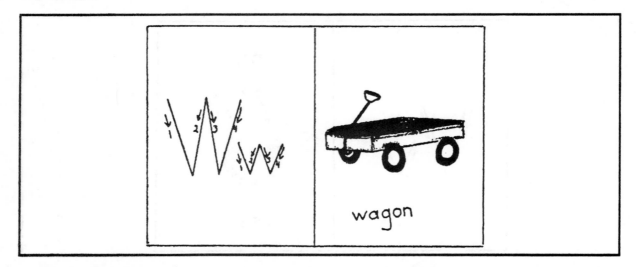

wagon

Make a Ww puppet and draw a wagon to use as a picture clue in identifying the initial sound of the word "wagon." Print the word "wagon" in lower case letters under the picture. Allow the child to color the wagon any color he chooses, but ask the child to identify the color that he chooses to ensure that he can recall the color name.

The chant for the letter puppet that the child may enjoy saying is: "Ww is for wagon that rolls right along. When I am in it I'll sing a song." Allow the child to pretend to be in a wagon as he chants the Ww chant with the puppet. A cardboard box large enough for the child to fit inside can be used for the wagon. Paper plates can be attached to the box with brass paper fasteners or glue to resemble the wheels. A cardboard strip or a string can be attached in the front to be used as a handle for pulling the cardboard wagon.

The alphabet puppets may then be carried in the wagon. Perhaps the child can choose special letter puppets to ride in his wagon. For example, only those upper case (big) letters with straight lines can ride in the wagon. The letters that can ride are A, E, F, H, I, K, L, M, N, T, V, and W. The letters X, Y, and Z may be added after they have been introduced in the next three weekly activities.

At another time, the child may enjoy choosing the lower case (small) letters that have tails to ride in his wagon, i.e., those that hang below the line. They are: g, j, p and q. The lower case "y" may be added after it is introduced in the weekly activity that emphasizes that letter.

If the child is especially interested in selecting special letter puppets to ride in his wagon, he may enjoy choosing the letters whose names sound alike. i.e., they rhyme. These letters are Bb, Cc, Dd, Ee, Gg, Pp, Tt, Vv and Zz (when Zz is introduced in the weekly activity that emphasizes that letter).

The child may make other suggestions in choosing special letter puppets to ride in his wagon such as the letter puppets with all curved lines such as Cc, Oo and Ss. Letters on the puppets with partly straight lines and partly curved lines such as Bb, Dd, Gg, Jj, Mm, Nn, Pp, Qq, Rr, and Uu may also be selected to ride together in the wagon. These special activities should be encouraged so that the child becomes well aware of the letters, their sounds, their configurations, those that rhyme and any other way that the child may choose to separate the letter puppets for a particular purpose.

This activity develops

- awareness of the letter Ww
- skill in identifying most of the letters
- more awareness of letter sounds
- skill in using visual clues to distinguish the letters
- more awareness that letter names sound alike
- role playing
- skill in making a decision in sorting special letters

Age 4 – Week 32

The Musical Xylophone

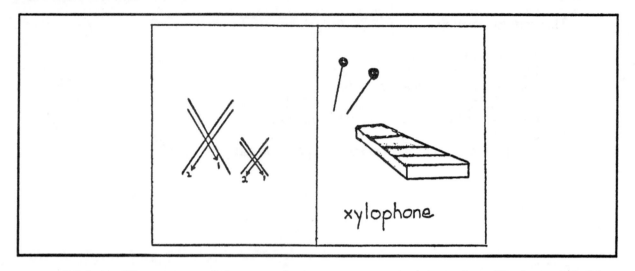

xylophone

Make an Xx puppet and draw a xylophone to use as a picture clue. The letter "Xx" has no true sound of its own and borrows the sound from the letter "Zz" except when it says its name in a word, such as in the word x-ray. Write the word "xylophone" in lower case letters under the picture. Tell the child to color the keys of the xylophone using the colors of the rainbow. Check to see that the child chooses red, orange, yellow, green, blue and purple. If the child has difficulty with any of the color names, make a note of it and work with the color identifications at another time.

The suggested chant for the letter "Xx" is: "Xx is for xylophone that I can play. Listen closely to what it will say." Encourage the child to repeat the chant several times.

Assemble a shoe box with the lid removed. Stretch several large different colored rubber bands around the shorter sides of the empty shoe box to resemble a xylophone. Show the child how to pluck the "strings" of the pretend xylophone. Encourage the child to sing the "Alphabet Song" or the xylophone chant. The child may even enjoy trying to produce the same sound as the rubber bands make when they are plucked on the pretend xylophone.

If you have a real xylophone, show it to the child and explain that a real xylophone has wood, metal or plastic pieces that make a sound when they are tapped with a mallet.

This will be a good time to introduce the different kinds of musical instruments to the child. Some instruments make music when a person blows and controls air, others make music when special strings are plucked or moved, while others make music when something is tapped on a special material. Show the child some pictures of different kinds of musical instruments. A dictionary or encyclopedia usually have small pictures of most musical instruments.

Sing or chant the "Alphabet Song" with the child and stop when you get to the letter "Xx." Ask the child what letter comes next. The child may enjoy doing this with other letters. For example, sing or chant the alphabet and stop at a given point and ask the child what letter comes next. This will serve to help the child to better understand alphabetical sequence.

This activity develops

- awareness of the letter Xx
- more awareness of the colors of the rainbow
- eye-hand coordination in moving the shoe box "strings"
- awareness that the letter Xx sounds like the letter Zz
- skill in predicting what comes next by association
- confidence in letter and sound recall

Age 4 – Week 33

Wind the Yarn

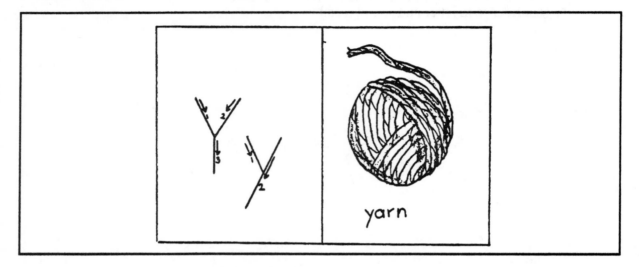

yarn

Make a Yy puppet and draw a ball of yarn to use as a picture clue to emphasize the initial sound of the letter "Yy" in a word. Write the word "yarn" in lower case letters under the picture. Allow the child to choose a crayon and color the yarn on the picture. Check for the identification of the chosen color.

The suggested chant for the letter Yy puppet is: "Yy is for yarn to wind in a ball. But it will unwind if you let it fall." Allow the child to chant the rhyme several times. Emphasize the initial sound of Yy as in the word yarn. Avoid telling the child at this time that the letter Yy has different sounds at the end of some words. For example, the "y" in baby sounds like an "e," the "y" at the end of the word fly sounds like "i." It is better to deal primarily with the initial (beginning) sounds of words at this age.

Show the child some yarn and allow him to wind it into a ball. When he finishes let him rewind the yarn. This is a very good coordination skill for a young child. He may also enjoy saying the Yy chant and allow the yarn ball to fall. He will then be able to observe the yarn as it unwinds. However, be certain to encourage him to rewind it before he has a mess of tangles.

At another time, play an alphabet game with the child such as those that have been suggested for the previous letters. Allow the child to suggest one, or choose one that you think he will enjoy. Children of this age often select the same game; therefore, encourage him to try to recall other games. You can name or show the child a letter and wait to see if he can recall the game suggested for that letter. If not, perhaps you can give him some clues to help him with him memory recall. Naming the letter puppets at random is a good game to play. Make a separate pile for the letter puppets that the child has difficulty naming. At another time, ask the child to recall the initial sound of each letter as the letter puppet is presented to him. Again take note of the sounds that need reinforcement and emphasize those letter sounds later.

This activity develops

- awareness of the letter Yy
- more skill in letter recognition
- eye-hand coordination in winding yarn
- skill in using picture clues to identify sounds
- confidence

Age 4 – Week 34

Zero

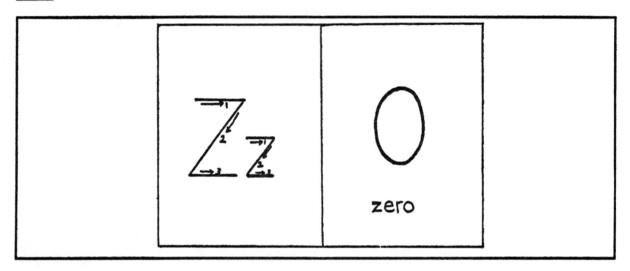

Make a Zz puppet and write a "O" to use as a picture clue in identifying the letter sound. Print the word "zero" in lower case letters under the symbol. Tell the child that zero comes before one in counting. It means nothing and it is a beginning point before we count to one. Illustrate this by showing him a ruler. Show him the end of the ruler on the left. Then point to the marking for one inch. Move your hand and show the child two inches, three inches and continue up to twelve inches. Then go back to the beginning and touch the left ruler edge which is "point zero," then move your hand to show one inch and continue to twelve inches again. Allow the child to repeat this independently if he seems to understand. If not, try again later.

The chant for the letter "Zz" is: "Zz is for zero where we begin. But when using letters, its name's at the end." Repeat the chant for the child several times and then encourage him,to say it. Show him an alphabet chart and point out that the letter "Zz" is the last letter. Use the chart and say the letters slowly. Encourage the child to say them with you.

For general interest, point out to the child that the words, zoo, zebra and zipper begin with the letter Zz. Allow the child to zip a zipper. Show him a picture of a zebra and talk about what a zoo is.

Empty all of the alphabet puppets from the shoe box and tell the child to put them in alphabetical order. Be certain to give him an alphabetical chart or write a letter at a time on a piece of paper and tell the child to look for that letter. It will be helpful, before beginning this activity, if the puppets are arranged in several rows. The child can be instructed to move his eyes from left to right in each row as he searches for the correct letter. This method will serve to avoid confusion because it is an organized way to look for a specific letter.

At another time, the letter puppets can be used with the pictures facing up. The child can then be instructed to put the pictures in alphabetical order. Allow the child to use the alphabetical chart and assist the child if necessary. Use the picture clues to help reinforce the initial sounds of the letters. Tell the child that we use these letters and sounds to help us to read, write and spell.

This activity develops

- The awareness of Zz as a letter and the last letter of the alphabet
- more skill in visual discrimination
- awareness of the meaning of zero
- skill in listening for initial sounds
- awareness of the use of letters and sounds
- confidence

Age 4 – Week 35

Finger Writing

For this activity, obtain an old shirt, which when buttoned backwards can be used as a smock to protect the child's clothing. In addition, you will need a can of shaving cream and a smooth washable working area such as a counter top, table or a large old tray.

Spray some of the shaving cream on the work area. Allow the child to smooth the cream out with his hands and explore. After this, show the child how to move his index finger through the cream to form a circle. Name the other shapes, one by one, and help the child draw the square, triangle, rectangle and oval.

Show the child how to combine the shape drawings to create objects that are familiar to him such as a wagon, a teddy bear, a flower, a house, a butterfly, etc.

At another time, use the same materials and show the child how to print the alphabet. The letter puppets can be used, one at a time, for the child to use as a model (visual clues) to copy the letter. The index finger can be guided to form the letter correctly in the shaving cream on the work area. If the child makes a mistake, just smooth the cream and start again. If the cream seems to disappear, add more so that the child has enough to feel the cream as he forms the letters. This activity can be continued at various times throughout the weeks until the child is comfortable in forming the letters.

If you prefer not to use shaving cream, try a thin flour paste, wet sand or something slippery that will fascinate the child, yet is safe for him to use. Children find that even a wet window glass is fun to write on.

This same activity can be expanded to teach the child how to write the numbers. It is more difficult for a child to hold a pencil and write than it is to finger write. The feel in forming the letters and numbers helps the child to build a better foundation for memory recall.

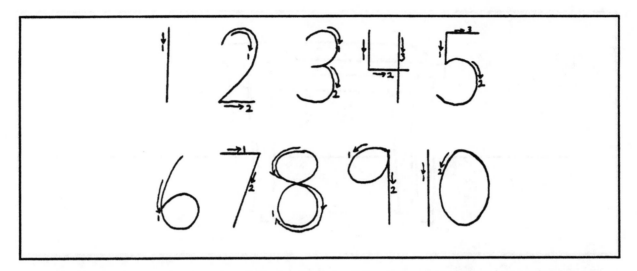

Simple rhymes to use in forming the numbers adds interest and help children to recall how to write numbers correctly. I do not know the origin of the following rhymes, but I used them in teaching kindergarten children to write numbers. I have heard different versions and have modified the following rhymes to suit my purpose:

- A straight line 1 is fun.
- Around and back on a railroad track 2-2-2.
- Around a tree and around a tree, that's the way to make a 3.
- Down and over and down once more, that's the way to make a 4.
- Down and around and put a flag on top and see what you have found. (5)
- Down through a loop, a 6 rolls a hoop.
- Across the sky and down from heaven, that's the way to make a 7.
- Make an S but do not wait, come back up to make an 8.
- An ellipse and a line is 9.
- A straight line one and an ellipse again, that's the way to make a 10.

This activity develops

- eye-hand coordination
- free exploration
- skill in forming shapes
- skill in forming letters
- skill in forming numbers
- tactile enhancement (feeling letter and number formations)
- more awareness that shapes can be used in drawing
- confidence

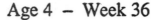

Age 4 – Week 36

Labeling

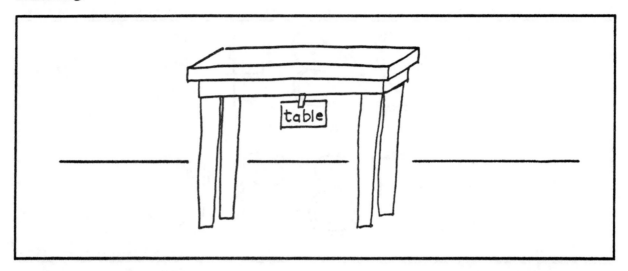

Use small index cards or something similar in size and print in lower case letters the names of a few familiar household items on the cards. Some suggestions to start with are: bed, desk, television, sofa, stove, table.

Read one of the words to the child and ask him to show you where to put the "label" on that object. Use masking tape to attach the word to the correct object. Ask the child to tell you the letters in the word. Point to the left of the word so that the child will recall the letters in the proper order. Follow the same procedure for the other objects. When the child can recall letters on the labels with confidence, add one or two more words. Continue doing this as long as the child is interested. A new word can be added each day if the child seems to be especially interested.

The child may attempt to read some of the labels, but it is more important to emphasize the letters and the beginning sounds at this age. Encourage the child to recall letters in books, labels on foods, magazines, license plates, buildings, the newspaper, etc.

As an extension of this activity, try naming familiar words and ask the child to listen and identify the beginning sound. Avoid words that begin with sh, ch, wh, and th. These are digraphs and the sound of the combination letters is different from isolated sounds of consonants. Words beginning with vowels should be short vowel sound words such as those introduced with each letter puppet in Aa, Ee, Ii, Oo and Uu.

This activity develops

- more awareness of letters and words
- skill in listening for sounds
- skill in identifying initial sounds
- skill in recalling letters in words
- skill in associating words and objects
- confidence

Age 4 – Week 37

More Ball

A child of this age should develop coordination in basic gross motor activities (large muscle skills). The ball is fun to use and the child can develop some basic skills with it. An inflated rubber ball that bounces easily is recommended. It should be the size that is easily handled by a child this age such as that introduced at the age 3, week 1 activity.

Mark a place with tape or chalk on the floor or sidewalk. Tell the child to drop the ball on that mark, watch the ball and catch it when it bounces back up. The child should use both hands to grasp the ball and avoid using his body to help in catching the ball. This activity should be practiced often. Counting each time the ball is dropped, adds interest to the skill being developed. The child can hear the bounce and the counting. This helps him to understand a use of counting.

Another skill with the ball is tossing. Show the child how to toss the ball up gently and to catch it when it comes down. Allow the child to toss the ball up and instruct him to keep his eyes on the ball and be ready to catch it when it comes down. The child should remember to avoid using his body to help him to catch the ball. The hands and arms must be slightly away from the child's body when he attempts to catch the ball. Counting can also be done each time the child catches the ball when it is tossed up.

You and the child can practice rolling the ball back and forth to each other in either a standing or sitting position. The rolling activity was introduced earlier but a child needs much practice in controlling a ball. The child may also enjoy rolling a ball to a wall with a slight push or force so that it will roll back for him to catch.

This activity develops

- better gross motor coordination
- skill in keeping the eyes on a moving target
- skill in the timing of when to catch the ball
- confidence
- skill in counting

Age 4 – Week 38

More Actions

Skipping is fun, but it is difficult for some four year olds. Practice is essential. If the child was not coordinated well enough when skipping was first introduced at age 3, week 2, then he needs more preliminary instruction and much practice. The basic steps of skipping are to instruct the child to start by placing one foot forward, then hop on that same foot forward. The foot that is not touching the ground or floor during the first hop should then step forward as the first hop is being completed. The second foot that is now forward should then hop as the first foot prepares to take another step and hop forward. The rhythm to say with the child is, "Step, quick hop." Remind the child to be ready to change feet as soon as the hop is completed. Continue to encourage the child to practice at various times. The child may feel more confident if he can practice independently, i.e., without an adult being present. Sometimes children are intimidated by the presence of an adult, especially when they are practicing a skill that seems difficult for them. However, praise from you will do wonders in encouraging a child to practice.

Children enjoy trotting. Tell the child that trotting is done with short alternating hops as he moves his body forward. Attaching jingle bells to the child's wrists or feet will add interest as he pretends to be a trotting horse or pony. Coordination in trotting is much easier for the child and can be substituted after a skipping practice.

Galloping was introduced earlier. To refresh your memory, this activity is accomplished by instructing the child to start on one foot. Tell the child that this foot will always be in the front and will be called the leading foot. As the child's leading foot moves forward, he should hop quickly while the other foot comes forward behind the leading foot. The leading foot again steps forward and the process is repeated. The child can pretend to be a galloping horse.

Once the child can skip, trot and gallop well, play a listen and do game with him. To begin the game, allow the child to skip in a circle. It would be helpful to use objects, tape or draw a circle to mark off a circular boundary. The reason for this is that children tend to skip, gallop and trot in small circles unless there is a given boundary for them to move outside of. As the child continues to skip around the circle say, "Trot." On that command, the child must then change from a skip to a trot. Allow the child to trot in the circle briefly. Then change the action to a gallop. Continue changing the actions until the child appears to be tired. Repeat this activity at various times because it teaches the child to listen, think and react.

This activity develops

- gross motor coordination
- skill in listening for a change in action
- confidence

Age 4 – Week 39

Listen and Name

This activity involves listening, thinking and responding verbally. The child may be able to give more than one answer for each statement. Encourage the discussion as much as possible and feel free to add to this list of statements. This is a good traveling or quiet game that can enrich the child's language development and his thinking processes, as well as extending his knowledge of the various things that are named during this activity.

- Name something that walks.
- Name something that sleeps.
- Name something that swims.
- Name something that floats.
- Name something that stings.
- Name something that rolls.
- Name something that flies.
- Name something that sails.
- Name something that melts.
- Name something that hurts.
- Name something that cuts.
- Name something that burns.
- Name something that trots.
- Name something that sticks.
- Name something that digs.
- Name something that opens.
- Name something that rings.
- Name something that moves.
- Name something that shines.
- Name something that eats.

This activity develops

- skill in listening and understanding concepts
- skill in thinking and associating
- language enrichment
- confidence

Age 4 – Week 40

Rope Jumping

Place a piece of old clothesline (rope) or a regular jump rope on the floor or ground. Tell the child to jump over the rope. Tape, tie or secure one end of the rope to a chair, table leg or something else so that the end of the rope is approximately four inches from the floor or the ground. Hold the other end of the rope at a four-inch level so that it is parallel to the floor or ground. Tell the child to jump over the raised rope. Allow the child to jump back and forth at this level until he is confident in jumping.

The height of the rope can be gradually increased. It can be secured with a stack of books, bricks or something else heavy. Continue to increase the height gradually until it is as high as the child can jump over comfortably.

At another time, choose a comfortable height for the child to jump over while one end of the rope is secured. Slowly swing the rope back and forth for the child to watch so that he can safely jump over the rope successfully. Encourage the child to practice this until he loses interest or appears tired. This activity should be repeated often until the child is secure in jumping over a rope in motion.

Choose a jump rope that is the proper length for the child and show him how to hold the jump rope with both hands. Instruct the child to place the rope behind him and move the rope slowly over his head, allow the middle of the rope to fall and touch the floor or ground. At that point, instruct the child to jump over the middle of the rope and bring the rope back up behind him as he did when he began. Tell the child to repeat this action very slowly at first, and as he becomes more confident, increase the movement of the rope. With practice the child should be able to develop skill in turning and jumping over the rope. Most children enjoy jumping rope independently at this age. However, some children do not develop this skill until they are in school.

When the child has developed some skill in jumping rope, count how many times he can jump without missing a jump.

The child can also practice jumping with a hoola hoop by holding it with both hands, turning it like the jump rope and jumping. The child can also count how many times he can jump in this manner without missing a jump.

This activity develops

- more skill in jumping
- gross motor coordination
- more awareness of the concept "over"
- skill in watching a moving object and reacting at the precise moment
- more skill in counting
- confidence

Age 4 — Week 41

Feel and Tell

Place at least five different items in a shoe box with a lid. Cut a hole in the lid, just large enough for the child's hand to go through. The items should be small enough to go through the hole in the box and suitable for the child to grasp easily. Some suggested items are a spoon, a rock, an empty plastic film can, a small toy and a large button.

Show the items to the child and allow him to feel and name the objects as you place them in the shoe box. Name one of the objects and tell the child to reach in the box, feel for the shape of the named object and pull it up through the hole in the shoe box. Praise the child if he is successful. If he has difficulty selecting the object, try to give clues as to the shape or feel of the object. If this does not help, retrieve the object and talk about it and allow the child to feel it again. Replace the object and name another object for the child to retrieve. Continue with this activity until the child succeeds most of the time. Change the objects and repeat this activity at another time.

As an extension of this activity, choose three things that are smooth and three things that are rough, such as a piece of smooth plastic, a button, a smooth feeling toy, a rough bottle cap, a piece of sandpaper and a rough feeling rock. Place these items in the shoe box with the hole in the lid and tell the child to feel in the box for something that is smooth or rough. Do this until the box is empty of the smooth and rough objects. Then encourage the child to feel and tell you things that are smooth and rough in the house. The child will enjoy feeling pieces of furniture for smooth and rough areas. He will also enjoy moving throughout the house discovering and talking about the feel of the various things that he feels. He may then identify some other names for the feel of things such as soft, fluffy, scratchy, bumpy, sticky, lumpy, etc.

At another time the same procedure, with the shoe box and the hole in the lid, can be repeated with soft and hard objects. Some suggested items are a cotton ball, a piece of cloth, a deflated balloon, a piece of wood, a spoon, bottle lid, etc. When the box is empty, the child may enjoy finding hard and soft objects within the home and telling you about them.

This activity develops

- further awareness of tactile sensations
- skill in recalling the objects' names by feeling
- skill in distinguishing rough and smooth
- skill in distinguishing hard and soft
- skill in decision making
- language enrichment
- confidence

Age 4 – Week 42

Foods

Children of this age should be made aware that good eating habits are essential. This activity is designed to identify the basic kinds of foods for the child. It is intended to interest the child enough so that he will have the desire to eat correctly.

Assemble four paper plates. Help the child to select and cut from a magazine a picture of the following foods: bread, cereal, meat, milk, cheese, fruit, and vegetable. Tell the child to glue the bread and cereal on one plate, the meat picture on the second plate, milk and cheese on the third plate and the fruit and vegetable on the fourth plate.

Place the four paper plates in a row. Encourage the child to name the foods on each plate. Tell the child to be healthy he must eat some of each of these kinds of foods everyday. Also, tell the child that people who do not eat the correct foods do not feel well and get sick more often.

Encourage the child to look at pictures of other foods in old magazines and to cut them out. The child can then place the food pictures in the correct food group plate.

At another time, the child can be motivated to select (with your guidance) his own menu. He can choose a picture of a food from each of the four food groups and cut them out. He should be encouraged to choose pictures that resemble a regular serving of a food. A paper plate can then be divided into four sections by using a felt marker to mark off the four sections. This will make the child aware of the four different food groups. The child can then either lay the chosen foods in the four sections of the plate or he may wish to glue them in place. Perhaps there will be enough interest for the child to select other menus for himself at various times.

At meal time, the child should be able to identify the foods on his plate and tell to which food group each food belongs. Hopefully this will encourage the child to be interested in eating a variety of foods.

This activity develops

- awareness of different food groups
- awareness that proper foods are necessary for good health
- language enrichment in identifying foods
- skill in classifying or grouping foods
- confidence
- an interest in making food selections
- fine motor coordination in cutting and gluing

Age 4 – Week 43

Jumping a Distance

Lay two ropes or two pieces of yarn parallel to each other and very close together. Tell the child to pretend that the space between the two ropes or yarn is a very narrow river. Instruct the child to jump over the very narrow river. Tell the child that he can jump over that river and not get wet because it is so narrow.

Move the ropes a little farther apart but close enough so that the child can successfully jump over the ropes. Tell the child that this river is wider than the narrow river. Instruct the child to jump over the river and to be careful not to fall in and get wet. If the child is unable to jump successfully over the wider river, allow him to try again or move the rope or yarn closer together. If he jumps successfully, tell him that he is a good jumper and did not get wet.

Move the two ropes a little farther apart. Make it wide enough so that the child may not be able to jump over the two parallel ropes or yarn. Tell the child this river is very wide. It is the widest of the three rivers. Encourage the child to try to jump over the widest river. If the child cannot jump over the two parallel ropes say, "Oops, you got wet." If the child can jump across say, "You can jump the widest river and you did not get wet."

Review the words, narrow, wider, and widest with the child. To reinforce the concept, tear a sheet of paper into three strips so that one is narrow, one is a little wider and the other one much wider. Play the game of "Pick Up" with the child. Instruct the child to pick up one of the three that you name, which should be called the narrow one, the wider one or the widest one. Whenever possible, try to use these words to reinforce the concepts with the child.

This activity develops

- gross motor coordination
- skill in jumping a given distance
- skill in distinguishing narrow, wider, widest
- skill in following directions
- listening skills
- confidence

Age 4 – Week 44

Number Stairs and Counting

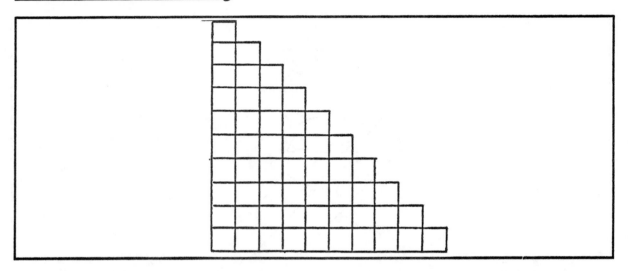

If available, assemble 55 shirt or similar buttons that are approximately the same size. Bottle caps, beans, small pebbles or uniform-sized paper squares may be used instead of buttons for this activity.

Instruct the child to place one button on a flat work area. Then instruct the child to place two buttons in a row under the one button. Add three buttons under the row of the two buttons. Do the same for the subsequent rows adding one more for each row until there are ten rows. This arrangement should consist of ten straight uniform rows that resemble stairs with the one at the top and the row of ten at the bottom. Count the items, on the diagonal, with the child as he moves his index finger down the "stairs" and then up the "stairs." The child may also enjoy counting the total number of objects that were used to form the rows that resemble stairs.

At another time, write the numbers 1 to 10 on individual index cards, paper rectangles or use small paper plates. Mix the cards, rectangles or paper plates and place them in a stack with the numbers facing down. Encourage the child to turn over one, read the number on it and count out that many buttons (or similar items) and place them on the card, rectangle or plate. Assist the child in identifying the number and in counting. This activity should be continued until all of the numbers have been turned over and all of the 55 buttons or pieces, that were used to make the "stairs" have been counted and placed correctly.

The child will need much practice in identifying numbers and counting objects correctly. In counting the objects, it will be helpful if the child will move each small object as he counts. Then he should move each piece to a different position to make a new pile. If the child omits a number in counting, ask him to begin again and count slowly so that he will not make a mistake. Give the child assistance if he does not know what number comes next when he is counting.

At another time the numerical cards, rectangles or paper plates can be placed in order from 1 to 10. Old playing cards may be substituted, but make sure that the child understands the "Ace" must be called "one." Whichever cards you decide to use may then be placed in numerical order. If you use an entire deck of old cards, the child may enjoy matching the cards with the same number. Then these piles may be placed in numerical order.

This activity develops

- more awareness of counting consecutively
- more awareness of one more as numbers increase
- skill in placing numbers in numerical order
- skill in counting objects to match the correct number
- confidence

Age 4 – Week 45

The Clock

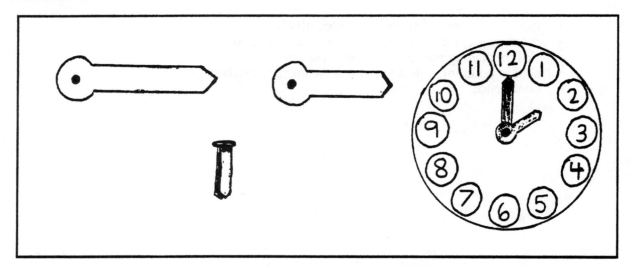

Use a penny to trace around and draw twelve small circles around the inside edge of a large paper plate. It will be easier to space the small circles if you draw the top and bottom circles first, then the middle, left and right circles. This will leave room to space evenly the rest of the twelve circles. Write the numbers 1 to 12 with a fine felt tip marker in the proper circles to represent the numbers on a clock. Draw two cardboard pieces to represent the clock hands. Cut one shorter than the other and trim the edges of one end of each clock hand to resemble a point. Fasten the hands with a brass paper fastener to the center.

Most children are familiar with a digital clock and very few have paid attention to an ordinary analog clock. Tell the child there are two kinds of clocks. If possible, show the child the difference. A child at age four may be able to count to sixty, but he probably will not understand the number concepts that high. Therefore, the paper plate clock is a good way to explain the concept of time. The child should understand the concept of hours, but minutes and seconds are too overwhelming for most children this age. Once the child is confident in identifying hourly time, minutes can be explained by watching a second hand go all the way around once on the face of a clock or watch.

To begin this activity, show the child the paper plate clock. Point to the numbers in the circles as you count from 1 to 12. Ask the child which hand of the clock is longer. Tell the child to put the longer (big) hand on the number 12. Make certain that the child knows the longer hand is called the big hand and the shorter hand is called the little hand. Instruct the child to point the little hand to the 1 o'clock position. Tell the child the clock shows that it is 1 o'clock. Tell the child to move the big hand all the way around once. Make sure that the child understands that it takes one hour of time for the big hand to move all the way around and back to the same place. Instruct the child to move the little hand and point it to the 2. Ask the child what time it is. Tell the child if he does not understand. Allow the child to continue to move the big and little hands and identify the correct hour as the hands are moved.

It is not necessary to explain morning and afternoon and a twenty-four hour day until the child has had much practice in moving the clock hands and recalling the correct hour.

It will be very helpful if a real analog clock can be placed in full view of the child for a period of time. In this way, the child can observe the second hand, as well as observe the slower pace of the minute (big hand) and the hour (little hand) as they slowly change positions.

As an extension of this activity, mark off 12 spaces with masking tape on the floor in a circle or use 12 rocks for markers outside to represent the number spaces on a clock. Allow the child to help you count out twelve paper plates or sheets of paper. Encourage the child to tell you what number to write on each plate, which should have the numbers 1 to 12 written on them. Ask the child to help you place the paper plates or numbered papers in the correct position to resemble a large clock. These pieces may then be secured with masking tape.

Allow the child to walk around clockwise using the paper plates or paper pieces as stepping stones. The child should be encouraged to say the correct number as he steps on each numbered plate or paper piece. This will reinforce the positions of the numbers that represent the hours and orientate the child to the meaning of moving clockwise.

For interest, the child can walk counter-clockwise and identify the numbers. This, too, will assist the child in number placement and an understanding of counter-clockwise.

This activity develops

- more awareness of the numbers 1 - 12
- awareness of a clock
- awareness of time and hour
- awareness of the spatial positions of the numbers on a clock
- more awareness of the concepts, big and little and long and short
- awareness of clockwise and counter-clockwise
- confidence

Age 4 – Week 46

Patterns

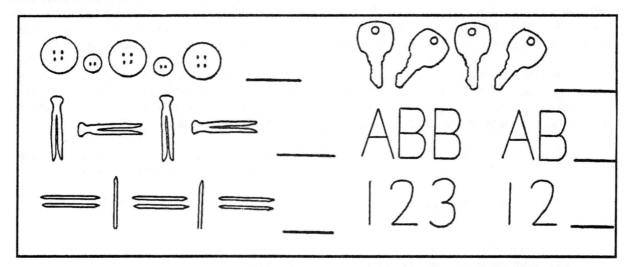

A pattern is a way of doing something and repeating it. Your child may not understand the word repeat. Therefore, I suggest that you use the term "do it again." Many different materials can be used to make a pattern or design. The idea is to show the child a pattern and ask what comes next with the pattern as it is extended or continued. This indirectly is a prerequisite to spelling, i.e, predicting or determining what letter comes next in a word.

Some suggested materials for making patterns are: buttons, clothespins, toothpicks, a large collection of keys, colored paper strips, etc. The pattern schemes for these materials are as follows:

- A button pattern can be made with big and little buttons. The child should then be asked what comes next in the pattern. Then the child can continue the pattern.

- A clothespin pattern can be read with one straight up and one placed on its side. The child can then be asked what comes next in the pattern and then continue with the pattern.

- A toothpick pattern can be arranged so that two toothpicks are laid parallel and one is placed straight up. The child can then be asked what comes next and continue with the pattern.

- A key pattern can be made by placing two keys with the points touching to form a "V" shape. The child should then be able to continue the pattern.

- A colored strip pattern can be formed with red, blue, red, blue colors. The child should then be encouraged to continue the pattern.

- A letter pattern can also be developed. It can read ABB, ABB. The child should then be able to repeat this pattern indefinitely.

- A number pattern can be 1-2-3, 1-2-3. By this time the child should be able to repeat this pattern and continue indefinitely.

- Encourage the child to make a pattern with tableware.

More complex patterns can be developed with various materials. Clapping out rhythms or tapping the feet or a combination of these, in addition to slapping the thighs or touching the head, can be developed into patterns. The child can be encouraged to repeat what you do and continue with it.

Make the child aware of the many patterns within the home such as floral, plaids, stripes or other design patterns on cloth, dishes, silverware, lamps, floor tiles, carpets, jewelry, furniture, wallpaper, etc.

This activity is one that can be extended indefinitely. It develops

- awareness of patterns
- skill in reading patterns
- skill in predicting or determining what comes next in a pattern
- visual or observational skills
- an appreciation of designs and patterns

Age 4 – Week 47

Picture Puzzles

Wooden and cardboard puzzles are expensive and children soon tire of working the same puzzles. Therefore, you may want to consider making your own puzzles. Puzzles are designed to develop some basic skills. They serve to develop eye-hand coordination, understanding the parts of a whole, positioning of pieces in a given area, problem solving and skill in manipulating the pieces for small muscle development. Adding a variety of picture puzzles should develop more interest for the child. Large colorful interesting pictures can be cut from magazines, old calendars, coloring books or pictures that you draw and color can be used to make puzzles. One or two puzzles at a time is all that is necessary to motivate the child to work puzzles. When the child develops more skill, smaller puzzles can be made from old greeting cards. Whenever you choose to make puzzles, keep in mind that a child of this age is capable of working puzzles with at least eight to ten pieces and can advance to work puzzles with fifteen or more pieces. However, the pieces should be large enough so that the child can hold and contain enough of a picture clue and shape for the child to problem solve and manipulate to complete the puzzle.

Puzzles can be made by gluing securely large colorful pictures to cardboard or heavy poster board. The top and bottom can be covered with clear contact paper, but this is not necessary. If you are handy with a jig saw in the workshop, then glue the pictures to wood and seal them with a puzzle-fixer glue or clear sealer. Once the child works a puzzle several times his interest usually wanes. Therefore, it is not necessary to make elaborate puzzles.

Once the glue or sealer has dried, draw the shapes of the pieces on the puzzles. Use large curves and indentations when developing a puzzle. Sharp pointed pieces are difficult for the child to place. Cut the pictures into puzzles pieces and label the back of each piece with a letter, number or other symbol to identify the pieces of a given picture. This will help to keep the pieces separated. Store each puzzle in a plastic bag. Allow the child to choose a puzzle to work and encourage him to put that puzzle away in the plastic bag before attempting to work another one.

If the child has difficulty working puzzles, use a separate blank piece of cardboard underneath the puzzle. Draw around each puzzle piece in its proper place on the blank cardboard. This will leave the shape of each puzzle piece and will serve as a guide for the child in working the puzzle.

This activity develops

- eye-hand coordination
- more of an understanding of the parts of a whole
- problem solving
- skill in manipulating the puzzle pieces
- visual skills (looking for detail)
- confidence and independence

Age 4 – Week 48

My Name

A child's name is very special to him and at this age he should be able to recognize his own name in print. Print the child's first name on an index card and ask him to name the letters in his name. It is important to use an upper case letter at the beginning of the child's name and to use lower case letters for the remainder of the letters in the name. The kindergarten teacher will have to "unteach" the child if all upper case letters are used in the child's name. It may be easier for the child to form upper case letters, but a child of four is not expected to hold a pencil correctly and write his name formally. This activity is designed to make the child aware of what his name looks like in print.

At this time, you may wish to use shaving cream on a flat smooth surface and print the child's name with your index finger. Shaving cream drawing and printing were introduced in the age 4, week 35 activity. If you do not wish to use shaving cream, use a thin flour paste spread on wax paper that is taped with masking tape to secure it. Encourage the child to recall the letters in his first name. Carefully print each letter again so that the child can observe as you form the letters.

Guide the child's index finger over the letters of his first name and call each letter by name as you do this. Repeat this procedure several times and then encourage the child to trace over each letter just as you guided his finger. Then tell the child to try to print his own name with the shaving cream and his index finger. It may be necessary to replace the shaving cream supply on the work area. The cream seems to disappear after being exposed to the air. The child may need you to print each letter separately with your index finger while he uses his finger to form the same letter below yours. With practice, the child will soon learn to write his first name. If he is very interested, show him how to print his last name. This activity can be repeated many times to improve the child's letter formation skills. Printing this way is fun because mistakes can easily be erased. When using paper and pencil, it is difficult to make mistakes disappear completely.

The child may enjoy using clay to form the letters in his name. Homemade play dough (clay) can be rolled in long "snakes" or rolls and the child can use a plastic picnic knife or old scissors to cut the lengths to form the letters. Cooked spaghetti can also be used to form the letters.

The child may enjoy attempting to learn to print all of the letters of the alphabet. The letter puppets may once again be retrieved and the child can use the letters as guides to print in shaving cream, print in clay or print with spaghetti. If the child becomes especially skilled in letter formation, make dots in the shape of a letter on a sheet of paper and encourage the child to connect the dots with a crayon to form the letter. The child may also enjoy printing with chalk on a chalk board.

This activity develops

- skill in recognizing the letters in a name
- eye-hand coordination
- skill in recalling the letters in a name in sequence
- tactile sensation of printing with different materials,
  such as shaving cream, clay, spaghetti, crayon and chalk
- confidence

Age 4 – Week 49

Listen

The purpose of this activity is to further develop the child's listening skills. Below is a list of words, two of which, are the same word. The child should listen carefully to the three words that are read to him and repeat only the two words that are the same. The words are listed below.

- house-lamp-house
- damp-door-door
- cook-cook-look
- box-table-box
- paper-paper-dress
- rug-carpet-rug
- blue-red-red
- fish-green-green
- yellow-yellow-orange

- pot-pan-pan
- boy-boy-girl
- lick-pen-pen
- black-brown-black
- tell-tell-sell
- sofa-chair-sofa
- three-three-two
- nine-line-line
- child-name-child

This activity can be used as a traveling game. Any three words can be substituted. Use the concept of "same" until you are certain that the child is confident. Then at another time, the child can repeat only the word that is different. However, do not interchange the concepts of "same" and "different" during a single activity. It may frustrate and confuse the child. Letters and numbers may also be used such as A-A-S, B-C-C, 1-2-2 or 3-4-3.

This activity develops

- keen listening skills (listening for a purpose)
- following directions
- more awareness of the concepts, same and different
- language enrichment
- confidence

Age 4 – Week 50

Clothing

The child should be aware that different kinds of clothing are worn for special reasons. Our finest clothes are usually worn on special occasions such as weddings, church, parties or special family gatherings, etc. Other clothing is suitable for work, play, leisure, sleeping, swimming, etc. These types of clothing vary as to the season, in places where seasonal changes are apparent. There are some clothes that keep us warm and some clothes that help us feel cooler when it is hot. A child of this age should be able to classify clothing as to the need.

Perhaps making seasonal books would be of interest to the child. Make four booklets with five or six pages stapled together for each booklet. Write the name of a season on each of the four booklets. They should be labeled Summer, Fall (Autumn), Winter and Spring. Read the names of the seasons in order of occurrence to the child. Allow the child to choose one of the booklets to use first or you may suggest that the child begin with the current season.

Encourage the child to look through old magazines or shopping catalogs and choose clothing that is suitable for the season that was chosen with which to work. Cut the pictures out and glue them in the booklet. Discuss briefly the chosen season with the child; at another time, read a story about that season.

At three other convenient times, follow the same procedure for the next three seasons. Make certain that the child understands the need for different kinds of clothing.

When the booklets are completed, invite the child to look at them with you. Allow the child to name each piece of clothing that is in the booklet. Assist the child if necessary. Print the name of the clothing on the page and invite the child to recall the letters in the word. The child may enjoy naming the colors that he sees in the clothing. The color words may then be added to the labeled picture of the clothing.

The child may want to make a special occasion or a night clothing booklet. The same procedure can be followed if the child wishes or he may suggest another way to design his booklet. In either case, encourage him to do so. This will expand his knowledge of clothing names, letters, colors, picture detail, improve his cutting and gluing skills and increase confidence in himself.

As a further extension of this activity, you can ask the child to tell you during what season he should wear a certain kind of clothing such as a coat, cap, bathing suit, boots, gloves, jacket, shorts, sweater, shirt, suit, vest, mittens and sandals.

Some skills that will serve to prepare your child to be more independent should be considered at this time, because the child will soon begin his formal education. A child of this age should be able to dress himself. He should be able to put on a jacket and zip or fasten it. He should be able to put on his boots and mittens without your help. A plastic bag placed over each shoe will make it easier for the child to slip on his boots. He should begin to learn to lace his shoes and be instructed how to tie them. Practice all of these skills with the child so that he will not need you to do them for him when he goes to school. Some parents do everything for their children because it seems easier at the time. With patience, the child can become self-sufficient and independent.

322

This activity develops

- awareness of the proper clothing to wear
- awareness of the seasons
- skill in making a decision
- listening and associating skills
- eye-hand coordination in cutting and gluing
- naming and letter recall

Age 4 — Week 51

ABC Actions

Review the alphabet with the child. Tell the child that you have an action for him to do or pretend to do that goes with each letter. Write the letters Aa through Zz on a separate index card and the action words on the back of each card. The actions to write on the back of the cards are listed below:

Aa - ask a question	Bb - bat a ball	Cc - clap your hands
Dd - dance around	Ee - empty a box	Ff - fish for a fish
Gg - giggle	Hh - hop on one foot	Ii - pretend to itch
Jj - jump up high	Kk - kick your foot	Ll - look up high
Mm - march in place	Nn - pretend to nap	Oo - get on and off
Pp - push something	Qq - quack	Rr - run in place
Ss - skip	Tt - tap your foot	Uu - get under something
Vv - vibrate	Ww - walk in place	Xx - exercise
Yy - yawn	Zz - zip your jacket	

Place the cards in a box or bag and mix them up. Allow the child to draw a card, read the letter on the card and hand the card to you so that you can tell him what to do. Read the action for that letter and allow the child to perform the action. Assist the child if necessary. Some actions will be quick and some will require the child to make a noise. If the child has difficulty, perform the action for him and allow him to imitate you. The child may be interested in doing only a few at a time or he may enjoy going through the entire alphabet.

The purpose of this game, the puppet games and the other alphabet games is to ensure that the child will be very confident with the letter names and sounds before he enters kindergarten.

The ABC action game can be used as a family charades game. Other members of the family can act out the actions and the child can attempt to identify the letters. At another time, the child can do the action and a family member can attempt to identify the letter for that action.

Another way to play the game is to name the action and have the child tell the letter that corresponds to the action. The letter can be named for the child and he can then verbally identify the action for it from memory.

Some of the actions can be changed for a given letter, such as in the letter, Pp, the action could be "push something," Ww could be to "wiggle." Allow the child to try to think of actions to match a letter.

This activity develops

- more of an awareness of the alphabet
- skill in identifying the letters
- gross motor activity
- listening skills
- following directions
- skill in associating the letter with the action
- confidence

Age 4 – Week 52

The Traveling Bag

The child will delight in assisting you in preparing a special bag for him to take with him whenever the family goes on a short or a long visit or trip.

Choose an overnight bag or shopping bag and allow the child to hold it. Tell the child it is empty and it is light in weight. Also tell the child that you will help him to choose some things to put in the bag. Emphasize that when you are ready to go away, there will be very special things in the bag for him to use.

Some suggested items are: crayons, a tablet of paper, old playing cards, a small flannel board with different colored felt shapes to make shape-pictures, a stuffed animal, pipe cleaners, a small doll or car, a yarn or sock ball and a plastic container with special small items enclosed such as keys, buttons, little plastic animals, etc.

The flannel board can be made by covering a piece of corrugated cardboard that is approximately 8 1/2 x 11 inches with a piece of plain colored flannel. Light green, blue or yellow are recommended colors. The loose ends can be attached in the back with masking tape. The felt pieces can be cut from scrap or bought squares into various sizes of geometric shapes. The child can be very creative and develop interesting pictures with the shapes. The loose pieces can be stored in a plastic bag.

When the bag is filled, allow the child to hold it. Ask the child why the bag is not empty and is heavier. Talk about why there is a difference. Can the child recall some of the things in the bag? If not, empty the bag and name each thing as you place the items back into the bag. This is good training for the child's memory recall.

Before you leave home with the bag, try to add a small snack for the child such as raisins, a small closed bag of cookies or animal crackers. A packaged sealed drink would also be a welcomed surprise for the child. Feel free to vary the contents of the bag, but be certain to always keep a bag packed. Believe me, it can be a life saver.

This activity develops

- more awareness of the concepts, empty and full
- more awareness of the concepts, light and heavy
- memory recall
- awareness of preparing for activities away from home
- language interaction

SLOW AND STEADY, I AM READY!

NOTES

NOTES

NOTES

To Order
Fill in the form below:

Slow and Steady, Get Me Ready
It's the perfect gift for
new parents and grandparents!

To order

_____
Name

_____
Address

_____
City, State, Zip Code

Price includes shipping and handling

Books	Unit Price	Quantity ordered		
1	$19.95	Subtotal		
2	$17.95	VA residents add sales tax		
5	$16.95	Total enclosed		
For additional discount rates and information, write or call		Get an early start! Don't delay, order today.		
(703) 323-6142				

Enclose a check or money order for the correct amount and send your order to:

Bio-Alpha, Inc.
Box 7190
Fairfax Station, VA 22039